PELICAN BOOKS

THE PSYCHOLOGY OF CONSCIOUSNESS

Robert E. Ornstein is a graduate of Queens College of the City University of New York and of Stanford University. He now teaches at the University of California Medical Center in San Francisco and is a research psychologist at the Langley Porter Neuropsychiatric Institute. In 1969 Professor Ornstein received the American Institutes of Research Creative Talent Award. He is author of *The Mind Field* and *On the Experience of Time,* coauthor with Claudio Naranjo of *On the Psychology of Meditation,* and one of the authors of *Symposium on Consciousness.* Professor Ornstein is also the editor of *Common Knowledge: Or Can of Foot Powder Elected Mayor of Ecuadorian Town* and *The Nature of Human Consciousness: A Book of Readings.*

The Psychology
of Consciousness

by Robert E. Ornstein

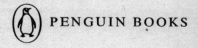

PENGUIN BOOKS

Penguin Books Ltd, Harmondsworth,
Middlesex, England
Penguin Books, 625 Madison Avenue,
New York, New York 10022, U.S.A.
Penguin Books Australia Ltd, Ringwood,
Victoria, Australia
Penguin Books Canada Limited, 2801 John Street,
Markham, Ontario, Canada L3R 1B4
Penguin Books (N.Z.) Ltd, 182–190 Wairau Road,
Auckland 10, New Zealand

First published in the United States of America by
W. H. Freeman and Company 1972
First published in Great Britain by Jonathan Cape Ltd 1975
Published in Pelican Books 1975
Reprinted 1977, 1978, 1979, 1980

Copyright © W. H. Freeman and Company, 1972
All rights reserved

Printed in the United States of America by
Offset Paperback Mfrs., Inc., Dallas, Pennsylvania
Set in Linotype Times Roman

To my house: Faith
David
Lisby
Di
Clif

For the trust
For the love
For the help

Contents

Acknowledgments

Grateful acknowledgment is made to the following for permission to quote selections from their books.

George Allen & Unwin, Ltd., for *The Persian Sufis* by Cyprian Rice; W. H. Allen & Co., Ltd., for *The Sufis* by Idries Shah; The Bodley Head and Simon & Schuster, Inc., for *A Separate Reality* by Carlos Castaneda; Jonathan Cape, Ltd., Collins-Knowlton-Wing, Inc., Idries Shah, and A. P. Watt, for *The Exploits of the Incomparable Mulla Nasrudin*, copyright © 1966 by Mulla Nasrudin Enterprises, Ltd., *The Pleasantries of the Incredible Mulla Nasrudin*, copyright © 1968 by Mulla Nasrudin Enterprises, Ltd., *Tales of the Dervishes*, copyright © 1967 by Idries Shah, *Thinkers of the East*, and *The Way of the Sufi*, copyright © 1968 by Idries Shah, all by Idries Shah; Chatto & Windus, Ltd., for *The Doors of Perception* by Aldous Huxley; Citadel Press, Inc., for *Spiritual Practices of India* by Frederic Spiegelberg; Faber & Faber, Ltd., for *Writings from Philokalia, on the Prayer of the Heart*, translated by E. Kadlovbovsky and G. E. H. Palmer; Faber & Faber, Ltd., and Harcourt Brace Jovanovich, Inc., for "Burnt Norton," from *Four Quartets* by T. S. Eliot, copyright © 1943 by T. S. Eliot; Victor Gollancz, Ltd., for *The Teachers of Gurdjieff* by Rafael Lefort; Grove Press, for *What the Buddha Taught*, copyright © 1959 by W. Rahula; Harper & Row, Publishers; Harvard University Press, for *On Knowing: Essays for the Left Hand* by Jerome Bruner; Hobbs, Dorman & Co., Inc., for *Psychosynthesis* by Roberto Assagioli; Hoopoe, Ltd., for *Documents of Contemporary Dervish Communities*, edited by R. Davidson; The Julian Press, Inc., for *Fundamentals of Yoga* by Rammurti

Mishra; M.I.T. Press, for *Language, Thought and Reality: Selected Writings of Benjamin Lee Whorf*, edited by J. B. Carroll; The Octagon Press, for *Caravan of Dreams* and *Oriental Magic*, both by Idries Shah; Pantheon Books, for *The Way of Zen* by Alan Watts; Princeton University Press; *Psychosomatic Medicine*, for "Codifications of Reality: Lineal and Nonlineal" by Dorothy Lee (Vol. 12, April–March 1950); Routledge & Kegan Paul, Ltd., for *The I Ching: or Book of Changes*; and John Weatherhill, Inc., for *The Three Pillars of Zen* by Philip Kapleau.

Preface

I suppose many people who read this book have asked themselves, "What is consciousness?" only to end up unsure of the answer and a bit confused. In my own wonderings, I began to read psychology and philosophy, hoping to find the answer there. Instead, I encountered a bewildering array of ideas, beginning with a definition of consciousness as "awareness of awareness," on up to facile cosmic pronouncements, and down to those who maintain that these wonderings are not meaningful. To ask "What is consciousness?" does not appear to be unreasonable; yet the question does not seem to be fully answerable in reasonable terms. So, along with questions like "What is God?" and "What is life?" we generally rule out consciousness from scientific inquiry.

After long searching for answers in many places, I have come to feel that these compelling questions *can* be answered, but, unfortunately, not fully within the mode of reason or intellection. There is no way to simply write down the answer, as we might give a textbook definition. The answers must come personally, experientially.

Then what of *The Psychology of Consciousness*, if many of its essential questions cannot be fully answered within a book? I have tried to do two things at once here: to write what can be written within science, without pretending that such an approach is a complete answer, just as a biologist does not really need a fully agreed-on definition of life in order to study it; and to point to a second stream of knowledge directed toward methods of answering these questions which scientific method excludes, the esoteric traditions of the Middle and Far

East. As Roger Bacon wrote 700 years ago, "There are two modes of knowing, those of argument and experience." They are complementary to one another; neither is reducible to the other; and their simultaneous working may be incompatible. One mode is verbal and rational, sequential in operation, orderly; the other is intuitive, tacit, diffuse in operation, less logical and neat, a mode we often devalue, culturally, personally, and even physiologically.

This book is a look ahead, an attempt to push beyond the immediate scientific evidence, in order to reach a new perspective.[1] It relies in part on a convergence of evidence from diverse sources: research in the functions of the two hemispheres of the brain; the ancient Chinese *I Ching*; current scientific analyses of the processes of cognition and perception; esoteric texts; research on how rats can control their blood flow; reports on Yoga. I have set out to present neither a problem-solving, advanced scientific treatise nor a step-by-step esoteric manual. The emphasis here is on a synthesis of two major streams of knowledge, and not on individual, unconnected states or techniques, such as the analysis of dreams, drug experiences, or the rich literature of hypnosis. I feel that a consideration of what lies behind the states and the experiments and the techniques is most important and most needed at the moment. So this is a book of what *could be* in psychology rather than of what is at present: an instrumental work, a means to an end, including speculation where that is appropriate, analysis of data in its proper place.[2]

Then what is in the book? The first chapter considers the inherent limits of a purely descriptive, behavioristic psychology. The second chapter attempts to integrate a great deal of modern research in perception and cognition, as it relates to the construction of individual consciousness and to biological survival. The third chapter introduces research which indicates that the two hemispheres of the brain are specialized for different modes of consciousness, one rational, one intuitive, which work in complement. Then a major dimension of consciousness, time, is considered along these lines; one mode, of duration, of the clock, of causality, is analyzed as a construction useful to the workings of a complex society, and a second mode, acausal, of events as "patterned wholes," is introduced. The fifth chapter is an introduction to the esoteric psychologies of intuition. The sixth chapter attempts to explore the reasons why people meditate, the communalities of all the varieties of meditation techniques, how meditation exercises can alter consciousness.

The seventh chapter, looser in content than any except the tenth, tries to open up for consideration many ideas that are largely ignored in the west, of subtle body energies, of sound influencing the brain, of a special use of oral literature. As in the sixth chapter, the emphasis is on the communality of the techniques of the esoteric tradition, as an education of that other, intuitive mode. I hope this emphasis will allow their sober consideration in science, and give an idea of the limits of a purely logical approach to understanding consciousness.

The eighth chapter, like the fifth, is a prelude, to a new synthesis of the two psychologies. The ninth chapter considers one example of this synthesis, biofeedback training, and explores its possibilities within science. The tenth chapter is again loose and more speculative. It concerns techniques and phenomena that are only beginning to be considered in western science, the effects of the geophysical surroundings, research on "paranormal" communication, new possibilities for psychotherapy, and a contemporary projection of the esoteric traditions. The chapters necessarily differ in level of analysis, more or less as is appropriate to the content of each.

Since I here attempt to bridge a chasm in research and thinking, I have asked for a great deal of help in this book. Far, far too many people aided me for me to be able to thank them all, but my gratefulness to David Sobel is overwhelming. We worked for days and days and days together, thinking, writing, and discussing the book, until it is now difficult to tell which part of the book stems from which of us. It was one of those rare instances, or so it felt to me, in which something larger than either or both of us emerged out of working together, and we are both grateful for it. Indeed, at one point we felt that, even if the book never reached anyone else, we had learned enough in doing it to justify all the time, the energy, and the pain. Although there was so little pain . . . My life is filled with Davids. The other one, David Galin, has been a thoughtful and helpful collaborator for the past four years, and out of our work together comes much of the basis of this book. Yet the responsibility for the speculation and the theoretical approach is mine, not either of the Davids'. Finally, Elizabeth Lloyd Mayer was patient and kind enough to help with the rewriting of many of the chapters. And to Faith Hornbacher for chapter-opening drawings (1, 2, 6, and 7), and for her trust, love, and support, and to the many others, thank you.

Robert Ornstein
San Francisco
April 1972

*The Psychology
of
Consciousness*

Chapter 1

Toward
a Complete Psychology

Is There Any Number Higher Than 100?

A man, having looted a city, was trying to sell an exquisite rug, one of the spoils. "Who will give me 100 pieces of gold for this rug?" he cried throughout the town.

After the sale was completed, a comrade approached the seller, and asked, "Why did you not ask more for that priceless rug?"

"Is there any number higher than 100?" asked the seller.[1]

It is easy to smile over the mistake of our friend the rugseller. And yet, we are like him, for each day our own conceptions of what is possible limit our awareness and action. This story reflects a process common both to everyday life and to scientific endeavor. Conceptions often act as barriers to understanding; they may stand in the way of higher possibilities, as the number 100 here blocks higher numbers from view. To give an example: Once it was considered impossible for a man to run a mile in less than four minutes. The "four-minute mile" became a real barrier to many, as if effort of another order was required to run a mile in 3:59.99 instead of four minutes. Then one man broke this barrier, and quite soon many others were able to perform what was once considered impossible. We all seem to set limits on possibility and to work within these assumed limits.

A similar process limits ordinary consciousness. We screen out much of our surroundings because we do not believe that certain events occur. Once a friend unwittingly emphasized this to me by reversing an ordinary saying: "I'll see it when I believe it!" If an object or sensory input appears which does not fit our set of categories, we may ignore it. The psychologist Jerome Bruner and his associates carried out the following experiment, which demonstrated this phenomenon.

One of our shared societal assumptions concerns the suits of playing cards. Through years of experience, we have learned that spades and clubs are black, hearts and diamonds are red. Normally, each deck of cards we see confirms this assumption. Bruner asked his observers to look at some cards through a tachistoscope—a device which allows visual materials to be flashed on a screen for an exact, short time. Intermixed with the ordinary cards were several "anomalous" ones: a *red* ace of *spades,* a *black* four of *hearts,* for instance. Many of the observers in this experiment did not "see" the unusual cards as they were. Rather, they "corrected" them, and reported a red six of spades as a six of hearts. Assumptions can limit the contents of awareness. At one point in the experiment, it was suggested to the observers that, although hearts are usually red, such usualness does not logically imply that they will *always* be red. With this new input extending their category system, some observers were then quickly able to see what was in front of them.[2]

Our "ordinary" assumptions about the nature of the world are generally useful to us. As we attempt to achieve a stable consciousness, we continuously "bet" about the nature of reality. We immediately assume that our rooms are "really" rectilinear, that a piece of coal is "really" black, that one person is intelligent, another aggressive. As Bruner's experiment and the preceding examples suggest, our assumptive world is conservative. It is quite difficult for us to alter our assumptions even in the face of compelling new evidence. We pay the price of a certain conservatism and resistance to new input in order to gain a measure of stability in our personal consciousnesses.

Any community of people holds in common certain assumptions about reality. Our language itself is a set of common assumptions, shared for the convenience of easy discourse. "No one can run a mile in less than four minutes" was another. Each scientific community, of physicists, mathematicians, psychologists, or others, shares an additional set of implicit assumptions, called the *paradigm* by Thomas Kuhn. The paradigm is the shared conceptions of what is possible, the boundaries of acceptable inquiry, the limiting cases.[3]

The working of the scientific paradigm is similar to the working of an individual's assumptions about reality. Personal categories are by their nature conservative of effort. Given our stable category system, we do not have to measure the walls on entering every new room to determine whether they are really rectilinear, or to inspect our friends at each meeting to determine whether they are really the same people we saw yesterday. Within science, a paradigm allows a similar stability of knowledge, again at the price of a certain insensitivity to new input. If several researchers hold a paradigm in common, this enables them to explore jointly one well-delimited area of inquiry and to coordinate effort. A shared paradigm allows them to communicate in a specialized language about an area, as the residents of one town may have their own local phrases and local jokes.

The development of a successful paradigm, then, enables a scientific community to maintain and share criteria for the selection of problems which might be amenable to solution. It allows a number of "local road maps" to be drawn up, tested, and validated by many independent researchers. But there is a danger here: parochialism. Just as the residents of a certain community may become smug about their town and consider it the "only" place in the world, so the scientist working under a successful paradigm may begin to lose sight of any possibilities beyond his own particular set of assumptions.

Psychology began as the science of consciousness, developing as a synthesis of natural philosophy and nineteenth-century science. One of its earliest practitioners, Gustav Fechner, invented the method of "psychophysics" in an attempt to correlate mental and physical events. Research on consciousness proceeded in the nineteenth century, spearheaded by a group at Cornell University under E. B. Titchener. This group sought evidence on consciousness through "introspection." In their research strategy, the observer attempted to analyze the contents of his personal consciousness and to compare his analysis with that of others, but the observers did not often find much agreement. To remedy this lack of a common ground, the introspectionists found it necessary to limit their field of inquiry. In the act of introspection it became "forbidden" for an observer to report seeing "a book," for example. He was only allowed to report seeing a brown object, of a certain size and shape. This and other limitations soon led to a sterility in the contents of psychology. Controversies of only academic import (in the worst sense of the term) arose, due to the limitations placed on inquiry. One, for instance, concerned whether "thoughts without images" could or could not occur. The concerns of psychologists drifted further and further away from the original ones. Soon their questions were of interest only to themselves, and it was evident that this paradigm was more of a restriction than an aid.

John Watson opened the gates once again with his suggestion that psychology could study action, which was, after all, verifiable and testable. This paradigm change allowed psychologists to study relevant problems once more. For instance, Watson could include such phenomena as personality in his textbook, while Titchener could not.[4] This movement, which came to be called *Behaviorism,* soon swept psychology. It was "objective" and "scientific," and encouraged the study of major problems that had been left out of the introspective paradigm. Behaviorism stimulated an unusual amount of productive research, especially in the realms of learning and of the motivation of behavior. But a similar problem arose with this approach: the scope of inquiry within psychology soon became unduly narrowed to processes which were amenable to solution by behavioristic methods. Psychologists began to ignore and even deny the existence of phenomena which did not fit into the dominant scheme. "Consciousness" itself was ignored in research for many years; some even denied that it existed. There was here an almost fatal confusion of "behaviorism as a useful tool" with "behaviorism as the total extent of knowledge." "Objective" factual knowledge was emphasized, to the exclusion of any question not subject to a verbal, logical answer. The *reductio ad absurdum* of this position was that of the "Logical Positivists," who maintained that any question not amenable to a perfectly logical answer should *not even be asked.*

This entire process, of course, parallels the workings of ordinary consciousness. We stabilize around a set of concepts (about cards, friends, the speed one can run) and hold them dear until we are overwhelmed by new evidence. Then our conceptions change once more, to include new possibilities (a red ace of spades, for instance). Similarly, scientific knowledge progresses by a complementary functioning of paradigm buildup and paradigm change. A successful paradigm serves to create stable, conservative knowledge within the scientific community, until the restrictions of the paradigm become too great and it proves to limit research unduly.

Science as a mode of knowing involves a limitation on inquiry. The essence of a good experiment is successful exclusion. One factor may be manipulated while a very few other processes are measured. If, for example, we want to study the response of cells in the brain to visual stimuli, we would be considered mad if we also monitor the blood flow to the feet, the temperature of the room, the phase of the moon, the growth rate of mushrooms outside, or any one of the millions of available possibilities. But, in psychology of late, the limitations of the successful behavioristic paradigm have proven to outweigh the advances. To give one example, until recently psychologists have tended to ignore some evidence (from sources as diverse as Yoga and animal experiments) that man is capable of a high degree of self-mastery of his internal physiology. Further, we have not incorporated evidence that the linear, verbal-intellectual mode of knowing is not the only mode available to man.

It is incomplete to hold that knowledge is exclusively rational. Even scientific inquiry, that most rational and logical of our pursuits, could not proceed without the presence of another type of knowledge. As an example, two scientific researchers may meet and discuss their ideas. Perhaps an experiment will emerge, to be written up in a journal and still later in a textbook. Those writings are generally as orderly and well-reasoned as the scientist can make them. The *entire process*, however, is not exclusively linear and rational. Scientific investigators act on personal knowledge, biases, hunches, intuition. It is the genius of the scientific method that the *a*rational thought becomes translated into the rational mode and made explicit, so that others can follow it.

The rational, verbal mode is primarily a method of communication. Experimental reports are made as explicit and logical as possible, so that any qualified reader can repeat the procedure. But this method of communication should not be misunderstood as implying that the experiment was *conceived* in a linear and rational manner. We leave the scruffy aspects of our thought, the hunches, the insights, out of public scientific writing. And yet without these wonderings, these "night-time" questions, we probably would not do science at all. A researcher may spend time thinking "What is the most important experiment to do?" or "How does this damn thing work?" and, after much more of such scratching about, may try performing an experiment which will aid his understanding. But the reliance on verbal rationality has caused many to feel that it is the only way in which knowledge is gained, a conception that writers of textbooks often reinforce.

The scope of psychology as it has been defined in texts, in the teaching of psychology, and in the bulk of research reports, has been unduly limited to one *special* case of man, one *special* method of study, one *special* manner in which consciousness can operate. Just as John Watson found it necessary to alter the paradigm of the introspectionists in order to open up inquiry, so we are faced with a similar situation today, a need to return to a psychology whose scope was well-stated by William James: "Our normal waking consciousness, rational consciousness as we call it, is but one special type of consciousness, whilst all about it, parted from it by the filmiest of screens, there lie potential forms of consciousness entirely different." [5]

In performing research, we are often unaware of the full effect of our tools, be they physical instruments or doctrines such as behaviorism. We often imagine that tools, like sensory organs, serve exclusively to extend awareness, but in fact we are wrong. Both serve to limit as well as extend. Abraham Maslow, commenting on the effects of a strict behaviorism in psychology, said, "If the only tool you have is a hammer, you tend to treat everything as if it were a nail." [6] A corrective needs to be applied, one which can open up the scope of psychological inquiry to the relevant questions once again. Even if all the "simple" questions cannot be fully answered at the moment by available methods, the perspective will not be lost. Part of this change involves the explicit recognition that, all too often, the *method* of psychology has itself become the goal; this confusion has led, in the past sixty years, to a "radical underestimation" of the possibilities, to use Jacob Needleman's phrase.[7]

Contemporary psychology has just recently progressed beyond such a limited conception as is exemplified by our rugseller. A new and extended conception of man is beginning to emerge, one which includes many capacities beyond the "normal" limits.

There are many recent developments that have begun to extend the scope of psychology. Psychologists are people of their culture, and our particular culture is in the midst of profound change. There exists a "counter-cultural" community opposed to Science, and exhibiting a tremendous distaste for rational thought and its products—logic, machines, computers, technology. And, although science ought not summarily to abandon the tools that have been so brilliantly developed in the past century, this radical distaste does result from a certain excess within the scientific community and within modern psychology as well. Some aspect of the complementary mode of knowledge, which is *a*rational, nonlinear, and personal in nature, could be incorporated into a more complete psychology, both on a personal and on a scientific level.[8]

A second input comes from the widespread interest in consciousness-altering drugs, such as the psychedelics. These drugs have experientially demonstrated to many, as they did to William James, that ordinary consciousness is not the only way in which consciousness can operate.

Perhaps much more importantly, many "esoteric" disciplines have become available and popular in the United States in recent years. They range from the merely bizarre and degenerate to the accumulated work of thousands of years of personal investigation into the problems of psychology. These more-developed traditions include Zen Buddhism, the Buddhism of Tibet, Sufism, and some aspects of Yoga. These disciplines have not yet been fully integrated into the West, although involvement with them has already shown many people that consciousness can be extended into areas beyond those defined as the current limits of contemporary psychology.

In concert with a shift in cultural interest, as more and more sophisticated research tools are developed, new areas of investigation open up to "legitimate" science. A purely descriptive, behavioristic approach is no longer the sole option available to experimental psychologists. For instance, electrophysiology researchers are able to detect subtle changes in brain and eye activity during sleep which signal the advent of dreaming. With this technological development, dreams can be researched objectively. Then, scientific psychology is able to admit the study of dreams, once that most private and "mentalistic" of phenomena, into the main current of science.

The problem, though, goes deeper. Many in this culture have observed that the contents of science have become extremely overrefined, more and more difficult for the general public to understand, more and more remote from their concerns, more and more specialized and abstract. In psychology, the attempt at methodological refinement these last sixty years has caused us to discard much of essential importance. Consider the process of refining wheat. Refined wheat is much more easily packaged and stored than whole. Refined wheat does not spoil as quickly as whole wheat. But refined wheat has lost much of the nutritional value of whole wheat—its essence. In psychology we, too, have discarded much of the essence—consciousness—in the process of refining the methods.

I think it now necessary to restore our psychological endeavors to completeness. However, awareness of this necessity has been lacking in some recent efforts. The position of many involved in conventional scientific investigation is depicted in a famous story.

Several blind men attempt to investigate an elephant. One who has the trunk says, "It is long and soft and emits air." Another, holding the legs, says, "It is massive, cylindrical, and hard." Another, touching the skin, "It is rough and scaly." All are misinformed. All generalize from partial knowledge.

For a psychology of consciousness, the major import of this story should be to make us recognize clearly that more than one way of knowing is possible. Each person standing at one part of the elephant can make his own limited, analytic assessment of the situation, but we do not obtain an elephant by adding "scaly," "long and soft," "massive and cylindrical" together in any conceivable proportion. Without the development of an over-all perspective, we remain lost in our individual investigations. Such a perspective is a province of another mode of knowledge, and cannot be achieved in the same way that individual parts are explored. It does not arise out of a linear sum of independent observations.

The intent of this book is to document the existence in man of two major modes of consciousness: one is analytic, the other holistic. The first is analogous to the process of viewing the individual parts of the elephant, the second to viewing the whole animal. They are complementary; both have their functions. Another way to convey the dichotomy is to point to the difference between the "rational" and "intuitive" sides of man. In our intellectual history, we have separated these two modes of knowing into separate areas of specialization, into Science and Religion, for example. Those who use one approach have rarely commerced with the other. With the breakup of organized religion as a major cultural force, science has become the dominant influence in our culture. It is natural, then, that the textbook ideal of scientific knowledge has become a dominant mode of knowledge within our culture. This mode is largely analytic, verbal, linear, and rational.

We deemphasize and even devalue the *a*rational, nonverbal modes of consciousness. Education consists predominantly of "readin', 'ritin', and 'rithmetic," and we are taught precious little about our emotions, our bodies, our intuitive capabilities. A strict emphasis on verbal intellectual knowledge has screened out much of what is or could be legitimate for study in contemporary psychology—"esoteric" systems of meditation are much misunderstood; the existence of "nonordinary realities" is not studied because they do not fit into the dominant paradigm, and neither, of course, do phenomena named "paranormal." Yet there are reports in popular and scientific circles of "paranormal" capacities—of yogis learning to control their hearts and metabolism, for instance, or of telepathy during dreams. These have not yet been fully explored, just as our friend at the beginning of the chapter is not able to conceive and use a number higher than 100.

Suppose there were two completely independent groups of investigators; one group (scientists) works exclusively during the day, the other (the mysterious "esoteric" psychologists) works exclusively at night, neither communicating well with the other. If those who work at night look up and see the faint starlight in the sky, and concentrate on the movements of the stars, they may produce documents which predict the positions of the stars at any given time, but these writings will be totally incomprehensible to someone who experiences only daylight. The brilliance of the sun obscures the subtle light of the stars from view.

A modern scientific psychologist may read in an obscure esoteric book about the existence of these "points of subtle light" and attempt to locate them, by his usual means of investigation—during the daytime. No matter how open and honest the investigator, and how dutiful his observations, he will be simply unable to find the "subtle light" in the brilliance of the day. The failure of many scientific investigators to locate the "subtle light" will only strengthen their conviction that the "stars" do not exist. The methods of science, then, have largely focused on one mode of knowing—identified with daytime. Contemporary science has developed methodology and discovered laws which are valid, and which have proven essential to the development of our civilization, but which may be only a special case, as, say, Newtonian mechanics is to Einsteinian.

As the esoteric disciplines of other cultures become accessible to the West, they emerge as *psychologies* which have specialized in that inward, receptive space of the "night." Their often-misunderstood techniques are exercises designed to alter the human nervous system, in an analogous manner to turning off the brilliant light of the day until the faint stars are perceptible.

Until quite recently, communication between the two types of psychology has been very limited. Western science has tended to ignore, and even to deny, the existence of these "faint signals," since they are not visible under normal observation conditions. On the other side, certain "mystics," and others of the esoteric traditions, have compounded the problem by labeling ordinary consciousness an "illusion"— which it may be to him who never enters the daylight. Then, of course, each side has its inevitable internal arguments, and overconcern with local color and methodology, be it commitment to a maze-learning experiment with all its rituals, or a particular kind of meditation exercise with all *its* ritual and stylized behavior.

Communication has begun to open up in our culture, so that it now appears that neither view is complete; the day is incomplete without the night. Each is a special case with its own laws.

This book is an attempt to redress the balance, to begin to integrate the rational and intuitive approaches to knowing, and to consider the essential complementary of these two modes of consciousness as they are manifest in science in general, in psychology in particular, and within each person psychologically and physiologically. A growing body of evidence demonstrates that each person has two major modes of consciousness available, one linear and rational, one *a*rational and intuitive.

Our highest creative achievements are the products of the complementary functioning of the two modes. Our intuitive knowledge is never explicit, never precise in the scientific sense. It is only when the intellect can begin to process the intuitive leaps, to explain and "translate" the intuition into operational and functional knowledge that scientific understanding becomes complete. It is the function of the verbal-scientific intellect to fit the intuition into the linear mode, so that ideas may be explicitly tested and communicated in the scientific manner. The linear, rational mode is not the only way in which we understand, but it is a way in which we can clarify and communicate that which we understand.

Current psychology is undergoing the first stirrings of a synthesis of the two modes. These may form the beginning of a more complete science of human consciousness, with an extended conception of our own capabilities. This "new" conception of possibility is the ancient one of the traditional, esoteric psychologies, but it is beginning to be combined with the methods and technology of contemporary science.

It is time, once again, to open up psychology as a discipline, to return to its primary business—an examination of conscious experience, with the new tools which have been so painstakingly developed during this past century. It would be premature to try to delimit, or quantitatively define, this new area. Rather, it is a time to redefine psychology itself and, once again, to extend the boundaries of our own possibilities.

For further reading

Thomas S. Kuhn. *The Structure of Scientific Revolutions.* Chicago: University of Chicago Press, 1962.

W. I. B. Beveridge. *The Art of Scientific Investigation.* New York: Random House, 1950.

Abraham Maslow. *The Psychology of Science.* Chicago: Henry Regnery, 1966.

William James. "The Scope of Psychology," in *The Principles of Psychology,* I, 1–8. New York: Dover Publications, 1950. Original copyright, 1890. Also reprinted in Robert Ornstein, ed., *The Nature of Human Consciousness.* San Francisco: W. H. Freeman and Co. New York: The Viking Press. 1973.

Thomas R. Blackburn. "Sensuous-Intellectual Complementarity in Science," *Science,* 172 (June 4, 1971), 1003–1007. Also reprinted in Ornstein, *The Nature of Human Consciousness.*

Liam Hudson. *The Cult of the Fact.* New York: Harper & Row. London: Jonathan Cape. 1973.

Chapter 2

"Ordinary" Consciousness: A Personal Construction

Seeing Double

A father said to his double-seeing son, "Son, you see two instead of one."

"How can that be?" the boy replied. "If I were, there would seem to be four moons up there in place of two." [1]

We can begin the study of consciousness with ourselves. Consider your own normal consciousness, and reflect for a moment on its contents: you will probably find it a mixture of thoughts, fantasies, ideas, and sensations of the external world. Objects appear, such as trees, books, chairs. We are aware of people, as bodies in space, as personalities, as voices. We move in tridimensional space and actively manipulate perceived objects—we may turn the page of a book, sit in a chair, speak to someone, listen to a lecturer. Normally, our personal consciousness is our whole world, and this equation can be considered successful to the extent that it enables us to survive.

But although we are sure that the world we experience has some physical validity, we usually go a bit further. At each moment of each day, we make the same mistake as the double-seeing son—we consider that our own personal consciousness *is* the world, that an outside "objective" reality is perfectly represented by our experience. Most people never realize there is an issue here, since for ordinary purposes our experience is reality.

Some early Walt Disney cartoons portrayed such an understanding. In some episodes a Little Man at a switch-board in the brain projected physical "pictures" of the world on a Consciousness Screen. The pictures, of course, were a perfect reflection of the external world.

A moment's thought, though, will show that the idea of a personal consciousness as a perfect mirror of an external reality cannot be true. If there were a Consciousness Screen, who could see it? Does the Little Man have another Little Man inside him? And sometimes we do experience objects which are *not* physically present. We hallucinate, imagine, distort. Each night we dream and experience events and objects which are totally produced by ourselves.

Consider also the enormous variety of physical energies

which impinge on us at each moment. To take one instance, "the air," or more properly, the geophysical environment, carries energy in the electromagnetic band: visible light, X-rays, radio waves, infrared radiation. In addition, there is mechanical vibration of the air, containing the information of sound; the constant energy from the gravitational field; pressure on the body; gaseous matter in the air. We also generate our own internal stimuli—thoughts, internal organ sensations, muscular activity, pains, feelings, and much more. These processes all occur simultaneously, and continue as long as we are alive; yet we are certainly not aware of each process at each moment. Our personal consciousness, then, cannot fully represent the external world or even our internal world, but must consist of an extremely small fraction of the entire "reality." We do not even possess the sensory systems to receive many energy forms.

Many questions arise once we realize that our personal consciousness is extremely limited. "How do we ever manage to maintain a stable consciousness in the face of all the stimuli which impinge on us?" "What is the nature of our experience of the world?" "Why is it necessary for our personal consciousness to be limited?"

Personal consciousness is outward-oriented, involving action for the most part. It seems to have been evolved for the primary purpose of ensuring individual biological survival, for which active manipulation of discrete objects, sensitivity to forces which may pose a threat, separation of oneself from others, are very useful. We first *select* the sensory modalities of personal consciousness from the mass of information reaching us. This is done by a multilevel process of filtration, for the most part sorting out survival-related stimuli. We are then able to *construct* a stable consciousness from the filtered input.

If we can realize, from the outset, that our ordinary consciousness is something we must of necessity construct or *create* in order to survive in the world, then we can understand that this consciousness is only *one* possible consciousness. And if this consciousness is a *personal* construction, then each person can change his consciousness simply by *changing the way* he constructs it. The psychologist William James compared this process to that of a sculptor carving a statue out of marble—the process largely involves selection and limitation, but each sculptor's statue is unique, as is each person's consciousness.

We see that the mind is at every stage a theatre of simultaneous possibilities. Consciousness consists in the comparison of these with each other, the selection of some, and the suppression of others, of the rest by the reinforcing and inhibiting agency of attention. The highest and most celebrated mental products are filtered from the data chosen by the faculty next beneath, out of the mass offered by the faculty below that, which mass was in turn sifted from a still larger amount of yet simpler material, and so on. The mind, in short, works on the data it received much as a sculptor works on his block of stone. In a sense, the statue stood there from eternity. But there were a thousand different ones beside it. The sculptor alone is to thank for having extricated this one from the rest. Just so the world of each of us, however different our several views of it may be, all lay embedded in the primordial chaos of sensations, which gave the mere *matter* to the thought of all of us indifferently. We may, if we like, by our reasoning unwind things back to that black and jointless continuity of space and moving clouds of swarming atoms which science calls the only real world. But all the while the world we feel and live in will be that which our ancestors and we, by slowly cumulative strokes of choice, have extricated out of this, like sculptors, by simply rejecting certain portions of the given stuff. Other sculptors, other statues from the same stone! Other minds, other worlds, from the same monotonous and inexpressive chaos! My world is but one in a million, alike embedded and alike real to those who may abstract them. How different must be the world in the consciousness of ants, cuttlefish, or crab! [2]

How, then, do we take the chaos and "make sense" out of it? Each of us selects and constructs a personal world in several ways. Our sense organs gather information which the brain can modify and sort. This heavily filtered input is compared with memory, expectations, and body movements until, finally, our consciousness is constructed as a "best guess" about reality.

THE SENSES AS DATA-REDUCTION SYSTEMS

We normally consider that our senses are the "windows" to the world—we see with our eyes, hear with our ears. But such a view, though it is certainly valid, is not entirely true, for a primary function of sensory systems taken as a whole is to discard "irrelevant" information, such as X-rays, infrared radiation, or ultrasonics. Aldous Huxley most elegantly stated this idea. In *The Doors of Perception*, Huxley quotes C. D. Broad:

> The function of the brain and nervous system is to protect us from being overwhelmed and confused by this mass of largely useless and irrelevant knowledge, by shutting out most of what we should otherwise perceive and remember at any given moment, leaving only that very small and special selection that is likely to be practically useful.

And then Huxley comments:

> According to such theory each one of us is potentially Mind at Large. But insofar as we are animals our business is at all costs to survive. To make biological survival possible, Mind at Large has to be funneled through the reducing valve of the brain and nervous system. What comes out at the other end is a measly trickle of the kind of consciousness which will help us to stay alive on the surface of this particular planet. To formulate and express the contents of this reduced awareness man has invented and endlessly elaborated those symbol-systems and implicit philosophies that we call languages. Every individual is at once the beneficiary and the victim of the linguistic tradition into which he has been born—the beneficiary inasmuch as language gives access to the accumulated records of other people's experience, the victim insofar as it confirms him in the belief that

reduced awareness is the only awareness, and as it bedevils his sense of reality, so that he is all too apt to take his concepts for data, his words for actual things. That which, in the language of religion, is called "this world" is the universe of reduced awareness expressed and, as it were, petrified by language. The various "other worlds" with which human beings erratically make contact are so many elements in the totality of awareness belonging to Mind at Large. Most people most of the time know only what comes through the reducing valve is consecrated as genuinely real by their local language. Certain persons, however, seem to be born with a kind of bypass that circumvents the reducing valve. In others temporary bypasses may be acquired either spontaneously or as the result of deliberate "spiritual exercises" or through hypnosis or by means of drugs. Through these permanent or temporary bypasses there flows, not indeed the perception "of everything that is happening everywhere in the universe" (for the bypass does not abolish the reducing valve which still excludes the total content of the Mind at Large), but something more than, and above all something different from, the carefully selected, utilitarian material which our narrow individual minds regard as a complete, or at least sufficient, picture of reality.[3]

Consider the most important avenue of personal consciousness, the eye. It responds to radiant electromagnetic energy in the visible spectrum. If we consult a chart of the electromagnetic spectrum, we note that the "visible" spectrum is but one tiny slit in the entire energy band. The entire spectrum ranges in wavelength from less than one billionth of a meter to more than a thousand meters; yet we can "see" only the tiny portion between 400 and 700 billionths of a meter. In addition to electromagnetic energy, many other forces arrive at the eye—pressure, mechanical vibrations in the air, gaseous matter, etc.—but the eye is "by design" ignorant of these.

We cannot possibly experience the world as it fully exists—we would be overwhelmed. We are restricted by our physical evolution to only a few sensory dimensions. If we do not possess a "sense" for a given energy-form, we do not

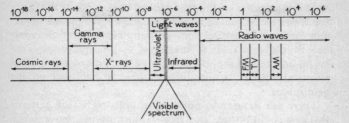

Figure 2.1
The electromagnetic spectrum.

experience its existence. It is almost impossible for us to imagine an energy-form or an object outside our normal receptive range. What would infrared radiation or an X-ray "look" like? What is the "sound" of a one-cycle note? Or, as in Zen, what would be the sound of one hand clapping? These questions may be difficult to grasp. It may be easier if we descend a bit on the evolutionary scale and examine an animal whose sensory systems, evolved for its survival, limit even more than do ours, ignoring dimensions of the external world which are a part of our own experience.

Perhaps the clearest relevant research has been on the visual system of the frog. The eye of the frog was studied by Lettvin, Maturana, McCulloch, and Pitts at the Massachusetts Institute of Technology. They were interested, essentially, in the same point made by Huxley, that sensory systems serve mainly for data *reduction*.[4]

They devised an experiment in which visual stimulation could be offered to one eye of an immobilized frog. The frog was so situated that its eye was at the center of a hemisphere seven inches in radius. Small objects could be placed in different positions on the inner surface of this hemisphere by means of magnets, or they could be moved around in the space inside the hemisphere. The investigators implanted microelectrodes into the frog's optic nerve to measure, as they called it, "what the frog's eye tells the frog's brain"—the electrical impulses sent to the brain by the eye. Since the frog's eye is somewhat similar to our own, these investigators hoped that electrical recording from the optic nerve would discriminate the different kinds of "messages" that the eye sends to the brain, and reveal the relationship of the evoked patterns of electrical activity to the different objects displayed on the hemisphere.

There are thousands, millions, of different visual patterns that one could present to a frog—colors, shapes, movements, in various combinations—choosing them from the almost infinite richness of the visual world of which humans are normally aware. However, in presenting many different objects, colors, movements to the frog, the investigators observed a remarkable phenomenon: from all the different kinds of stimulation presented, only four different kinds of "messages" were sent from the retina to the brain. In other words, no matter what complexity and subtle differences are present in the environment, the frog's eye is "wired up" to send only a very few different messages. The frog's eye presumably evolved to *discard* the remainder of the information available.

The structure of its eye limits the frog's awareness to only four different kinds of visual activity. Lettvin and his co-workers termed the four related systems *sustained contrast detectors, moving-edge detectors, net dimming detectors,* and *net convexity detectors.* The first provides the general outline of the environment; the second seems to enhance response to sudden moving shadows, like that of a bird of prey; the third responds to a sudden decrease in light, as when a large enemy is attacking. These are systems which have presumably evolved to extract information relevant to survival and to discard the rest, in the manner described by Huxley.

The fourth type of "message," conveyed by the net convexity detectors, is the one most obviously related to the frog's biological needs and is the most interesting system. The net convexity detectors do not respond to any general change in light or to contrast; they respond only when small dark objects come into the field of vision, and move quite close to the eye. It is quite clear, then, how the frog gets its food, how it can see flying bugs even with its limited visual system. The frog has evolved its own subsystem, which is wired up to ignore all "irrelevant" information and to notice only that of bugs flying around close to it—a very specialized "bug-perceiving" subsystem.

So, out of the complexity and richness of the information presented to the eye, the frog seems to select only four different classes of events. Higher-level animals exhibit similar selectivity, but in a much more complicated way. This type of electrophysiological analysis has been extended to cats and monkeys by David Hubel and Torsten Weisel at Harvard University, and now by many other investigators, who have determined that different cells in the cortex of mammals respond to different types of sensory stimulation. They found that certain cells detect edges and corners, others respond to movement on the retina, etc. Although vision has been the sensory system most often studied (since it is relatively easy to record from the visual system and to specify the stimulus dimension), one would also expect other sensory modalities to show the same kinds of relationships.

It is the function of sensory systems, then, by their physiological design to reduce the amount of "useless and irrelevant" information reaching us and to serve as selection systems. The information input through the senses seems to be gathered for the primary purpose of biological survival. The frog is a clear physiological demonstration of this highly evolved selective system.

All human beings are similarly evolved to select certain common aspects of the physical universe: we possess eyes which receive radiant electromagnetic energy; ears which receive mechanical vibrations; a nose; touch sensors; taste. It is easy, then, to assume that these exhaust the extent of the real known world. After all, there is "consensual validation"— friends agree that there is a tree "out there," a bird in song, a dinner on the table. It is important to realize that this kind of "validation" is limited to the con-sensual—with the senses. Our "agreement" on reality is subject to common shared limitations that evolved to ensure the biological survival of the race. All humans may agree on certain events only because we are all similarly limited in our very structure as well as limited in our culture. Like the double-seeing son, it is very easy for us to confuse our common agreement with an external reality. If everyone "saw" double, for instance, we would believe that two moons existed. As can well be imagined from the limited nature of our senses, our agreement covers but a small portion of what actually exists, as the noontime is to an entire day-night cycle.

HIGH-LEVEL SELECTIVITY "TUNING"

Ascend the evolutionary ladder from the frog, and consider more and more complex organisms. The avenues of sensation become more complex, multimodal. More importantly, though, the *flexibility* of the sensory systems themselves becomes much greater, because of the increasing programmability of the central nervous system. To make use of familiar machine analogies, the sensory systems of some animals are like permanently wired-up, simple machines. In a mousetrap or a pencil sharpener, or even in a telephone or an automobile, a change in one part throws everything else out of adjustment, since the machine has no built-in capacity for internal reorganization. As we consider more complicated animals, more and more advanced all the way up to man, their nervous systems seem to be more computer-like—machines, to be sure, but ones that can alter the relationship between input and performance by a change in the program. The higher mammals can be regarded as machines that are capable of reprogramming themselves in accordance with alterations in the external environment. This is not to say that there are no limits to their performance. Even the most sophisticated current computer has its physical limitations. No matter how the computer alters its own programs, it will never learn to fly all by itself—it has no wings. But a computer can alter itself within the limits of its own structure, as can we.

We can personally experience this computer-like, higher-level selectivity and tuning. At a party (or someplace) where several people are talking at the same time, close your eyes and listen to just one person speaking, then tune him out and listen to another person. Perhaps you will feel surprised at how easy it is to tune your attention in this way. Actually, we have little reason to be surprised at this ability, since we tune ourselves continuously to suit our needs and expectations, but the surprise comes because we are not usually *aware* of such self-tuning. The selection process is programmable, within the fixed sensory limits. When we perspire during the summer, we like the taste of foods that are more salty than usual. We don't think consciously that we need salt, and that we should take more salt in our foods; we *simply like* foods that at other times we would consider quite oversalted. Also, we continuously "set" ourselves to see objects. The character in the middle of Figure 2.2 can be seen either as a number or as a letter, depending on the context.

Figure 2.2

Many contemporary psychologists have investigated our programmability. Some have used the tachistoscope, which allows figures, objects, pictures, to be presented for short and measurable periods of time. One interesting series of experiments with the tachistoscope demonstrated that we recognize familiar objects or words in less time than unfamiliar ones. A coherent sentence, for instance, is recognized much more quickly than a random sequence of words. Our past experience "tunes" us to have some idea of what should follow what, and we need much less information to construct an image. Jerome Bruner calls this "going beyond the information given."

One naive view of the brain and nervous system has stimulated some useful research in psychology. (Recall first that the lens of the eye reverses input light energy from left to right and up to down.) A common question reflects this view: "If the eye reverses the input, then why do we see the world right-side up, when the image on the retina is upside down?" The answer, of course, is that "right-side up" and "upside down" have no meaning biologically. Since we do not see *what exists,* the question is meaningless. All we need in order to "see" is for a *consistent* relationship to exist between the external object and the pattern of excitation on the retina. In man, this pattern can be "upside down," "reversed," or any other consistent transform of the stimulus.[5]

If the visual world of a goldfish is inverted by surgical rotation, it never adapts to the alteration in input, swimming in circles forever. It may even starve, unable to reach food.[6] In contrast, if a human being or monkey's visual world is optically altered, adaptation is quite quick. In a few weeks, a man can pedal a bicycle through a crowded town wearing specially designed inverting lenses.[7] Our naive view cannot be correct. We never see the world *right-side up;* we select from the input, and construct our personal consciousness from what we have selected. So, if the visual input is inverted, there is of course an initial disturbance in the input and output systems of the brain. The normal and consistent relationship between external objects and the pattern of sensation on the retina is upset. It takes some time for us to learn the new correspondences. In reaching toward an object, we may move in the wrong direction initially, then overreach, then hit it. But gradually, in the same manner as we initially learned to see, we begin to learn the newly appropriate correspondences between input and objects. The consistency of the selection is once again restored, and we are able to ride a bicycle and see objects "right-side up."

Our eyes are also constantly in motion, in large eye

movements *(saccades)* as well as in eye tremors *(nystagmus)*. We blink our eyes almost every second, move our eyes around, move our heads and our bodies, and follow moving objects. The view of an object is never constant, and the very receptive fields on the eyes are changing all the time; yet our visual world remains quite stable. If we walk around a horse, for instance, our view is constantly changing—we sometimes see the tail, sometimes the back, or a side view, or a three-quarter view, or a straight front view—yet we always see the *same* horse. If we "saw" an "image" on our retina, the visual world would be different each second, sometimes one object, then another, sometimes a blur due to the eyes moving, sometimes darkness due to blinks. We must then *construct* a personal consciousness from the selected input, and in this way achieve some stability of awareness out of the rich and continuously changing flow of information reaching our receptors.[8]

AUTOMATIZATION

If at each moment we were aware of each quantum of energy reaching us, we would probably be overwhelmed by the flood of irrelevant information. We might not be able to discriminate enough to notice impending dangers, a tree about to fall, a truck approaching. Because we must discriminate between continuous, "safe" stimuli and survival-related ones, we have evolved sensory systems which respond primarily to alterations in the external environment. The cells in the visual cortex and the retina, for example, are specialized to detect *changes* in input and to ignore constancies (see Figure 2.3).

To take another example: there is a spot in our visual field which we can never "sense" because of the anatomy of the eye (see Figure 2.4). At the exit of the optic tract, no light energy can stimulate the retina. There is a "hole," always present in our world; our little exercise in Figure 2.4 merely makes it explicit. But since this gap in perception is always present, we *never* notice it, since we are specialized to notice change.

Further back in the central nervous system, higher levels of

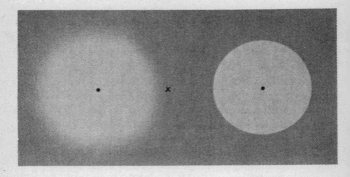

Figure 2.3

Look steadily at the left dot; the light circle disappears. You can make it reappear by looking at the X. The right-hand circle will not disappear if you stare at it, although it is as light in the center as the other circle. The visual system, like other sensory systems, is maximally sensitive to sharp changes.

Figure 2.4

To find the blind spot, close your right eye and stare at the circle. Hold the book 10 to 12 inches from the eye, and move it toward you and away until the square disappears. Notice that this "hole" is *always* present in your visual world.

brain organization allow us to respond automatically, "unconsciously," to the more complex constancies of the environment. Let us consider several examples of such constancies.

First, try this: say the word "need" over and over to yourself one hundred times. It becomes "strange," loses meaning, and it no longer seems like the same word.

That is, mere repetition of a stimulus will cause a change in consciousness.

While we are learning a new skill, like skiing, all the complex adjustments and motor movements are somewhat painfully in our awareness. As we progress, as skill becomes "automatic," the movements no longer enter consciousness. Compare the first time you tried to drive a car, especially one with a gear shift, with how it feels to drive a car now, after you've learned.

After you have learned to drive, when you travel along a road for the first time, everything appears quite new and interesting—a red house, a big tree, the road itself—but gradually, as you drive the same route over and over, you "get used" to everything on the way. You stop "seeing" the trees, the bridges, the corners, etc. You have become automatized in your response to them.

When you enter a room and a fan is turning, creating a buzzing sound, you are aware of it for the first few moments, but then the sound disappears from your awareness; you have stopped paying attention to it.

We quickly adapt to the constancies of the world; hence we constantly need new stimulation. When we buy a new phonograph record, we play it over and over again for a while, then leave it on the shelf unplayed. We get bored with it; the record no longer seems "new"; it is out of our awareness, on "automatic." Most consumer products are periodically changed slightly (automobiles, for instance), so that we begin to notice them once again, and presumably buy them.

In psychology and physiology the phenomenon we have been describing is termed "habituation." It is one of the physiological components of the "orienting reaction" to new stimuli, the reaction that is involved in our registering of input. The physiological indicators of such reaction often include a blocking of the alpha rhythm of the electroencephalogram, an increase in heart rate, and a drop in skin resistance. Suppose we measure the resistance of the skin, for example, and repeat a click every five seconds. The first click will cause a sharp drop in skin resistance. A smaller drop will be caused by the second click, still less by the third, until, depending on the parameters of the particular experiment, the skin resistance no longer drops with each click. The response of the skin to this stimulus has been habituated. After we hear the sound of a clock ticking, when the sound is turned off, we no longer show the orienting or registering reaction. This is not merely a simple process of raising the threshold for stimuli entering into awareness and thus tuning the click out. Our nervous system is capable of a more sophisticated selective tuning. It is true that if we substitute a louder click, we will begin to hear it again. But if we substitute a *softer* one, the orienting reaction also returns, and we will hear it again. If we change the interval between the clicks—if a click appears a little later than we expect or a bit sooner—it returns to awareness, and the orienting reaction reappears.

Karl Pribram has pointed out another example of this phenomenon, which he called the "Bowery El" effect. An elevated railroad once ran along Third Avenue in New York City. At a certain time, late each night, a noisy train ran. The train line was torn down some time ago, with some interesting aftereffects. Many people in the neighborhood called the police to report "something strange" occurring late at night—noises, thieves, burglars, etc. The police determined that these calls took place around the time of the former late-night train. What these people were "hearing," of course, was the *absence* of the familiar noise of the train. We have such an experience, although often a much simpler one, whenever a noise that has been continuing suddenly stops.[9]

If we look at the same object over and over again, we begin to look at it in the same way each time. We do this with the constancies of our world, our ordinary surroundings, such as the pictures in our house, or the routes we drive every day. Charles Furst has studied the effect of repeated viewing of the same picture on the way we look at it. He found that eye movements tend to become more and more stereotyped as the same visual stimulus is presented. When we see a new image, our eyes tend to move in a new pattern around it, but as we see it again and again, as we see the rooms in our house, we tend to look in a fixed way at fixed portions of it and ignore or tune out the rest.[10] The "Bowery El" effect, the "Furst" effect, and other studies on habituation suggest that we tune out the recurrences of the world by making a "model" of the external world within our nervous system, and testing input against it. We somehow can program, and continuously revise or reprogram, our models of the external world. If the input and the model agree, as they do most often for the constancies of the world, then the input stays out of consciousness. If there is any disagreement, if the new input is recognizably different, slower, softer, louder, different in form or color, or even absent, we become aware of the input once again. This programming forms an additional, active selection process imposed on the data that gets through the relatively fixed reducing valves of the senses. In everyday situations there is more tolerance than in these laboratory demonstrations; much more discrepancy can be tolerated, although how much depends on the situation.

OUR ASSUMPTIVE WORLD

Perhaps the clearest and most striking trend in the psychology and physiology of perception in the past few years has been our increasing understanding of the interactive and constructive nature of ordinary awareness. One of the leaders in this field of investigation, Jerome Bruner, has emphasized that perception involves acts of categorization.[11] As we mature, we attempt to make more and more consistent "sense" out of the mass of information arriving at our receptors. We develop stereotyped systems, or *categories,* for sorting input. The set of categories we develop is limited, much more limited than the input. Simple categories may be "straight," or "red." More complex ones may be "English," or "in front of." In social situations, the categories may be personality traits. If we categorize a person as "aggressive," we then consistently tend to sort all his actions in terms of this category.

Previous experience with objects and events strengthens

personal category systems as it does a scientific paradigm. We expect cars to make a certain noise, traffic lights to be a certain color, food to smell a certain way, and certain people to say certain things. But what we actually experience, according to Bruner and others, is the *category* which is evoked by a particular stimulus, *not* the occurrence in the external world.

The anomalous-card experiment that Bruner and his associates carried out was an attempt to demonstrate the effects of our well-learned categories on the contents of awareness. Our past experience with playing cards evokes categories in which the colors and the forms of playing cards are "supposed" to fall. The import of these and others of Bruner's demonstrations is that at each moment we construct a model of the world, expect certain correspondences of objects, colors and forms to occur, and then experience our categories.

THE TRANSACTIONALISTS

About the time Bruner was studying the effects of categories, another group of psychologists, led by Adelbert Ames, was exploring the nature of awareness. Ames characterized ordinary awareness as a "transaction" between the perceiver and the environment. In spite of the overflow of information available to our sense organs at any given time, *relevant* information is often lacking. Color information, for instance, is directly present on the retina, but we cannot determine tridimensionality directly. We cannot immediately know whether a room is "really" rectangular or not, or whether a given chair is physically closer than others, since we do not possess a direct monocular sense of distance. There are, however, perceptible dimensions usually associated with closeness of objects. If we assume that two objects we are looking at are the same size, then the one that looks larger would be closer to us. That is, if we are trying to determine closeness, we "bet" that the "larger" object is the closer. However, this "bet" is not a conscious process of correction. We *directly experience* the larger object as closer. The Ames group set out to demonstrate the nature of the "bet" we make with the environment.[12]

By manipulating "unconscious inference," as Helmholtz called it, we can become aware of the bets or, in Bruner's term, the categories that constitute our awareness. To give another example, when we see a line drawing of a room as in Figure 2.5, A, we "bet" that in a top view it would be shaped like a rectangle. But a rectangle is only one of the many possible forms that could be derived from the two-dimensional drawing. One side may not be parallel with the other, so the top view might look like Figure 2.5, C, or 2.5, D, or might be some other shape entirely. We bet that the room is rectangular because almost all the rooms in our experience have been rectangular. But if the room is in fact not rectangular, our bet causes us to "see" objects or people in the room in a very strange way (see Figure 2.6).

George Kelly pursued a similar line of investigation, concerned more with the psychology of ordinary experience and with clinical psychology. His conception was that each person *creates* his own world by means of his "personal constructs." He considered these "constructs" similar to scientific hypotheses, in that they are generated on the basis of our past experience and are applied to new experiences as long as they seem to work. So, for Kelly, our experience of the world consists of our constructs, as it consists of categories for Bruner and of transactions for the Ames group. Kelly was a psychotherapist, and his therapy was based on the belief that a patient's problems were in large part due to his poor construction of the situation. The treatment involved a "prescription" of new constructions that the patient could apply to his life.[13]

HOW THE BRAIN CONTROLS ITS INPUT

Since we can tune ourselves in terms of our category systems, there must be physiological mechanisms that allow this tuning to take place. Karl Pribram and Nico Spinelli have set out to demonstrate a physiological analog of this process.

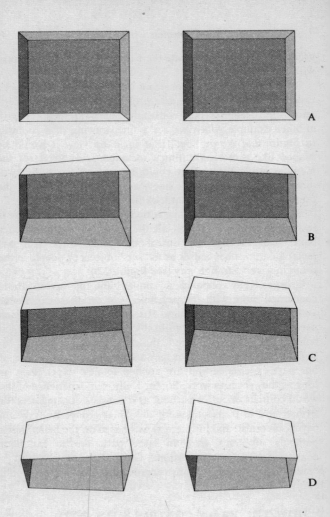

Figure 2.5
If we look at the top figures, we immediately assume that they are
rectilinear. However, many shapes can give rise to the impression of
rectilinearity, as this drawing illustrates: as the front of each box tilts
downward, we can see that they are not rectilinear at all.

Figure 2.6
A photograph of the "distorted room" at the Exploratorium, San Francisco.

They recorded from cells in the frontal cortex of the brain while stimulating the retina, and showed that the patterns in which the receptive fields of the retina respond to external stimuli can be altered by the brain. That is, the way in which stimuli are received, even on the retina itself, can be reprogrammed from moment to moment, and this ability can be demonstrated physiologically.[14] These and other experiments demonstrate that the motor-output system of the brain (efference) has an effect on the input (afference): the brain "selects its input."

The investigation of the active role of the brain's output in determining the contents of awareness has been a recent major trend in the psychophysiology of perception. The work of Bruner, of the transactionalists, and of Kelly demonstrate this active role on a psychological level; that of Pribram and Spinelli on the physiological. Some investigators have been explicitly concerned with how the relationship between the input processing and the output systems of the brain affects the contents of awareness. There is a test we can try: Close one eye, and push the other eye gently from the outside corner. The visual world seems to shake a bit, to jump about discontinuously. But if we move the eye in the usual manner over the same space, the world does not seem to shake. This difference indicates that in constructing our awareness we must also take our own movements (motor output of the brain) into account and correlate them with the changes in input. If we did not possess records of our efference (in this case, our eye movements), the visual world would be constantly jumping around.

Some researchers have even argued that consciousness depends *solely* on the output of the brain, no matter what the input is that keys off a given output. Roger Sperry has emphasized this point, and after him Leon Festinger and his associates have provided some experimental demonstrations of this idea.[15] Their contention, that awareness depends solely on output regardless of input, is consistent with Bruner's contention that the category activated will determine awareness. For example, if you are "ready" to see a black ace of spades or a red ace of hearts when a red ace of spades is shown, you will see one of the two choices you have set for yourself. Or, if you are "ready" to make a straight eye movement in response to a curved line, you will see the curved line as straight.

TRANSITORY CHARACTERISTICS
OF PERSONAL CONSCIOUSNESS

The very physiology of our senses and central nervous system in large part determines the characteristics of our personally constructed worlds. However, we have further limitations on our perceptions. We are each subject to moment-to-moment changes in our personal worlds. We each have a specific personal history, and have undergone training which can partially program consciousness (schooling, jobs, special interests, etc.). Moreover, all of us, within a given culture, share a set of "unconscious" assumptions given us by the very organization of the culture and by our possession of a common language.

Individual consciousness is not wholly stable: biases and assumptions shift, as do our needs and intents. We are sometimes hungry, sometimes full, sometimes sexually attracted, sometimes sated, sometimes tired, sometimes alert. Our consciousness is constructed differently on these occasions. When hungry, we seem to notice food, aromas, and restaurants more than when we are full. Awaiting the arrival of a friend, we may immediately tune ourselves to notice anyone who remotely resembles him or her. When we are interested in the opposite sex, we perceive them differently than when we are not. The thirteenth-century Persian poet Jallaludin Rumi noted this phenomenon when he wrote: "What a piece of bread looks like depends on whether you are hungry or not."

For this area, as for many other important dimensions of personal consciousness, some of the most relevant psychological experiments have been performed by Jerome Bruner and by the transactionalist group. In one experiment, Bruner studied poor and well-to-do children. Noting that need may alter the characteristics of consciousness, Bruner found that children from poor homes tended to think a given coin larger than their more fortunate peers did. In addition, the poor children thought nickels were worth more than dimes.[16] What money looks like depends on whether you are poor or not.

Albert Hastorf and Hadley Cantril studied an event at a Princeton-Dartmouth football game. A football game is a suitable place to observe the transitory influences on consciousness caused by the extreme biases which may be called up by an emotional involvement with one side or the other. In this particular game, the star quarterback of the Princeton team was injured. Hastorf and Cantril asked two groups of spectators to record their experiences at the game on a questionnaire. The Princeton fans reported undue violence and aggressions directed unfairly toward their quarterback; the Dartmouth fans experienced the game as rough, but fair.[17] What an injury looks like depends on whether you are from Princeton or not.

THE STREAM OF THOUGHTS

Our thoughts are transitory, fleeting, moving from one idea, object, image to another; yet it is always the same consciousness that flows from experience to experience. More than any other factor, thoughts are the foundation of normal consciousness. We maintain and refresh our personal construction through continued thoughts. William James presents the most suitable metaphor.

> Consciousness then does not appear to itself chopped up in bits. Such words as "chain" or "train" do not describe it fitly, as it presents itself in the first instant. It is nothing jointed, it flows. A "river" or a "stream" are the metaphors by which it is naturally described. *In talking of it thereafter, let us call it the stream of thought, of consciousness, or of subjective life.*[18]

ENDURING CHARACTERISTICS OF PERSONAL CONSCIOUSNESS

Each person is a unique individual, with a certain family history, training, profession, interests. These background factors deeply influence the differences in our personal consciousnesses. Any given event of "spacetime" is infinitely rich in itself; but this richness will be perceived variously, depending on the perceiver. Consider a scene in a park on a Sunday afternoon. An artist walking through may note the quality of the light, the colors of the leaves on the trees, the geometric forms of the landscape. A psychologist might notice the people present, their mannerisms, interactions, speech patterns. A physician, looking at the same people, might notice not their interactions, but their body structures and their health. A botanist might ignore the people, to focus on the flowers. One woman may remember words, another gestures. One man may be fascinated by a particular smell in the air, while another may be too immersed in his own thoughts and fantasies to register anything about the external environment.

Whole lives can be spent directing personal consciousness to one small portion of the world. One person's attention can be occupied by sailboats, becoming an expert on the winds, rigging, hull design; another is concerned with taste and smell, learning to discriminate a 1947 red Bordeaux wine from a 1949 of the same chateau.

It seems that one of the most basic differences between individuals is between those who tend to employ the linear, verbal mode and those who are less verbal and more involved in spatial imagery. The scientist, the writer, the mathematician are examples of the culturally "dominant" verbal-rational mode. The visual artist, the craftsman, the musician, the teacher of body movement may be examples of another mode. Of course, each of us works in both modes: almost everyone speaks and reads; we all move in three-dimensional space. However, some people are more specialized in one mode of operation than others, which often makes communication difficult between, say, husband and wife, if one is a scientist, the other an artist.

Cultural Characteristics

A primary motivation in life is biological survival, both of the individual and of the species. To survive individually, man adopts a mode of active manipulation of the external environment. This mode could be considered an *analytic* position toward the world, involving an attempt to separate oneself from other people, other living organisms, and other objects. At times this separation may be essential for an individual's survival. If man had put up no boundaries between a personal identity and the remainder of creation when, say, a wild animal approached, the race might not have survived.

This mode of individual survival is active, geared to the consciousness of external events, to analysis, and to linearity. By linearity, I largely refer to the consciousness of events enduring in time, in sequence, of causes and effects. Such linearity is essential in the development of an organized culture. It is necessary for planning into the future, for taking the lessons of past history into account.

Language and science can be considered quite refined aspects of this mode. They allow us to dissect, discriminate, and divide the external environment into consistent segments which can be actively manipulated. They enable us to record experience cumulatively, to transmit information at a distance, and even to partake of the wisdom of those long dead.

To use a language is to use a set of ready-made categories that must help shape individual consciousness. Contemporary Americans possess only a few words for snow, the Eskimo many. We use one word for love, the mystic many. According to Benjamin Lee Whorf, language is an organ of the mind.[19] Within a linguistic community, the common language provides an almost unconsciously agreed-on set of categories for experience, and allows the speakers of that language to ignore experiences excluded by the common category system: "Is there any number higher than 100?" Similarly, our eye allows us to perceive radiant electromagnetic energy in the band between 400 and 700 billionths of a meter, but forces us to ignore everything else.

Science as a Mode of Knowing

Personal consciousness is a continual process of selection and construction, at each stage becoming more and more conservative. As a refinement of the active, personal mode, science is one of the most restricted and sure forms of knowledge available to man. Our senses limit; our central nervous system limits; our personal and cultural categories limit; language limits; and beyond all these selections, the rules of science cause us to further select information which we consider to be true. By a slow, conservative process of construction, science gradually builds a stable core of knowledge. Science is the very essence of the analytic mode, one of meticulously charting causes and effects, of radically restricting the conditions of observation in order to attain precision. It constitutes another highly specialized development of consciousness, at once its most conservative, yet its most reliable.

Most cultures are fundamentally based on this active, linear mode—the way of language, science, and history. Ours is so thoroughly based on it that many have almost forgotten that other constructions of individual consciousness, other cultural styles, are even possible.

The anthropologist Dorothy Lee studied the people of the Trobriand Islands and reports that their lack of linearity is evident even in language. In lieu of a sequential construction, the Trobrianders have a total present-centeredness, in which every action exists only in the present. Lee contrasts our dominant mode with this alternative.

> The line is found or presupposed in most of our scientific work. It is present in the *induction* and *deduction* of science and logic. It is present in the philosopher's phrasing of means and ends as lineally connected. Our statistical facts are presented lineally as a *graph* or reduced to a normal *curve.* And all of us, I think, would be lost without our diagrams. We *trace* a historical development; we *follow the course* of history and evolution *down* to the present and *up from* the ape. . . . Our psychologists picture motivation as external, connected with the act through a line, or, more recently, entering the organism through a lineal channel and emerging transformed, again lineally, as response. . . .
>
> When we see a *line* of trees, or a *circle* of stones, we assume the presence of a connecting line which is not actually visible. And we assume it metaphorically when we follow a *line* of thought, a *course* of action, or the *direction* of an argument: when we *bridge* a gap in the conversation, or speak of the *span* of life or of teaching a *course,* or lament our *interrupted career.* . . .
>
> But the Trobrianders do not describe their activity lineally; they do no dynamic relating of acts; they do not

use even so innocuous a connective as *and.* Here is part of a description of the planting of coconut. "Thou-approach-there coconut thou-bring-here-we-plant-coconut thou-go thou-plant our coconut. This-here-it-emerge sprout. We-push-away this we-push-away this-other coconut-husk-fiber together sprout it-sit together root." We who are accustomed to seek lineal continuity, cannot help supplying it as we read this; but the continuity is not given in the Trobriand text; and all Trobriand speech, according to Malinowski, is "jerky," given in points, not in connecting lines.[20]

THE PROCESS
OF PERSONAL CONSCIOUSNESS

Our normal personal consciousness is not a complete, passive registration of the external environment, but a highly evolved, selective, personal construction that is aimed primarily at individual biological survival. But if this consciousness is something we each personally construct, how is it that we seem to agree on events? Personal consciousness has been called an illusion in the yogic tradition. This may be far too strong a word, but, to adopt it for a moment, we could say, "Yes, personal consciousness may be an 'illusion,' in that only a 'measly trickle' of the available external information is ever present in consciousness. But if it is an illusion, it is a *constrained* illusion." The constraints are that we select the *appropriate* survival-related objects and events to be the contents of personal consciousness. Alternative illusions have (presumably) disappeared in the course of evolution. Further, the constraints make consensual validation possible. All humans have evolved with identical sense organs, which select only certain aspects of the flux of available stimulation.

Let us trace this process. The sense organs discard most of the input information reaching us. The brain further limits input, by selectively inhibiting the sensory activity, sending down efferent signals which can modify stimulation even in the receptor itself. Our senses and central nervous system select by responding primarily to changes. We quickly learn to "habituate" to the constancies of the world. Further, we sort the input into categories that depend on transitory needs, language, our past history, our expectations, and our cultural biases. Finally, we must *construct* a stable consciousness from the heavily selected input, as does James' sculptor.

We do not, for instance, "see" with our eyes. More properly, the eyes participate in the whole process of visual experience. There is no image or copy of the external world on the retina, nor is one transmitted to the brain to be seen by a little man.

The experience of an infant, according to William James, is a "blooming, buzzing, confusion!" It is so partly because the infant lacks a suitable category system in which to sort experience consistently. As we learn to construct a socially acceptable personal consciousness, we learn to consistently associate, say, the experience of light with external objects. As we mature, this correlation is reinforced. Whenever a particular pattern of excitation is produced in the nervous system, we become more and more likely to be conscious of light energy from outside events. Our world becomes relatively stable; we become able to avoid danger successfully and to manipulate objects. We survive.

But it is quite important here to consider that "light" is a dimension of human consciousness. In physical fact, the only difference between "visible light" and the nearby portions of the electromagnetic spectrum is in wavelength. Nothing sacred occurs in nature between the electromagnetic wavelengths of 390 and 400 billionths of a meter, yet we can perceive one and not the other. It is only the receptive characteristics of our eye which give a special place to a wavelength of 400 billionths of a meter, but not to one of 390.

Furthermore, we do not even need the presence of external light to "see." If "seeing" is a certain pattern of excitation in the central nervous system, then anything which produces that pattern will result in visual experience. Obviously, the vast majority of visual experiences occur in the normal way: light enters the eye, which then sends electrophysiological impulses through the optic tract to the brain, contributing to the construction of a certain visual experience. However, this system can be interrupted at several points. Close your eyes, and press your eyeball for a moment. You will experience a greenish flash of light. No light energy, but merely the pressure of the finger, was transmitted to the retina. Here we have "tricked" the visual system, causing the retina to fire by means of pressure rather than stimulation by light. *Any* stimulus which causes the retina to fire will give rise to the experience of light, be it pressure or some more subtle form of electrical or chemical stimulation.

Wilder Penfield, among others, has demonstrated that the experience of vision can also be evoked by electrical stimulation of the central nervous system. Penfield performed brain surgery on patients with epilepsy and, as part of this procedure, electrically stimulated various areas of the brain; his patients often reported conscious experiences without any other input at all.[21] For instance, many surgeons have found that electrical stimulation of the occipital cortex usually leads to the experience of vision. We can understand, then, that seeing is a process which takes place not *in* our eyes, but rather *with the help* of our eyes. It is a process that is constructed in the brain, one largely determined by the category and output systems of the brain.

At other times, hallucinations may be caused by unusual functioning of the nervous system, for example, if the brain is stimulated by drugs which alter the normal relationships between external input and consciousness. Also, we dream each night and enter visual worlds which do not exist outside personal consciousness. Similar analyses would hold for other senses as well. Ordinary consciousness is each individual's own private construction. This insight has been more elegantly expressed by philosophers and poets. Alfred North Whitehead said:

Nature gets credit which in truth should be reserved for ourselves, the rose for its scent, the nightingale for his song, and the sun for its radiance. The poets are entirely mistaken. They should address their lyrics to themselves and should turn them into odes of self-congratulations on the excellence of the human mind. Nature is a dull affair, soundless, scentless, colorless, merely the hurrying of material, endlessly, meaninglessly.[22]

The poet T. S. Eliot, similarly: "We are the music while the music lasts."

THE NATURE OF ORDINARY INDIVIDUAL CONSCIOUSNESS

Ordinary consciousness is an exquisitely evolved personal construction, "designed" for the primary purpose of individual biological survival. Sense organs and the brain serve to select the aspects of the environment which are most relevant for survival. Our ordinary consciousness is object-centered; it involves analysis, a separation of oneself from other objects and organisms. This selective, active, analytic construction enables us to achieve a relatively stable personal world in which we can differentiate objects and act upon them. The concepts of causality, linear time, and language are the essence of this mode.

And yet this individual, active mode is not the only mode in which consciousness can operate, as the daylight hours do not constitute an entire day. If ordinary consciousness is a personal construction, then other constructions and other consciousnesses are potentially available to us. William James (as usual) put it best:

Our normal waking consciousness, rational consciousness as we call it, is but one special type of consciousness, whilst all about it, parted from it by the filmiest of screens, there lie potential forms of consciousness entirely different. We may go through life without suspecting their existence; but apply the requisite stimulus, and at a touch they are there in all their completeness, definite types of mentality which probably somewhere have their field of application and adaptation. No account of the universe in its totality can be final which leaves these other forms of consciousness quite disregarded. How to regard them is the question,—for they are so discontinuous with ordinary consciousness. Yet they may determine attitudes though they cannot furnish formulas, and open a region though they fail to give a map. At any rate, they forbid a premature closing of our accounts with reality.[23]

For further reading

W. H. Ittelson and F. P. Kilpatrick. "Experiments in Perception." *Scientific American* (Aug. 1951), pp. 50–55. Available from W. H. Freeman and Co. as Offprint no. 405.

Ulric Neisser. "The Processes of Vision." *Scientific American* (Sept. 1968), pp. 204–214. Offprint no. 519.

Albert H. Hastorf and Hadley Cantril. "They Saw a Game: A Case Study." *Journal of Abnormal and Social Psychology*, 49 (Jan. 1954), 129–134.

William James. "The Stream of Consciousness," from *The Principles of Psychology*, I, 224–290. New York: Dover Publications, 1950. Original copyright, 1890.

Aldous Huxley. *The Doors of Perception.* New York: Harper & Row, 1954.

Benjamin Lee Whorf. "Language, Mind, and Reality," in J. B. Carroll, ed., *Language, Thought, and Reality: Selected Writings of Benjamin Lee Whorf.* Cambridge, Mass.: The M.I.T. Press, 1951. London: The M.I.T. Press, 1956.

Selections from all the preceding have been reprinted in Robert Ornstein, ed., *The Nature of Human Consciousness.* San Francisco: W. H. Freeman and Co. New York: The Viking Press. 1973.

Lawrence Durrell. *The Alexandria Quartet: Justine, Balthazar, Mountolive, Clea.* London: Faber, 1957–60. New York: E. P. Dutton, 1960. A series of novels which explores consciousness as a personal construction.

Richard Held and Whitman Richards, eds. *Perception: Mechanisms and Models.* San Francisco and Reading, England: W. H. Freeman and Co., 1972.

Chapter 3

Two Sides
of the Brain

Never Know When It Might Come In Useful

Nasrudin sometimes took people for trips in his boat. One day a pedagogue hired him to ferry him across a very wide river. As soon as they were afloat, the scholar asked whether it was going to be rough.

"Don't ask me nothing about it," said Nasrudin.

"Have you never studied grammar?"

"No," said the Mulla.

"In that case, half your life has been wasted."

The Mulla said nothing.

Soon a terrible storm blew up. The Mulla's crazy cockleshell was filling with water. He leaned over toward his companion. "Have you ever learned to swim?"

"No," said the pedant.

"In that case, schoolmaster, all your life is lost, for we are sinking." [1]

The two characters in this story represent two major modes of consciousness: the verbal, rational mode is portrayed by the pedagogue, who is involved in and insists on neat and tidy perfection; the other mode is represented here by the skill of swimming, which involves movement of the body in space, a mode often devalued by the neat, rational mind of the pedagogue.

On one level, these two characters represent different types of people. The verbal-logical grammarian can also be the scientist, the logician, the mathematician who is committed to reason and "correct" proof. The boatman, ungraceful and untutored in formal terms, represents the artist, the craftsman, the dancer, the dreamer whose output is often unsatisfactory to the purely rational mind.

But other interpretations of this story are possible. These two characters can also represent major modes of consciousness which exist across cultures (comparing the Trobrianders with the West) and which simultaneously coexist within each person. Try the following exercise. Close your eyes and attempt to sense each side of your body separately. Try to get in touch with the feelings of the left and of the right side, their strengths, their weaknesses. When you are finished, open your eyes for a moment and reflect on one of these questions. Close your eyes and sense inside for the answer, then repeat the process with the next question.

1. Which side of you is more feminine?
2. Which is more masculine?
3. Which do you consider the "dark" side of yourself?
4. Which side is the "lighter"?
5. Which is more active?
6. Which is more passive?
7. Which side is more logical?
8. Which more "intuitive"?

9. Which side of you is the more mysterious?
10. Which side is the more artistic?

If you are righthanded, most likely you felt the right side of your body as more masculine, lighter, active, and logical, the left side as more feminine, dark, passive, intuitive, mysterious, and artistic. The psychologist William Domhoff asked a large number of people to rate the concepts *left* and *right* on several dimensions. His sample regarded *left* as "bad," "dark," "profane," and "female," while *right* was considered the opposite.[2]

The difference between the left and right sides of the body may provide a key to open our understanding of the psychological and physiological mechanisms of the two major modes of consciousness. The cerebral cortex of the brain is divided into two hemispheres, joined by a large bundle of interconnecting fibers called the "corpus callosum." The left side of the body is mainly controlled by the right side of the cortex, and the right side of the body by the left side of the cortex. When we speak of *left* in ordinary speech, we are referring to that side of the body, and to the *right* hemisphere of the brain.

Both the structure and the function of these two "half-brains" in some part underlie the two modes of consciousness which simultaneously coexist within each one of us. Although each hemisphere shares the potential for many functions, and both sides participate in most activities, in the normal person the two hemispheres tend to specialize. The left hemisphere (connected to the right side of the body) is predominantly involved with analytic, logical thinking, especially in verbal and mathematical functions. Its mode of operation is primarily linear. This hemisphere seems to process information sequentially. This mode of operation of necessity must underlie logical thought, since logic depends on sequence and order. Language and mathematics, both left-hemisphere activities, also depend predominantly on linear time.

If the left hemisphere is specialized for analysis, the right hemisphere (again, remember, connected to the left side of the body) seems specialized for holistic mentation. Its language

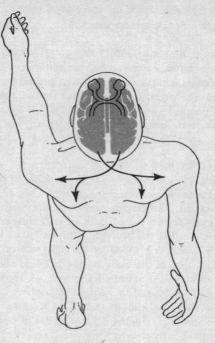

Figure 3.1

ability is quite limited. This hemisphere is primarily responsible for our orientation in space, artistic endeavor, crafts, body image, recognition of faces. It processes information more diffusely than does the left hemisphere, and its responsibilities demand a ready integration of many inputs at once. If the left hemisphere can be termed predominantly analytic and sequential in its operation, then the right hemisphere is more holistic and relational, and more simultaneous in its mode of operation.*

* This right-left specialization is based on righthanders. Lefthanders, who are about 5 per cent of the population, are less consistent;

For over a century, neurological evidence has been slowly accumulating on the differential specialization of man's two cerebral hemispheres. A very valuable part of this evidence has come from the study of people whose brains have been damaged by accident or illness, and from the surgery performed on them. It is, then, in the work of clinical neurology, and especially in the review paper of Joseph Bogen, that the primary indications of our hemispheric specialization are to be found.[3]

In 1864, the great neurologist Hughlings Jackson considered the left hemisphere to be the seat of the "faculty of expression," and noted of a patient with a tumor in the right hemisphere, "She did not know objects, persons, and places." Since Hughlings Jackson, many other neurologists, neurosurgeons, and psychiatrists have confirmed that two modes of consciousness seem to be lateralized in the two cerebral hemispheres of man. In hundreds of clinical cases, it has been found that damage to the left hemisphere very often interferes with, and can in some cases completely destroy, language ability. Often patients cannot speak after such left-hemisphere lesions, a condition known as "aphasia." An injury to the right hemisphere may not interfere with language performance at all, but may cause severe disturbance in spatial awareness, in musical ability, in recognition of other people, or in awareness of one's own body. Some patients with right-hemisphere damage cannot dress themselves adequately, although their speech and reason remain unimpaired.

Throughout the clinical and neurological reports, there exists a tendency to term the left and right hemispheres the "major" and the "minor," respectively. This seems more a

---

some have reversed specialization of the hemispheres, but some have mixed specialization—e.g., language in both sides. Some are specialized in the same way as righthanders. And even in righthanders these differences are not binary, but are specializations of each "half-brain." At least in very young people, each side does possess the potential for both modes; e.g., brain damage to the left hemisphere in young children often results in the development of language in the right side.

societal than a neurological distinction. The dominant or major mode of our culture is verbal and intellectual, and this cultural emphasis can bias observations. If an injury to the right hemisphere is not found to affect speech or reason, then this damage has often been considered minor. Injury to the left hemisphere affects verbal functions; thus it has often been termed the major hemisphere. However, the conception of the function of the two hemispheres is changing, largely because of the superb work of Bogen and the increasing evidence of the brain's lateral specialization. The position of the fussy pedagogue who devalues the nonverbal boatman becomes less and less tenable.

Each hemisphere is the major one, depending on the mode of consciousness under consideration. If one is a wordsmith, a scientist, or a mathematician, damage to the left hemisphere may prove disastrous. If one is a musician, a craftsman, or an artist, damage to the left hemisphere often does not interfere with one's capacity to create music, crafts, or arts, yet damage to the right hemisphere may well obliterate a career.

In more precise neuropsychological studies, Brenda Milner and her associates at McGill University in Montreal have attempted to correlate disorders in specific kinds of tasks with lesions in specific areas of the brain. For example, a lobectomy of the right temporal lobe severely impairs the performance of visual and tactile mazes, whereas left temporal-lobe lesions of equal extent produce little deficit. These researchers also report that lesions in specific areas of the left hemisphere are associated with specific kinds of language disorders: an impairment of verbal memory is associated with lesions in the anterior (front) left temporal lobe; speech impairment seems to result from lesions in the posterior (rear) left temporal lobe.[4] On less empirical grounds, the Russian physiologist A. R. Luria has reported that mathematical function is also disturbed by lesions of the left side.[5] Milner and her associates also report that the recognition of musical pitch seems to be in the province of the right hemisphere.

The clinical neurological research is intriguing, correlating the different functions of the hemispheres which are impaired by brain damage. More intriguing still is the research of Roger Sperry of the California Institute of Technology, and his associates, notably Joseph Bogen and Michael Gazzaniga. The two cerebral hemispheres communicate through the corpus callosum, which joins the two sides anatomically. Professor Sperry and his colleagues had for some years experimentally severed the corpus callosum in laboratory animals. This led to the adoption of a radical treatment for severe epilepsy in several human patients of Drs. Vogel and Bogen of the California College of Medicine.[6]

This treatment involved an operation on humans similar to Sperry's experimental surgery on animals—a severing of the interconnections between the two cerebral hemispheres, effectively isolating one side from the other. The hope of this surgery was that when a patient had a seizure in one hemisphere, the other would still be available to take control of the body. With this control available, it was hoped that the patient could ingest the proper medication or perhaps inform the doctor of his attack. In many cases, the severely disturbed patients were improved enough to leave the hospital.

In day-to-day living, these "split-brain" people exhibit almost no abnormality, which is somewhat surprising in view of the radical surgery. However, Roger Sperry and his associates have developed many subtle tests which uncovered evidence that the operation had clearly separated the specialized functions of the two cerebral hemispheres.

If, for instance, the patient felt a pencil (hidden from sight) in his right hand, he could verbally describe it, as would be normal. But if the pencil was in his left hand, he could not describe it at all. Recall that the left hand informs the right hemisphere, which does not possess any capability for speech. With the corpus callosum cut, the verbal (left) hemisphere is no longer connected to the right hemisphere, which largely communicates with the left hand; so the verbal apparatus literally does not know what is in the left hand. If, however, the patient was offered a selection of objects—a key, book, pencil, etc.—and was asked to choose the previously given object with his left hand, he could choose correctly, although he still could not state verbally just what he was doing. This situation resembles closely what might happen if I were privately requested to perform an action and you were expected to discourse on it.   ·

Another experiment tested the lateral specialization of the two hemispheres using visual input. The right half of each eye sends its messages to the right hemisphere, the left half to the left hemisphere. In this experiment the word "heart" was flashed to the patient, with the "he" to the left of the eyes' fixation point, and "art" to the right. Normally if any person were asked to report this experience, he would say that he saw "heart." But the split-brain patients responded differently, depending on which hemisphere was responding. When the patient was asked to *name* the word just presented, he or she replied "art," since this was the portion projected to the left hemisphere, which was answering the question. When, however, the patient was asked to point with the left hand to one of two cards on which were written "he" and "art," the left hand pointed to "he." The simultaneous experiences of each hemisphere seemed unique and independent of each other in these patients. The verbal hemisphere gave one answer, the nonverbal hemisphere another.

Although most righthanded people write and draw with the right hand, most can to some extent write and draw with their left. After surgery, Dr. Bogen tested the ability of the split-brain patients to write and draw with either hand. The ability to write English remained in the right hand after surgery, but this hand could no longer draw very well. It seemed to have lost its ability to work in a relational, spatial manner. Given a square to copy with the right hand, the patient might draw four corners stacked together: he could draw *only* the corners; the hand seemed no longer able to link the disconnected segments. The left hemisphere, which controls the right hand, seems to be able to operate well in an analytic manner, yet poorly in a relational mode. The performance of the left hand reversed that of the right. The left could draw and could copy spatial figures, but could not

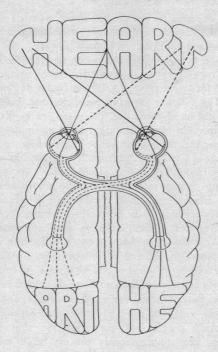

Figure 3.2

A simplified diagram of visual input to the two hemispheres of the brain. Images in the left visual field are projected to the right hemisphere, images in the right visual field to the left hemisphere. This schematic drawing illustrates one experiment performed on split-brain patients: note that the corpus callosum is cut. The "HE" and "ART" projections are, of course, fanciful, not anatomically correct.

copy a written word. It can operate holistically, but does not have very much capacity for verbal-analytic information processing. In these split-brain patients, the right hemisphere can understand some simple speech, though it has no capacity for verbal expression; we do not know whether this is an artifact of the surgery or whether it represents a rudimentary right-hemisphere capability in normal people.

A common test of spatial mentation requires the construction of a two-dimensional geometric figure using a set of cubes, each face painted with a different color or combination of colors. The patient's left hand could perform this task quite well; the right hand could not. Professor Sperry often shows an interesting film clip of the right hand attempting to solve the problem and failing, whereupon the patient's left hand cannot restrain itself and "corrects" the right—as when you may know the answer to a problem and watch me making mistakes, and cannot refrain from telling me the answer.

The split-brain surgery most dramatically delineates the two major modes of consciousness which seem normally to coexist within each person. Recent research with experimental split-brain monkeys indicates that the two hemispheres can function simultaneously as well as independently. At the same moment, a split-brain monkey can be trained on one learning problem with one eye-brain pair (the optic chiasm in monkeys is severed as part of the experimental procedure) and a second problem with the other eye-brain pair.[7] One experiment with the split-brain people has also indicated that their two hemispheres can simultaneously process more information than can those of a normal person. Dr. Sperry writes of the effect of the operation in humans: "Everything we have seen so far indicated that the surgery has left each of these people with two separate minds, that is, with two separate spheres of consciousness."[8]

The recognition that we possess two cerebral hemispheres which are specialized to operate in different modes may allow us to understand much about the fundamental duality of our consciousness. This duality has been reflected in classical as well as modern literature as between reason and passion, or between mind and intuition. Perhaps the most famous of these dichotomies in psychology is that proposed by Sigmund Freud, of the split between the "conscious" mind and the "unconscious." The workings of the "conscious" mind are held to be accessible to language and to rational discourse and alteration; the "unconscious" is much less accessible to reason or to the verbal analysis. Some aspects of "unconscious" communication are gestures, facial and body movements, tone of voice.

There are moments in each of our lives when our verbal intellect suggests one course and our "heart" or intuition another. Because of psychosurgery which has physically separated the hemispheres, the split-brain patients provide a clear example of dual response to certain situations. In one experimental test, Roger Sperry attempted to determine whether the right hemisphere could learn to respond verbally to different colors. Either a red or a green light was flashed to the left visual field of the patient, which is received on the right half of the retina and sent to the right hemisphere (see Figure 3.2). Sperry then asked the split-brain patients to guess verbally which color was flashed to them. Since the left hemisphere controls the verbal output and the color information was sent to the right hemisphere, it was expected that the patients would not be able to guess the answer beyond chance, no matter how many guesses were allowed. The side which was doing the guessing, after all, was disconnected from the side which knew the answer.

After a few trials, however, the patients' scores improved whenever the examiner allowed a second guess. What happened was this. If a red light was flashed and the patient guessed correctly by chance, this terminated the trial. If the patient guessed incorrectly, he might frown, shake his head, and then "correct" his answer verbally. The right hemisphere had seen the light, then heard the left make an incorrect answer. Having no access to verbal output, the right hemisphere used the means at its disposal, and caused a frown and a head-shake, which informed the left hemisphere that its answer was incorrect.

In a loose way, this is an analog of the conflict between "conscious" and "unconscious" processes which Freud so compellingly described. In the split-brain patients, the verbal, rational processing system, disconnected from the source of information, was countermanded by gestures and tone of voice, as when a person may insist "I am *not* angry," yet his tone of voice and facial expression simultaneously indicate exactly the opposite feeling.

A similar situation occurred when emotion-laden information was given to the right hemisphere while the verbal hemisphere remained unaware of it. A photograph of a nude woman was shown to the right hemisphere of a patient in the course of a series of otherwise dull laboratory tests. At first, the woman viewing the nude on the screen said that she saw nothing, then immediately flushed, alternately squirmed, smiled, and looked uncomfortable and confused. But her "conscious" or verbal half was *still* unaware of what had caused the emotional turmoil. All that was accessible to the verbal apparatus was that *something* unusual was occurring in her body. Her words reflected that the emotional reaction had been "unconscious," unavailable to her language apparatus. To paraphrase her, "What a funny machine you have there, Dr. Sperry."

In this instance a clear split was observed between the two independent consciousnesses that are normally in communication and collaboration. In such an experiment with split-brain patients, we can accurately localize the split of information in the system. A similar process, although much more difficult to localize, may underlie the classic Freudian symptoms of repression and denial, both situations in which the verbal mechanism has no access to emotional information in other parts of the system. In less pathological instances, when we perform an action "intuitively," our words often make no sense, perhaps because the action has been initiated by a part of the brain little involved in language.

But these spectacular split-brain and lesion studies are not the only evidence for the physiological duality in consciousness. In general, caution should be exercised in drawing inferences on normal functioning from pathological and surgical cases alone. In dealing with these cases we must recall that we are investigating disturbed, not normal, functioning, from which inference to how normal people function may be a bit tenuous. In cases of brain damage, it is never fully clear that one hemisphere has not taken over a function from the other to an unusual degree because of the injury. It is necessary to seek out evidence from normally functioning people, even if that evidence is more indirect, since we don't go poking inside the brains of our friends. In this, we are fortunate that recent research with normal people has confirmed much of the neurosurgical explorations.

If the right hemisphere operates predominantly in a simultaneous manner, it could integrate diverse input quickly. This mode of information-processing would be advantageous for spatial orientation, when the person must quickly integrate visual, muscular, and kinesthetic cues. In a carefully controlled experiment with normal people, the right hemisphere was found to be superior in depth perception to the left.[9]

When a tachistoscope is used to introduce information to only the right hemisphere and either a nonverbal or a verbal response is required, the nonverbal response comes more quickly than the verbal one. A verbal response requires the information to be sent across the callosum to the left hemisphere, which takes some time. This indicates that the normal brain does indeed make use of the lateral specialization, selecting the appropriate area for differential information-processing.[10]

Another experiment which confirms the differential specialization of the two hemispheres uses eye movements as an indicator. Ask a friend a question such as, "How do you spell Mississippi?" The chances are that he will shift his gaze off to one side while reflecting. Marcel Kinsbourne of Duke University, and Katherine Kocel, David Galin, Edward Merrin, and myself of our research group at the Langley Porter Neuropsychiatric Institute, have found that which direction a person gazes in is affected by the kind of question asked. If the question is verbal-analytical (such as "Divide 144 by 6, and multiply the answer by 7"), more eye movements are made to the right than if the question involves spatial mentation (such as "Which way does an Indian face on the nickel?").[11]

Kinsbourne has performed another experiment which deserves special mention. Ask a friend to balance a wooden dowel on the index finger of each hand, one hand at a time. Generally, the preferred hand is more adept at this balancing. Ask the person then to speak while balancing this dowel, and time the length of the balancing. In Kinsbourne's experiment, the balancing time of the right hand decreased, as would be expected, since the addition of a task interferes with perform-ance in most situations. But the balancing time of the left hand *increased* with concurrent verbalization.[12]

The right hand, recall, is predominantly controlled by the left hemisphere. When the left hemisphere is engaged in speech, its control of the right hand suffers. While the left hand is balancing, the left hemisphere may still intrude on its performance. When the left hemisphere is occupied in speech, it no longer seems to interfere with the left hand and the balancing time of the left improves.

The normal brain constantly exhibits electrical activity, in the form of very low voltages, as recorded at the scalp by the electroencephalograph or EEG. If the EEG is recorded from both hemispheres of a normal person during the performance of verbal or spatial information-processing tasks, different "brain-wave" patterns result. During a verbal task, the alpha rhythm in the right hemisphere increases relative to the left, and in a spatial task the alpha increases in the left hemisphere relative to the right. The appearance of the alpha rhythm indicates a "turning off" of information-processing in the area involved. As if to reduce the interference between the two conflicting modes of operation of its two cerebral hemi-spheres, the brain tends to turn off its unused side in a given situation.[13]

But how do these two modes interact in daily life? My opinion, and that of David Galin, is that in most ordinary activities we simply alternate between the two modes, se-lecting the appropriate one and inhibiting the other. It is not at all clear how this process occurs. Do the two systems work continuously in parallel, and merely alternate control of the body, or do they truly time-share the control? Clearly each of us can work in both modes—we all speak, we all can move in space, we all can do both at once; yet in skiing, for instance, an attempt to verbally encode each bodily movement would lead to disaster. The two modes of operation *complement* each other, but do not readily substitute for one another. Consider describing a spiral staircase. Most would begin using words and quickly begin to gesture in the air. Or consider attempting to ride a bicycle purely from a verbal instruction.

This lateral specialization of the brain seems to be unique to humans and related to the evolution of language. There is no evidence that the two cerebral hemispheres of other primates are specialized, although it would be reasonable to assume some evolutionary precursor of man's hemispheric asymmetry. Jerre Levy-Agresti and Roger Sperry have suggested that humans have evolved in this manner because the sequential information-processing which must underlie language, mathematics, and "rational" thought is not readily compatible with the more simultaneous mode of information-processing which underlies relational perception, orientation in space, and what our verbal intellect can only term "intuition." [14]

Within each person the two polarities seem to exist simultaneously as two semi-independent information-processing units with different specialties. There is some suggestive evidence that the modes of physiological organization may be different in the two hemispheres. Josephine Semmes, of the National Institute of Mental Health, has found that damage to the left hemisphere results in quite localized disturbance of function, whereas damage to the right interferes less focally with performance. Semmes and her co-workers studied 124 war veterans who had incurred brain injuries. They tested the effects of brain injury on simple motor reactions, somatosensory thresholds, and object discrimination—testing each hand-hemisphere pair separately. Studying the right hand, they found that injuries in quite specific areas of the left hemisphere interfered with performance of specific tasks, but no such focus of localization could be found with right-hemisphere lesions. [15] This evidence seems to indicate that the left hemisphere is more anatomically specialized for the discrete, focal information-processing underlying logic, and that the right hemisphere is more diffusely organized, which is advantageous for orientation in space and for other situations which require simultaneous processing of many inputs.

It is the polarity and the integration of these two modes of consciousness, the complementary workings of the intellect and the intuitive, which underlie our highest achievements. However, it has often been noticed that some persons habitually prefer one mode over the other, for example, our pedagogue at the beginning of this chapter. The exclusively verbal, logical scientist manifests a similar dominance, and may often forget and even deny that he possesses another side; he may find it difficult to work in the areas of the right hemisphere, in art, crafts, dance, sports. But this other mode, although less logical and clear, is important for creativity: "combinatory play" was Einstein's phrase. "Have you ever learned to swim?" asks the boatman.

This duality in human consciousness has long been recognized in other cultures. For instance, the Hopi Indians of the American Southwest distinguish the function of the two hands, one for writing, one for making music. The French word for Law, that most linear and rational of human pursuits, is *droit,* which literally means "right." For the Mojave Indians, the left hand is the passive, maternal side of the person, the right, the active father. William Domhoff concludes his interesting survey of the myth and symbolism of *left* and *right* by noting that the left is often the area of the taboo, the sacred, the unconscious, the feminine, the intuitive, and the dreamer. And we do find that the symbolism of the two sides of the body is quite often in agreement with these ideas. In myth, the feminine side is most often on the left, the masculine on the right.[16]

On this right-left duality, we have scientific evidence only for dreaming, and it is not too strong. In a report on three cases, Humphrey and Zangwill have found that damage to the right parietal lobe of the brain seems to interfere with dreaming. Bogen notes that his split-brain patients tend to report the absence of dreams after the operation, perhaps because of the disconnection of the verbal output from the right hemisphere. In a study with normal subjects, Austin reports that people who tend to specialize in analytic thinking (convergers) are less likely to recall dreams than those with the opposite bias (divergers), whom he characterized as more imaginative and more able to deal with the nonrational.[17]

In Vedanta, the duality in consciousness is said to be between intellect (Buddhi) and mind (manas). Such a distinction may be hard for us to state clearly, for when we say, "This person has a fine mind," we are usually referring only to the verbal and intellectual portion of the mind. The Chinese Yin-Yang symbol neatly encapsulates the duality and complementarity of these two poles of consciousness.

Figure 3.3
The Yin-Yang symbol.

Facing out, on the figure's left is the "night," the dark side named *K'un* in the *I Ching.* On the figure's right is the "day," the light, *Ch'ien,* the creative, sometimes translated as the active or the originating principle. Here are the two polarities of man (and all creation) as represented in the Wilhelm-Baynes translation of the *I Ching.*

Ch'ien, The Creative

The first hexagram is made up of six unbroken lines. These unbroken lines stand for the primal power, which is light-giving, active, strong, and of the spirit. The hexagram is consistently strong in character, and since it is without weakness, its essence is power or energy. Its image is heaven. Its energy is represented as unrestricted by any fixed conditions in space and is therefore conceived of as motion. Time is regarded as the basis of this motion. Thus, the hexagram includes also the power of time and the power of persisting in time, that is, duration.

K'un, The Receptive

This hexagram is made up of broken lines only. The broken line represents the dark, yielding, receptive primal power of yin. The attribute of the hexagram is devotion; its image is the earth. It is the perfect complement of *The Creative*—the complement, not the opposite, for the Receptive does not combat the creative but completes it. It represents nature in contrast to spirit, earth in contrast to heaven, space as against time, the female-maternal as against the male-paternal. However, as applied to human affairs, the principle of this complementary relationship is found not only in the relation between man and woman, but also in that between prince and minister and between father and son. Indeed, even in the individual this duality appears in the coexistence of the spiritual world and the world of the senses.[18]

Note that one pole is in time, the other in space; one is light, one dark; one active, one receptive; one male, one female.

It is the complementarity of these two modes of consciousness which is a central consideration of this book, as they manifest themselves on several levels simultaneously—within each person, between different persons, within different disciplines such as scientific inquiry (psychology in particular), and in the organization of cultures. In his review on the "other" side of the brain, Joseph Bogen clarified the concept by presenting a set of dichotomies between the two modes of consciousness. Following him, I present one such table, but only for purposes of suggestion and clarification in an intuitive sort of way, not as a final categorical statement of the conception. Many of the poles are, of course, tendencies and specializations, not at all binary classifications. Examination of the table may also make the Day-Night metaphor I am using a bit clearer.

The Two Modes of Consciousness: A Tentative Dichotomy

Who Proposed It?		
Many sources	Day	Night
Blackburn	Intellectual	Sensuous
Oppenheimer	Time, History	Eternity, Timelessness
Deikman	Active	Receptive
Polanyi	Explicit	Tacit
Levy, Sperry	Analytic	Gestalt
Domhoff	Right (side of body)	Left (side of body)
Many sources	Left hemisphere	Right hemisphere
Bogen	Propositional	Appositional
Lee	Lineal	Nonlineal
Luria	Sequential	Simultaneous
Semmes	Focal	Diffuse
I Ching	The Creative: heaven masculine, Yang	The Receptive: earth feminine, Yin
I Ching	Light	Dark
I Ching	Time	Space
Many sources	Verbal	Spatial
Many sources	Intellectual	Intuitive
Vedanta	Buddhi	Manas
Jung	Causal	Acausal
Bacon	Argument	Experience

Many different occupations and disciplines involve a concentration in one of the major modes of consciousness. Science and law are heavily involved in linearity, duration, and verbal logic. Crafts, the "mystical" disciplines, music, are more present-centered, aconceptual, intuitive. A complete human consciousness involves the polarity and integration of the two modes, as a complete day includes the daylight and the darkness.

The first chapter of this book restated the idea that even scientific knowledge, largely a linear and rational pursuit, also relies heavily on intuition for completeness. W. I. B. Beveridge, in his *The Art of Scientific Investigation*, stresses the need for the development of the intuitive side in scientists. He defines "intuition" in science as "a clarifying idea which comes suddenly to mind." Intuitive knowledge complements the normal, rational scientific knowledge, much as the paradigm change is the complement to the normal progress of scientific thought.[19]

According to Beveridge, intuitions have most often come to scientific investigators when the normal rational processes are temporarily suspended. The French mathematician Poincaré, after dismissing his work from his rational mind, went for a drive in the country. "Just as I put my foot on the brake, the idea came to me." Many others have stressed this point, that reason in science must be complemented by the "other" mode. Albert Einstein, for instance, said of his own creative processes, "The really valuable thing is intuition." The realm of the paradigm *maker* is the "other" side of science. The complete scientific endeavor, then, involves working in both modes.

To take a similar example quite close to hand. In the writing of this book, I have had vague idea after idea at different times: on the beach, in the mountains, in discussion, even while writing. These intuitions are sparse images—perhaps a connection which allows a new gestalt to form—but they are never fully clear, and never satisfactory by themselves. They are incomplete realizations, not a finished work. For me, it is only when the intellect has worked out these glimpses of form that the intuition becomes of any use to others. It is the very linearity of a book which enables the writer to refine his own intuitions, and clarify them, first to himself, and then if possible to the reader.

The process of building a house provides another example. At first, there may be a sudden inspiration of the gestalt of the finished house, but this image must be brought to completion, slowly, by linear methods, by plans and contracts, and then by the actual construction, sequentially, piece by piece.

The idea of the complementarity of two major modes of consciousness is hardly new. It antedates the *I Ching* and is found in many forms of philosophical, religious, and psychological endeavor. It was emphasized in physics by Robert

Oppenheimer and in metaphysics by many. What is new now is a recognition that these modes operate physiologically as well as mentally and culturally. With a recognition of the physiological basis of the dual specializations of consciousness, we may be able to redress the balance in science and in psychology, a balance which has in recent years swung a bit too far to the right, into a strict insistence on verbal logic that has left context and perspective undeveloped. Two contemporary psychologists stress this same integrative view, although neither refers to the two modes of the brain. The Italian psychiatrist Roberto Assagioli discusses the articulation of the two modes.

> We will consider intuition mainly in its cognitive function, i.e., as a psychic organ or means to apprehend reality. It is a synthetic function in the sense that it apprehends the totality of a given situation or psychological reality. It does not work from the part to the whole—as the analytical mind does—but apprehends a totality directly in its living existence. As it is a normal function of the human psyche, its activation is produced chiefly by eliminating the various obstacles preventing its activity. . . .
>
> The most important combination is that with a controlled mental activity and mental discrimination. To use an analogy, it is a necessary and difficult marriage. Often it is a stormy marriage which sometimes ends in divorce. First, there is a good number of those who do not even contemplate such a marriage. They are content to either use only the intuition or only the intellect. Even when this attempt at matrimony is begun, there are various difficulties: in some cases one of the partners is too imperative and devaluates and keeps in subjection the other—and it can be either one that makes this mistake, with all the drawbacks of repression, of overt or covert rebellion. In other cases there is an oscillation, a fight between the two in which temporarily the one or the other predominates.
>
> Many intellectuals are to a certain extent afraid when an intuition intrudes into their thought processes; they are diffident and treat it very gingerly; consciously or unconsciously, in most cases they repress it.

To speak more directly, and without metaphor, of the true relationship between intuition and intellect, intuition is the creative advance toward reality. Intellect [needs, first, to perform] the valuable and necessary function of interpreting, i.e., of translating, verbalizing in acceptable mental terms, the results of the intuition; second, to check its validity; and third, to coordinate and to include it into the body of already accepted knowledge. These functions are the rightful activity of the intellect, without its trying to assume functions which are not its province. A really fine and harmonious interplay between the two can work perfectly in a successive rhythm: intuitional insight, interpretation, further insight and its interpretation, and so on.[20]

The American Jerome Bruner, who has contributed much to our understanding of individual consciousness, elegantly summarizes the interplay of the two modes. He relates them both to the current problem in psychology and science, and to the two sides of the body.

Since childhood, I have been enchanted by the fact and the symbolism of the right hand and the left—the one the doer, the other the dreamer. The right is order and lawfulness, *le droit*. Its beauties are those of geometry and taut implication. Reaching for knowledge with the right hand is science. Yet to say only that much of science is to overlook one of its excitements, for the great hypotheses of science are gifts carried in the left.

Of the left hand we say that it is awkward and, while it has been proposed that art students can seduce their proper hand to more expressiveness by drawing first with the left, we nonetheless suspect this function. The French speak of the illegitimate descendant as being *à main gauche*, and, though the heart is virtually at the center of the thoracic cavity, we listen for it on the left. Sentiment, intuition, bastardy. And should we say that reaching for knowledge with the left hand is art? Again it is not enough, for as surely as the recital of a daydream differs from the well-wrought tale, there is a barrier between undisciplined fantasy and art. To climb the barrier requires a right hand adept at technique and artifice. . . .

One thing has become increasingly clear in pursuing the nature of knowing. It is that the conventional apparatus of the psychologist—both his instruments of investigation and the conceptual tools he uses in the interpretation of his data—leaves one approach unexplored. It is an approach whose medium of exchange seems to be the metaphor paid out by the left hand. It is a way that grows happy hunches and "lucky" guesses, that is stirred into connective activity by the poet and the necromancer looking sidewise rather than directly. Their hunches and intuitions generate a grammar of their own—searching out connections, suggesting similarities, weaving ideas loosely in a trial web. . . .

The psychologist, for all his apartness, is governed by the same constraints that shape the behavior of those whom he studies. He too searches widely and metaphorically for his hunches. He reads novels, looks at and even paints pictures, is struck by the power of myth, observes his fellow men intuitively and with wonder. In doing so, he acts only part-time like a proper psychologist, racking up cases against the criteria derived from a hypothesis. Like his fellows, he observes the human scene with such sensibility as he can muster in the hope that his insight will be deepened. If he is lucky or if he has subtle psychological intuition, he will from time to time come up with hunches, combinatorial products of his metaphoric activity. If he is not fearful of these products of his own subjectivity, he will go so far as to tame the metaphors that have produced the hunches, tame them in the sense of shifting them from the left hand to the right hand by rendering them into notions that can be tested. It is my impression from observing myself and my colleagues that the forging of metaphoric hunch into testable hypothesis goes on all the time. And I am inclined to think that this process is the more evident in psychology, where the theoretical apparatus is not so well developed that it lends itself readily to generating interesting hypotheses.

Yet because our profession is young and because we feel insecure, we do not like to admit our humanity. We quite properly seek a distinctiveness that sets us apart from all those others who ponder about man and the human condition—all of which is worthy, for thereby we forge an intellectual discipline. But we are not satisfied to forge distinctive methods of our own. We must reject whoever has been successful in the task of understanding man—if he is not one of us. We place a restrictive covenant on our domain. Our articles, submitted properly to the appropriate psychological journal, have about them an aseptic quality designed to proclaim the intellectual purity of our psychological enterprise. Perhaps this is well, though it is not enough.

It is well, perhaps because it is economical to report the products of research and not the endless process that constitutes the research itself. But it is not enough in the deeper sense that we may be concealing some of the most fruitful sources of our ideas from one another.[21]

For further reading

Jerome Bruner. *On Knowing: Essays for the Left Hand.* Cambridge, Mass.: Harvard University Press, 1965.

R. W. Sperry. "The Great Cerebral Commissure." *Scientific American* (Jan. 1964), pp. 142–152. Offprint no. 174.

Michael S. Gazzaniga. "The Split Brain in Man." *Scientific American* (Aug. 1967), pp. 24–29. Offprint no. 508.

Dorothy Lee. "Codifications of Reality: Lineal and Nonlineal." *Psychosomatic Medicine*, 12, no. 2 (1950), 89–97.

Arthur Deikman. "Bimodal Consciousness." *Archives of General Psychiatry*, 25 (Dec. 1971), 481–489.

Joseph E. Bogen. "The Other Side of the Brain: An Appositional Mind." *Bulletin of the Los Angeles Neurological Societies*, 34, no. 3 (July 1969), 135–162.

G. William Domhoff. "But Why Did They Sit on the King's Right in the First Place?" *Psychoanalytic Review*, 56 (1969–70), 586–596.

All of the preceding have been reprinted, in whole or in part, in Robert Ornstein, ed., *The Nature of Human Consciousness*. San Francisco: W. H. Freeman and Co. New York: The Viking Press. 1973.

Francis Schmidt, ed. *The Neurosciences: Third Series*. London: The M.I.T. Press, 1974. The first section contains a fairly comprehensive review of recent studies and thinking on the functions of the two cerebral hemispheres by such psychologists and psychobiologists as Sperry, Broadbent, and Teuber.

The Temporal
Dimensions
of Consciousness

Moment in Time

"What is Fate?" Nasrudin was asked by a scholar.

"An endless succession of intertwined events, each influencing the other."

"That is hardly a satisfactory answer. I believe in cause and effect."

"Very well," said the Mulla, "look at that." He pointed to a procession passing in the street.

"That man is being taken to be hanged. Is that because someone gave him a silver piece and enabled him to buy the knife with which he committed the murder; or because someone saw him do it; or because nobody stopped him?" [1]

Like the scholar in the story, we live our daily lives in a realm of causality, with a past and a future, in the province of the clock. The clock is the very embodiment of linearity and sequence. Inside a clock, the rotation of a wheel or the vibrations of a tuning fork are mechanically translated into movements of a pointer. These yield seconds, then minutes, then hours, as the movements add up. For any ordinary purpose, the more constant the internal mechanism of the clock the better, for one hour must be defined as the equal of any other in linear time, otherwise a consistent sequencing of events could not be maintained. According to the clock, one event follows another, one hour follows another, in a strict unchanging sequence; eight o'clock always follows seven and precedes nine. Spring is followed by summer, in time. The consistent linear sequence of time is so much a given part of ordinary consciousness that it seems a bit strange to examine it: could time operate in any other manner?

Consider, for a moment, this normal sense of time. Our normal consciousness consists of objects and people, who can only exist in time. Our experiences follow each other linearly, like the hours of the clock. We notice our friends growing up and growing old "in time." To paraphrase Benjamin Lee Whorf, we experience the stream of duration, which carries us out of the past and into the future. The normal modality is linear; it includes a past, present, and future, and consists of a sequence of enduring events, one following another.

This mode of temporal experience forms a basis of our personal and cultural life. The clock of hours, minutes, and seconds allows us to "time" meetings and races, to arrive at the moment when an event such as a lecture begins. This linear concept of time allows us to plan for a future, to arrange actions well in advance, to coordinate our individual and social lives with those of others. All in all, it forms an integral part of the sustaining, invisible fabric of normal life and normal consciousness. This mode of time is as much a necessary dimension of ordinary consciousness as vision is.

Linear time is so much a part of our lives that we can hardly comprehend how "time" could exist in any other manner. Words must follow a recognizable sequence to make sense; causes must precede effects for science to exist; if 5,000 people are to appear on schedule, the concept "three o'clock next Thursday" must have some real meaning.

Although the linear mode of temporal experience is necessary for the functioning of our daily lives, this mode does not exhaust the possibilities. In Chapter 2 we noted that the contents of normal consciousness are a personal construction; so now we must consider the possibility that the normal mode of experiencing time is only one particular personal construction of reality. There is nothing sacred about our clock. Many civilizations have existed without the clock as we know it.

The question here is not whether the clock, and the linear, sequential, enduring time which goes with it, are "successful" in terms of survival. They are. Indeed, they have become *necessary* for the functioning of a complex technological society. Nevertheless, other modes of experiencing time are available to us.

Each person, each day, moves in and out of the linear and nonlinear modes of experience. Let us resume the metaphor of two modes of consciousness, identified with the day and the night.

It is *daytime* which is governed by the clock and by linearity. The clock is quite important in our jobs, in our studies, in coordination of action. Clock time is an important element in the active mode of consciousness. To perform successful manipulative action, a precise and sequential construction of time is very helpful. In work, or at school, it is quite important whether we arrive at 9:00 A.M. or 9:17. In the former case we are "on time"; in the latter we are "late."

Precise timing of events underlies scientific inquiry. It necessarily governs any inference we make about causality. The more linear and objective the endeavor, the smaller the basic unit in which sequential time is measured. Western scientists define the second as "9,192,631,700 cycles of the frequency associated with the transition between the two energy levels of the isotope cesium 133." [2] The smallest sequential unit of our linear day is a second, unless we are "timing" a race, where we may employ a stopwatch which measures hundredths of a second. But many other cultures, less technically advanced and linearly organized, do not break time into such small units. One Indian culture uses the "time to boil rice" as the smallest basic unit. The Trobrianders and the Hopi Indians of the Southwest do not even seem to employ the linear construction. Theirs is a continuous mode of simultaneity and present-centeredness, the mode of the night.

Our *nighttime* existence is less "in time" than our daytime existence. To most people it matters less whether it is 4:00 A.M. or 4:17 A.M. on the clock than whether it is 9:00 A.M. or 9:17 A.M. The night belongs mainly to another mode of consciousness, the mode of the dreamer, in which linearity and sequence are more fluid, as they are reported to be in the world of the Hopi.[3]

The story which begins this chapter contrasts the two major dimensions of temporal experience. One polarity is the analytic mode typified by the scholar, similar to the pedagogue of the last chapter, who seeks a linear explanation for events (such as, "he did this because . . ."). The other pole is represented by Nasrudin: a holistic perception of events as intertwined entities, each reciprocally influencing the other. The stream of events can be broken into a linear sequence, and valid inferences made from this construction—this is the way in which we usually operate. But the events can also be construed as a "patterned whole," as the drawing at the beginning of this chapter so clearly indicates, with all action drawn in one single stroke. This is a useful graphic portrayal of the mode of consciousness of the *night* in our metaphor, of the *left* in symbol and myth, the cultural mode of the people of the Trobriand Islands. It does not postulate duration, a future or a past, a cause or an effect, but a patterned "timeless" whole.

In reviewing the differences between the modes of operation of the two cerebral hemispheres of the brain, Joseph Bogen observed that one of the most important differences between them is "the extent to which a linear concept of time participates in the ordering of thought." [4] As he and other neuropsychologists have pointed out, our two cerebral hemispheres seem neurologically specialized to process information in two different, complementary modes, the left more linearly than the right. The left hemisphere of the cortex, which subtends language and mathematics, seems to process information primarily in a linear, sequential manner, appropriate to its specialties. The right side of the cortex processes its input more as a "patterned whole," that is, in a more simultaneous manner than does the left. This simultaneous processing is advantageous for the integration of diffuse inputs, such as for orienting oneself in space, when motor, kinesthetic and visual input must be quickly integrated. This mode of information-processing, too, would seem to underlie an "intuitive" rather than an "intellectual" integration of complex entities.

TIME IN PSYCHOLOGY

Most psychologists, in considering time, have taken for granted that a "real" time, external to our construction of it, does exist, and that this time is linear. If this were the case, then we would possess a real "sense" of time just as we have a visual "sense." The implicit idea of many of these researchers has been that we, therefore, perceive a Real Time (identified with the clock) with a special organ of perception.

Even a little reflection will reveal, however, that the clock is not a time "receiver" but a special time *definer*. Nevertheless, linear clock time is so ingrained into our own personal constructions of reality that it has even influenced research paradigms, and has thus led to much confusion in psychology. In 1891, Henry Nichols wrote modern psychology's first review of the research performed on time experience, sounding a theme which was to become the *leitmotif* of many later reviews of such work.

Casting an eye backward we can but be struck by the wide variety of explanations offered for the time-mystery. Time has been called an act of mind, or reason, of perception, of intuition, of sense, or memory, of will, of all possible compounds and compositions to be made up of them. It has been deemed a General Sense accompanying all mental content in a manner similar to that conceived of pain and pleasure. It has been assigned a separate, special, disparate sense, to nigh a dozen kinds of "feeling," some familiar, some strangely invented for the difficulty. It has been explained by "relations," by "earmarks," by "signs," by "remnants," by "struggles," and by "strifes," by "luminous trains," by "blocks of specious-present," by "apperception." It has been declared *a priori,* innate, intuitive, empirical, mechanical. It has been deduced from within and without, from heaven and from earth, and from several things difficult to imagine as of either.[5]

With a tributary of research ideas so broad, yet so shallow, it was hardly surprising that the mainstream of psychological thought became less and less concerned with time as a dimension of consciousness. With John Watson's purging of "mentalism" from psychology in the early 1900's, time's tributary almost dried up. The flow of research on consciousness as a whole began to slacken, the work on time even more so.

The reasons why time research has been and remains so scattered and so offensive to an "objectively" minded psychology can be clearly seen. To perform an analysis of the experience of time, one can point neither to an *organ* of consciousness, such as the eye, nor to a physical continuum, such as the wavelength of light, for study by objective methods. There is no immediate physical or physiological point of departure for a scientific analysis of time experience. There is no process in the external world which directly gives rise to time experience, nor is there anything immediately discernible outside ourselves which can apprehend any special "time stimuli." It is therefore not too surprising that psychological research on time as a dimension of consciousness has been so diverse, so incoherent, and so easily forgotten.

Yet some researchers continue to overlook the lack of a time organ and try to approach temporal experience as if it really were a sensory process, as if we had a special time sense. In ordinary speech we often use the phrase "a good sense of time" to refer to someone who is consistent with respect to the clock, to someone who is "on time." This may be a useful everyday idea, but as a scientific concept it has seriously impeded an understanding of temporal experience.

Even within our ordinary experience, time has too many referents to be considered a unitary sense. The novelist Lawrence Durrell cites a few of the many times of experience: "One lies here with time passing and wonders about it. Every sort of time trickling through the hourglass, time immemorial, and for the time being, and time out of mind. The time of the poet, the philosopher, the pregnant woman, the calendar." [6]

The simple confusion of one construction of time with another has caused great difficulties for professional researchers in many disciplines, among them philosophy, biology, psychology, and physics. This confusion stems from the underlying, implicit belief that a "Real" linear time exists somewhere outside of man. To take one example, in *The Problem of Time*, Gunn points out that one stumbling block in physics has been the confusion of different time concepts, of physical time with either mathematical or clock time. [7] This mirrors the case within the psychology of consciousness, where the confusion has been between the time of experience and either biological time or the linear time of the clock.

Many psychological experiments have been performed to find out how "accurately" such "real" time is perceived. "Real time" is, of course, identified with the clock. To call the clock "Real Time" is somewhat like calling American money "real money": it is parochial at best. A useful psychological analysis should be concerned with time as a dimension of consciousness, as it exists in itself, not with how it relates to hours, days, burning rope, a sundial, or some other mode of defining time. It should answer the question, "How is linear time constructed?"

In considering time as a dimension of consciousness, we

must distinguish between the different modes of temporal experience, to be sure we will not confuse one mode with another. First, we will briefly consider the general dimensions of linear time: the present, duration, simultaneity, the concept of causality. Then we will undertake a closer analysis of duration, the mode which we usually experience, and consider one approach to understanding how this continuing experience is constructed. Finally, after a brief discussion of drug experiences, we will consider how else time might be experienced, especially the nonlinear mode, in which all action is experienced as a "patterned whole."

THE DIMENSIONS
OF LINEAR TIME EXPERIENCE

The Present

We continually experience the immediate present passing by, the time that is always NOW. This is the time of our immediate contact with the world, a very short, continually changing, fading away, forever being replaced by a new NOW. William James quotes an anonymous poet: "the moment of which I speak is already far away." In the linear mode, time is directional, a duration carrying us from the past into the future; the present is always fleeting away behind us as the poet laments. In the nonlinear mode, however, the present exists, and is all that exists.

In modern psychological research, the idea of a fleeting, immediate present seems to have held up under some rigorous experimental analyses. Peterson and Peterson, among others, have demonstrated the existence of an immediate memory process, fleeting and decaying quickly, that is distinct from the more permanent memory. George Miller and others have shown that the information-processing capacity of this immediate memory is fixed at a very low amount, and is difficult to modify by training.[8]

Duration

The other continuous mode in which we experience linear time is that of duration. This constitutes our normal experience of time passage, of hours lengthening and shortening, of a recent event seeming "a long time ago," of one interval passing more quickly for one person than another, or more quickly for the same person at one time than at another. Duration is the continuing, persevering, normal time of our lives. The short, decaying present is continuing, but always fading from consciousness. The experience of duration is malleable. One "hour" seems quite long, another brief. Our experience of duration seems to be constructed on the remembrance of things past—on retrospection.

It therefore may be that our linear experiences of time are divided along the lines of memory: the present (within these terms) constructed from short-term storage, the past or duration from the contents of long-term memory. There will obviously be a high correlation between these experiences if each involves memory, but, since not all experience enters our permanent store, the correlation will not be perfect.

Simultaneity

A less immediate dimension of our consciousness of time is its cultural definition. Our culture is largely linear, scientific, clock-oriented. We "break" time into small units, and "time" events precisely. But other cultures do not share this orientation. Some "break" the flow of events into larger chunks of simultaneity, and some dispense with the linear, sequential mode entirely.

When do we experience events as occurring "at the same time"? What *is* "at the same time"? Henri Bergson pointed out that this experience depends on one's frame of reference, on how fine one divides the "grain" of time experience, the basic unit of sequence.[9] The experience depends on the mode of consciousness employed as well. If we take the second as the basic unit, we must construct an experience of what occurred "at the same time" that is quite different from what we would construct if we consider all events within the time needed to boil rice as being "at the same time."

Causality

Causality can be inferred only within a linear mode of temporal consciousness. The information-processing of this mode breaks the flow of events into serial lists which can be sequentially analyzed, studied, and manipulated. Succession and duration are the underpinnings of causality, for without a concept of past and future, of discrete events following each other temporally, it would be impossible to perform scientifically meaningful analyses. Together with language and mathematics, this linear construction of temporal experience constitutes the essence of the active mode of consciousness.

THE CONSTRUCTION OF DURATION

It is duration more than any other continuing experience which underlies our lives. We continually experience the passage of time: we move out of the past into the future; we experience one hour passing quickly, another dragging on and on and on. Sometimes an entire year will pass with almost no notice, especially as we age; yet some years are so event-filled they seem to last forever.

Albert Einstein once jokingly explained, "When you sit with a nice girl for two hours, it seems like two minutes; when you sit on a hot stove for two minutes, it seems like two hours. That's Relativity." Many psychologists, ignoring the fact that ordinary temporal experience is personally and relativistically constructed, have searched for an internal organ of duration, rooted in one physiological process or another. This postulated "organ" has been termed a "biological clock." Again, this search follows from the sensory-process paradigm of how we experience time that is used by those who would try to determine the accuracy of our experience of time in relation to the ordinary clock. Such thinking confuses, once again, a convenient construction with Reality. A similar confusion was recently displayed by a group of farmers in the Midwest, who opposed the introduction of Daylight Savings Time on the grounds that the extra hour of sunlight would burn the grass.

Much difficulty results from trying to postulate an internal biological clock as the basis of ordinary temporal experience. A multiplicity of physiological processes, such as heart rate and basal metabolism, have been suggested as *the* clock, but many experiments have shown that these processes each seem to move at different rates. No single internal process which could be the clock has been found. There are, of course, many internal rhythmic processes which are quite important for consciousness, but these do not necessarily relate to time as it is experienced.

We seem to construct our experience of duration from the filtered contents of normal consciousness. When these contents are artificially restricted, as in sensory deprivation, our experience of duration shortens. Conversely, multidimensional complex experience causes duration experience to lengthen.

That our experience varies is, of course, not a new observation. It has strong antecedents in the work of the relativity-oriented time analysts, in Einstein's little joke, and in the work of the French philosopher Henri Bergson. Bergson noticed that duration is experienced differently by different people, and that it might even lengthen or shorten for one person relative to other experiences. The idea of a "sense" of time may be useful in ordinary discussion, when we might wish to compare experience to the clock, to discuss someone who is habitually not "on time," for instance, but as a scientific metaphor it has led to a search for a nonexistent organ of time experience and to an implicit acceptance of a linear Real Time as existing independently of our consciousness.

We can replace the "time sense" metaphor with a "construction of time" similar to our understanding of how the rest of normal consciousness is constructed. Temporal experience can then be studied without necessarily being tied to any process external to consciousness, be it a biological, chemical, or ordinary mechanical clock.

The Storage-Size Metaphor

To begin our thinking about physical memories, let us consider the computer. If we put information into a computer, and instruct it to store that information in a certain way, we can count the number of spaces in its memory that it uses to store that information. Using this approach, we can then relate our constructed experience of the duration of a given interval to the amount of information we remember about that interval. If more events, or more complex events, occur in that interval, the experience of duration should lengthen.[10]

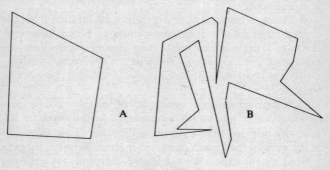

Figure 4.1

The more we experience and remember about a given situation, the longer our construction of its duration will be. Look at Figure 4.1, A, for thirty seconds, then look at Figure 4.1, B, for the same time. Chances are that your experience of duration was longer for the latter figure, even though you "knew" that the experiences were equal in clock seconds. A piece of music that contains 40 events per minute is experienced as shorter than one with 80 events per minute; the latter is experienced as shorter than one with 120 events per minute. If increasingly complex figures are displayed, such as those in Figure 4.1, A and B, the experience of duration lengthens, as it will for tapes that contain increasingly complex sequences of sounds. But it is ultimately memory on which we construct linear time. Suppose you go on an interesting vacation. Just before you return home, the period of vacation seems quite long. After you return and become immersed once again in your daily life, the duration of the vacation suddenly seems to collapse. When away, the memory of your experiences is complex: "We went to Waikiki beach, ate in that famous restaurant, listened to Dorman's orchestra, then traveled to another island, stayed here," etc. When you are home again, this complexity collapses: you merely code the experience as "I was in Hawaii for two weeks."

The psychologist Harton studied a similar phenomenon. He found that intervals containing successful events were estimated as shorter than those containing failures. He postulated that a successful experience becomes more organized in memory than a failure.[11] With increasing organization, the storage size of the interval is smaller (as when we know a code) and the duration experience lessens. In one of my own time experiments, the more organized was the memory of the shape of a line figure, the shorter was the experience of duration.

Duration experience, then, is malleable, a personal construction formed from the stored portion of normal experience. If we can understand that "duration" is only one possible way to construct a dimension of ordinary consciousness, not a sensory process reflecting a "Real" time existing independently of ourselves, then we can make some sense of the vast confusion in psychological research on time, and at least open up to consideration other possible ways in which our experience of time might be constructed.

DRUG EXPERIENCES AND TIME: A TRANSITION BETWEEN THE TWO MODES

Certain drugs, such as marijuana, LSD, DMT, and the amphetamines, including MDA, may radically alter the "reducing valve" of the normal sensory systems. If the dosage is relatively mild, the great increase in the contents of consciousness may produce an effect similar to increasing the amount of information reaching the person. Smokers of marijuana, for instance, typically report that their experience of duration lengthens during the period of intoxication, and also report that they experienced "more" during that interval than normal.

But with stronger drugs, the effect sometimes overwhelms the linear mode of consciousness entirely, and induces a nonlinear mode of experience. Very often this experience cannot be placed in linear coordinates, for it is outside this mode of operation, outside words, outside normal time. The best the verbal-logical mode can do to account for these experiences is to term them "timeless." These experiences, for many, represent the first significant break from a normal linear consciousness, normal reality, and normal time. For some, the break into a new area of experience is unsupported by the remainder of their lives and their training, and they may not be able to return to normal consciousness. The very discontinuity of these experiences is difficult for many to deal with.[12]

NONLINEAL TIME EXPERIENCE

During each complete day, our consciousness flows in and out of linearity. Each night we dream, and enter a world in which a linear sequence of time has less meaning. Events in the dream space seem fluid. When we recall dreams and try to place them in a linear mode, we often cannot decide whether one event preceded or followed another. At other times, almost randomly, moments come on each of us which are out of time. They are moments in which there is no future, no past, merely an immediate present. Our linear, analytic world is for the moment destructured. These moments naturally do not lend themselves to analysis, for analysis and language itself is based upon linearity. Often a word, spoken during such a moment, will be enough to return the experience to linearity, back into time as we ordinarily know it.

That we now lack a psychological framework for these

nonlinear time experiences means not that they should be ignored entirely, but that we must develop a suitable structure if we are to incorporate them into contemporary science. Perhaps one tentative step in that direction might be to regard these "present-centered" moments as shifts toward a right-hemisphere predominance. One approach to this problem could be in the study of the time experience of brain-damaged patients, or split-brain people. For instance it has been found that left-hemisphere damage interferes with the perception of sequence, while right hemisphere damage does not.[13]

These "timeless" experiences are often produced by psychoactive drugs, which overwhelm the linear construction and allow "an infinite present" to exist. The receptivity and present-centeredness of these experiences are sought in meditation, which also attempts to undo deliberately the "normal" process of constructing consciousness. It is to poets that we must look for any verbal celebration of this mode of time experience. One of the most successful attempts to discuss the indescribable mode of time is found in "Burnt Norton," a poem written about time by T. S. Eliot:

> Words move, music moves
> Only in time; but that which is only living
> Can only die. Words, after speech, reach
> Into the silence. Only by the form, the pattern,
> Can words or music reach
> The stillness, as a Chinese jar still
> Moves perpetually in its stillness.
> Not the stillness of the violin, while the note lasts,
> Not that only, but the coexistence,
> Or say that the end precedes the beginning,
> And the end and the beginning were always there
> Before the beginning and after the end.
> And all is always now. Words strain,
> Crack and sometimes break, under the burden,
> Under the tension, slip, slide, perish,
> Decay with imprecision, will not stay in place,
> Will not stay still. Shrieking voices
> Scolding, mocking, or merely chattering,

Always assail them. The Word in the desert
Is most attacked by voices of temptation,
The crying shadow in the funeral dance,
The loud lament of the disconsolate chimera.

The detail of the pattern is movement,
As in the figure of the ten stairs.
Desire itself is movement
Not in itself desirable;
Love is itself unmoving,
Only the cause and the end of movement,
Timeless, and undesiring
Except in the aspect of time
Caught in the form of limitation
Between unbeing and being.
Sudden in a shaft of sunlight
Even while the dust moves
There rises the hidden laughter
Of children in the foliage
Quick now, here, now, always—
Ridiculous the waste sad time
Stretching before and after.[14]

The distinction between these two modes of consciousness is well-represented in the drawing for "Moment in Time" at the beginning of this chapter. It depicts a situation that would be a linear sequence in "normal" consciousness as a unified "patterned whole."

The distinction between the two modes of time is also made in the Zen tradition. We ordinarily view events as sequence. We see a piece of burning wood *become* ashes. But to the present-centered consciousness,

When firewood becomes ashes
    it never returns to being firewood.
But we should not take the view
    that what is latterly ashes was formerly firewood.
What we should understand is that . . .
    firewood stays at the position of firewood.
There are former and later stages.

> We do not consider . . . that Winter
> *becomes* Spring or that Spring *becomes* summer.[15]

In this mode, all action occurs in an infinite present. There is no attribution of causality or construction of a sequence. All events occur simultaneously. Although the linear, analytic mode forms the basis for a complex, technological society, other societies have developed around the present-centered mode. It is the conflict between these two modes of consciousness which has caused much cultural and personal misunderstanding. A Westerner may wonder what the Zen monk is talking about when he speaks of "no time" existing. We wonder "why a person from India cannot seem to build a bridge 'on time.' " Yet this question is relevant only within our particular construction of reality, not in the nonlinear mode.

Recall the example in Chapter 2 of the Trobrianders, a culture which Dorothy Lee reports as based on nonlinearity and on present-centeredness.[16] To take an example similar to that of firewood and ashes, when we ordinarily view the process of the maturation of a plant (e.g., a yam), we see a sequence. We experience the *same* yam turning from ripeness to overripeness in sequential time. The Zen monk does not share our view, nor does the Trobriander. The ripe yam (which in the language of the Trobriander is called "taytu") *remains* a ripe yam. When an overripe yam appears, it is a different entity, not causally or sequentially connected with the ripe yam. It is another entity entirely and is even given another name, "Yowana." In Lee's words, there is no temporal connection between events in the world of the Trobriander, "no tenses, no distinction between past and present," as is also portrayed in the opening story. "What we consider a causal relationship in a sequence of connected events is to the Trobriander an ingredient in a patterned whole."

The two modes are personified by the scholar and by Nasrudin in the story: analysis in time is essential to the dominant mode in which consciousness is constructed in modern cultures; a "patterned whole" (or gestalt) and a total present-centeredness is likewise essential to the way in which the Sufi or the Zen monk constructs his consciousness, and seems to be a dominant mode of the people of the Trobriand Islands and of the Hopi Indians of the Southwest.

The temporal dimension is one key in a more complete science of consciousness. The recognition that the linear mode of time is but *one* possible construction opens up for consideration other modes of temporal experience, those associated with phenomena outside the range of the normal. For us, an event is considered "paranormal" if it does not fit within the coordinates of ordinary linear time. But if linear time is but one possibility, these unusual events, unusual communications, may in fact occur, even though they cannot be charted in the coordinates of linearity. The laws which govern such experiences may not be those which govern normal consciousness: the experience of the night is not that of the day.

The nonlineal mode is a daily part of the experience of each person. It is deliberately cultivated in "mystical" traditions, as a complement to ordinary consciousness. It is sometimes brought about by the administration of consciousness-altering drugs. It is the dominant cultural mode of the Trobriander and of the Hopi Indian. It is a mode associated with the intuitive, holistic side of ourselves.

For further reading

Robert E. Ornstein. *On the Experience of Time.* Harmondsworth, England, and Baltimore, Md.: Penguin Books, 1969.

Henri Bergson. *Time and Free Will.* New York: Harper & Row, 1960.

J. T. Fraser, ed. *The Voices of Time.* New York: George Braziller, 1966.

T. S. Eliot. *Four Quartets.* London: Faber. New York: Harcourt, Brace & World. 1943.

Carl G. Jung. "Synchronicity: An Acausal Connecting Principle." In *The Interpretation of Nature and the Psyche*, Bollingen Series LI. New York: Pantheon, 1955.

THE TRADITIONAL ESOTERIC PSYCHOLOGIES

Chapter 5

Introduction

In our society, those who are intrigued by such questions as how the mind works, or what is the nature of human consciousness, or what rules govern evolution, often become psychologists, philosophers, physicians, psychiatrists. In the cultures of the Middle and Far East, especially in the past, those similarly intrigued by consciousness and the questions that surround it have generally entered the relevant disciplines of *their* society, such as Buddhism, Yoga, or Sufism.

These traditional, "esoteric" psychologies have emphasized a personal, empirical approach to knowledge that is very different from our Western attempt to achieve an "objective," impersonal knowledge. Until quite recently, our culture lacked paradigms that could allow us to appreciate these esoteric traditions, just as our rugseller friend lacked the constructs necessary to appreciate numbers higher than 100. An impersonal, objective, scientific approach, with its exclusive emphasis on logic and analysis, makes it difficult for most of us even to conceive of a psychology which could be based on the existence of another, intuitive, "gestalt" mode of thought.

Our preceding analysis of consciousness within the modern framework does, however, give us a way to begin opening up these esoteric psychologies to consideration. From modern psychology, we learn that our normal, stable consciousness is a personal construction. Although this construction has been a success, it is not the only way in which "Reality" can be apprehended. Scientific knowledge is perhaps the highest development of the linear mode, but the linear mode is only *one* mode possible for us. We find that another major mode of consciousness manifests itself culturally, personally, and physiologically. It is a mode of consciousness which is *a*rational, in space but not in time; in the terms of the *I Ching*, it is receptive, as opposed to active. Such a mode is difficult to encompass within the lineal, verbal terms so dominant in our culture, but it is this mode of knowing which is cultivated in the esoteric traditions.

We are now for the first time in a position to begin seriously dealing with a psychology which can: speak of a "transcendence" of time as we know it; encompass *a*rational mentation; use exercises for control of the "autonomic" nervous system; develop techniques for entering a state of "void" or no mind; and employ procedures for inducing communication which is "paranormal" according to our ordinary conceptions of what is possible for man. Since these experiences are, by their very mode of operation, not readily accessible to causal explanation or even to linguistic exploration, many have been tempted to ignore them or even to deny their existence. These traditional psychologies have been relegated to the "esoteric" or the "occult," the realm of the mysterious—the word most often employed is "mysticism." It is the taboo area of inquiry, which has been symbolized by the Dark, the Left side of ourselves, the Night.

One meaning of "esoteric" is "deeply hidden, inaccessible, needing special training." There is, of course, much esotericism in modern science as well. In the past century, many academics and researchers have become exceedingly specialized, with many devoting their careers to the exploration of one approach to a part of a part of a problem. Many, if not most, psychologists can no longer fully understand all the research current in their field, since it includes everything from electrochemical analyses of single cells on the retina to demographic analyses of voting patterns.

Inaccessibility, difficulty, and an elitist "professionalism" are accretions which, unfortunately, form around almost every human endeavor. They have formed around the traditional esoteric psychologies as well as around modern scientific psychology. In each approach, a certain parochialism tends to creep in. For instance, a scientific psychologist may be interested in the relationship of consciousness to the brain and may become an electroencephalographer, measuring the tiny voltages which appear at the scalp, attempting to relate them to states of consciousness. In time, his vision may narrow to the complex problems of analysis of the EEG, and his interest may become focused on technique rather than content. A similar narrowing of vision occurred in psychology as a discipline since the advent of Behaviorism.

In the traditional psychologies, one group may find that a certain technique works well in a given situation. Its members may tend to apply it in situations where it is inappropriate, or with people for whom it is inappropriate. Because the technique works for them, they come to believe that it ought to work for everyone at all times. The technique becomes the end, and may become an obsession. Those who are involved in using such a technique, be it a particular meditation technique or a certain breathing exercise, can become fixated and restricted to what the technique has to offer. The adherents may set up schools to teach the "sacred" ritual, forgetting that any technique has its relevance only for a certain community at a certain time. Just as can happen with any scientific technique which is overextended or which persists for too long, the original application and intent of the esoteric technique may become lost, although the surface appearance of the enterprise is well-maintained. Religions construct cathedrals and design robes, just as scientists develop elaborate equipment and professional journals, but all too often the enterprise may become limited to a propagation of the means, with the original end, the desired objective, forgotten.

Within either the scientific or esoteric traditions, parochialism can lead to a disdain for others who employ another technique in an attempt to reach the same end. The very word "academic" has come to mean a distinction which has little real significance. Within the esoteric traditions, "religious" arguments mirror the process. A small stylistic difference in a "sacred" prayer or a meditation may cause a schism which may lead to lasting and sometimes violent disagreements.

The disdain is often greater between members of the modern and the traditional esoteric psychologies. Many Westerners see those of the Orient as following a path of self-indulgence, performing useless and ridiculous rituals, and withdrawing from life while many starve around them. From the other side come attacks on "materialism" and on the consciousness of Western man as a total "illusion."

Although the mutual disdain has at times bordered on the fanatic, the disdain does mark a certain imbalance in each of the major approaches when they are taken to extremes. On the one hand, many cultures seem unable to feed, clothe, and house their people adequately. They seem to lack a full measure of the skills needed to organize and coordinate effort. The underdevelopment of a linear causal mode of operation may in part contribute to these societal problems. On the other hand, the development of a purely logical, rational science, unbalanced by a perspective born of intuition, can proceed, if unchecked, close to the point of self-destruction. This lack of an over-all perspective can lead to a certain sterility and irrelevance in the content of scientific inquiry. At worst, science becomes technology for its own sake, the performance of experiments simply because they *can* be performed, or the building of a new highway simply because it *can* be built. In both cases, the imbalance contributes somewhat to major cultural problems.

For Western students of psychology and science, it is time to begin a new synthesis, to "translate" some of the concepts and ideas of the traditional psychologies into modern psychological terms, to regain a balance lost. To do this, we must first extend the boundaries of inquiry of modern science, *extend our concept of what is possible for man.*

It is the very esotericism of both systems which is an obstacle to this process. The language and procedures of the traditional esoteric psychologies seem difficult to comprehend, let alone practice. There is, too, our own tendency to want conclusive proof at once, in our own logical and causal terms. If, for instance, a man reports experiences which we consider "paranormal," we naturally want him to perform them in *our* laboratory under *our* strict conditions in *our* time-scale. The hazards of such impatience can at least be clarified by considering the following example.

Suppose we tell an illiterate peasant from Afghanistan that

human beings can construct space vehicles which can take them to the planets. He may at first simply dismiss the possibility from his mind, then later, if we say it often or compellingly enough, allow it some credence. He may become excited, since this concept is for him a radical extension of the possibilities open to him in his life. He now knows that Man is capable of building a spaceship.

But we must inform him that, to accomplish this feat, he must first learn an entirely new language, English, and then a new vocabulary, mathematics. After learning the basics of grammar, he will need to study technical manuals. He will also need the cooperation of many other similarly trained people who have interlocking skills and who want to help in such a complex project. There is also the question of money, and countless other considerations.

Our peasant knows nothing of this. He cannot see why, if it is indeed *possible* (as we claim) for man to fly to the planets, he cannot do it *now* in his own terms. If we try to be helpful, and give him a first book on English in order to allow him to make the necessary first step, he may be either offended or incredulous. "What do these stupid marks on paper have to do with the grandeur of a flight to the planets?" he may ask. He may, if he does not follow our advice, attempt to fly to Venus by means of his own primitive technology, intending to take along some friends who are similarly excited with the idea. When he fails, he will likely come to believe that "space flight" is really an impossibility, and that anyone who claims it to be possible is simply gullible, "unscientific," or even a liar.

It is similar tendencies in ourselves which we, as Western students of psychology, may need to overcome in investigating an area which is so new, so spectacular, and so unknown to us. And the problem for us is indeed great, for there is no other area of human experience, save perhaps sexuality, about which so much garbage has been written. The Sufi poet Rumi noted this process when he wrote, "Counterfeiters exist only because real gold does exist."

We are not about to write off Western science merely because, in some cases, it has committed excesses; so we should not ignore "Eastern science" because of its imbalances, or because of the misinterpretations heaped around it.

The next two chapters of this book are a preliminary attempt to encompass some of the concepts, techniques, and exercises of the traditional psychologies within a more conventionally Western framework—in hopes that the pace of the necessary synthesis may be quickened. These chapters are a bit longer and more discursive than the others in this book, since they introduce areas of inquiry largely unrepresented in contemporary psychology.

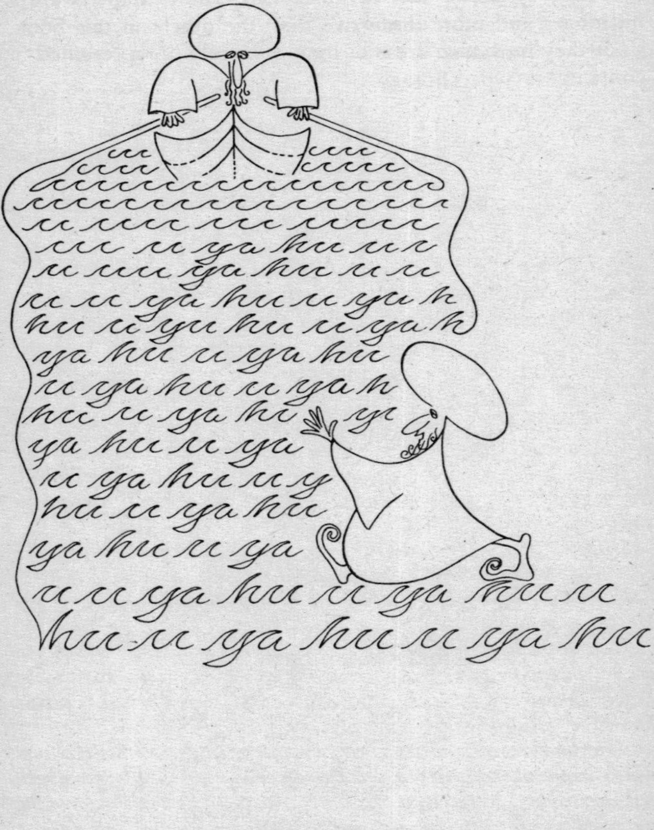

Chapter 6

Meditation Exercises

The Man Who Walked on Water

A conventionally minded dervish, from an austerely pious school, was walking one day along a river bank. He was absorbed in concentration on moralistic and scholastic problems, for this was the form which Sufi teaching had taken in the community to which he belonged. He equated emotional religion with the search for ultimate Truth.

Suddenly his thoughts were interrupted by a loud shout: someone was repeating the dervish call. "There is no point in that," he said to himself, "because the man is mispronouncing the syllables. Instead of intoning YA HU, he is saying U YA HU."

Then he realized that he had a duty, as a more careful student, to correct this unfortunate person, who might have no opportunity to be rightly guided, and was therefore probably only doing his best to attune himself to the idea behind the sounds.

So he hired a boat, and made his way to the island in midstream from which the sound appeared to come. There he found a man sitting in a reed hut, dressed in a dervish robe, moving in time to his own repetition of the initiatory phrase. "My friend," said the first dervish, "you are mispronouncing the phrase. It is incumbent on me to tell you this, because there is merit for him who gives and for him who takes advice. This is the way in which you speak it," and he told him.

"Thank you," said the other dervish humbly.

The first dervish entered his boat again, full of satisfaction at having done a good deed. After all, it was said that a man who could repeat the sacred formula correctly could even walk on the waves: something that he had never seen, but had always hoped–for some reason–to be able to achieve.

Now he could hear nothing from the reed hut, but he was sure that his lesson had been well taken. Then he heard a faltering U YA as the second dervish started to repeat the phrase in his old way.

While the first dervish was thinking about this, reflecting on the perversity of humanity and its persistence in error, he suddenly saw a strange sight. From the island, the other dervish was coming toward him, walking on the surface of the water.

Amazed, he stopped rowing. The second dervish walked up to him, and said, "Brother, I am sorry to trouble you, but I have come out to ask you again the standard method of making the repetition you were telling me, because I find it difficult to remember it." [1]

Many questions arise when one tries to consider the esoteric traditions, meditation exercises in particular. The interested student immediately discovers a bizarre and seemingly unconnected variety of techniques. Turkish dervishes spin in a circle. Buddhists concentrate on their breathing. Yogis may gaze at a mandala or at a vase. A person may be asked to contemplate a meaningless phrase, such as "Show me your face before your father and mother met." What do these diverse exercises have in common, in terms of how they work, and in terms of the experiences which they make possible?

Several aspects of meditation are even more confusing to the interested psychologist. What is a state of "no mind," or of a "mysterious darkness"? People meditate to change consciousness, to bring about what is often called a "mystic" experience. But what is the nature of this experience, and how do the meditation techniques bring it about? Is there any way that these techniques and these experiences can be integrated with a contemporary knowledge of the psychology of consciousness? What relevance do the techniques and the experiences have to contemporary psychology, and to individuals? It is these concerns I touch on in this chapter.

Meditation is among the most common and the most highly perfected of the techniques of the traditional psychologies. Such techniques have been employed in almost every culture, from that of ancient Egypt to that of the contemporary Eskimo.

Since they have recently gained some currency within our culture, meditation exercises (and their accompanying psychologies) have aroused much confused repulsion and attraction in the minds of many. In considering meditation, some devalue the entire process as one alien to the Western sensibility, while others are superficially attracted to the trivial and exotic aspects of the techniques.

Some of this results from simple misinterpretation. "Meditation" is often considered to be a form of directed thinking, as when we say "I'll meditate on that," meaning "I'll think about it, consider it, and come to a conclusion." If meditation is considered an exercise in reason or problem-solving, then some of the statements and claims of its Indian and Japanese practitioners seem incomprehensible. When they speak of "thinking of nothing" or of entering a "void" or "nirvana" or of achieving a state of "no mind," the techniques may only call forth disdain in the Western mind, for how could reason lead to nothingness? [2]

Also, the negative aspects of meditation can become salient. For instance, an obsessive overindulgence in these exercises may lead to a permanent withdrawal from life, a regression from and a devaluation of intellectuality. It is certainly true that, devoid of a proper context, meditation can and has become an empty technique, food for the literal-minded who insist on the "proper" procedure, but have forgotten its purpose. And yet it is the attitude and *attention* of the meditator which is important, rather than the specific form of his practice, as is emphasized in the story which begins this chapter.

But the exercises of meditation do not involve reason, and they cannot be understood by means of ordinary logic alone. They are, rather, techniques designed to cultivate a certain mode of operation of the nervous system, at a certain time, within a certain context. *This* is the use of "thinking of nothing."

The other side of our response to the esoteric psychologies is an attraction to the exotic for its own sake. Words like *koan, mantra,* and *karma* spice many conversations these days. The style of dress of the "Indian Holy Man" is now often adopted by the college student. A diet may be followed out of context, be it kosher or macrobiotic. To this type of mind, the more esoteric the technique, the better.

Some friends of mine recently made a hopeful journey to India. Attracted by the repute of a certain famous guru (teacher), they hitchhiked across country, found a very inexpensive trans-Atlantic flight, and then traveled overland, with great difficulty, all the way to the Himalayas in the Indian subcontinent.

Finally, after walking for days and days, they reached the ashram (a sort of "religious living association") of the guru. After allowing them some time to calm down, the guru saw them. Their hopes were high: perhaps they would receive a mysterious "secret initiation" or maybe even a genuine "magic word." When they had outlined their trek, their difficulties, their expectations, and their hopes, the guru instructed them: "Sit, facing the wall, and count your breaths. This is all."

My friends were crestfallen. To have come so far, to have undergone so much, to learn a technique so ordinary they "could have learned it at home." But few of them realized that this was the point of the demonstration.

An analysis of any experiential phenomenon in terms of science, here in terms of psychology and physiology, is naturally more limited, more restricted, and drier than the actual experience. When we try to bring any experience within the linear frame of reference of science, a great deal of its richness and complexity is unfortunately lost in our attempt to gain a measure of precision.

A story in Philip Kapleau's *The Three Pillars of Zen* provides us with a useful point at which to begin a psychological consideration of the practices of meditation.

> The importance of single-mindedness, of bare attention, is illustrated in the following anecdote:
> One day a man of the people said to the Zen master Ikkyu:
> "Master, will you please write for me some maxims of the highest wisdom?"
> Ikkyu immediately took his brush and wrote the word "Attention."
> "Is that all?" asked the man. "Will you not add something more?"
> Ikkyu then wrote twice running: "Attention. Attention."
> "Well," remarked the man rather irritably, "I really don't see much depth or subtlety in what you have just written."
> Then Ikkyu wrote the same word three times running: "Attention. Attention. Attention."
> Half angered, the man demanded: "What does that word Attention mean anyway?"
> And Ikkyu answered, gently: "Attention means attention." [3]

The concept "meditation" refers to a set of techniques which are the product of another type of psychology, one that aims at personal rather than intellectual knowledge. As such, the exercises are designed to produce an alteration in consciousness—a shift away from the active, outward-oriented, linear mode and toward the receptive and quiescent mode, and usually a shift from an external focus of attention to an internal one. If this alteration is isolated from the context needed to support it (as when, typically, Westerners try meditating), it can be meaningless, or even disruptive. But as a first step in many of the traditional psychologies, meditation is regarded as an extremely important preparation for a more comprehensive personal knowledge. For many, it may also demonstrate experientially that ordinary consciousness is a personal construction, that it can be extended to a new mode of operation.

In terms of one of the running metaphors in this book, meditation is a technique for turning down the brilliance of the day, so that everpresent and subtle sources of energy can be perceived within. It constitutes a deliberate attempt to separate oneself for a short period from the flow of daily life, and to "turn off" the active mode of normal consciousness, in order to enter the complementary mode of "darkness" and receptivity. It is an attempt to inhibit the usual mode of consciousness, and to cultivate a second mode that is available to man.

Since reliable information about the various forms of meditation has so far been rather hard to come by in the Western world, we should perhaps first set the background and review some of the general similarities of meditation exercises. Most involve separating the practitioner from the daily, ongoing activities. He usually sits alone, or with a small group, in a special, quiet room set aside for meditation, or, if outside, in a special place (perhaps constructed) in a naturally isolated area, sometimes near a waterfall. Generally, he attempts to keep all external sources of stimulation to a minimum, to avoid being distracted from his object of meditation. This isolation is felt to be especially needful in modern cities, where the many random sounds and human voices can be very distracting. In most forms of Yoga and in Zen, there is emphasis on maintaining a specific posture, the lotus position, in order to keep body movements to a minimum and therefore out of awareness during the meditation period. The straight back is said, traditionally, to lessen the possibility of drowsiness in the reduced stimulation setting.

The general instructions for most beginning meditation exercises are similar: pay attention closely and continuously to the meditation object (say, a vase). This exercise is more difficult than it sounds: most beginners lose awareness of the meditation object quite often. Each time one notices that awareness has shifted away from the object of meditation, one must return the attention to it. In many of the esoteric traditions, each session of meditation lasts about half an hour. In most, although not all, meditation may be practiced twice a day, often in the morning before the day's major work, and again in the evening. Beginners usually practice for less time and work up to about half an hour a day. As progress is made, more and more complicated exercises are usually given.

In terms of the psychology of consciousness, there are two general varieties of meditation: those exercises which involve restriction of awareness, focusing of attention on the object of meditation or on the repetition of a word (which Claudio Naranjo terms "concentrative meditation" [4]); and those which involve a deliberate attempt to "open up" awareness of the external environment. In the next, long section we will consider concentrative meditation, in the following one, the opening-up form.

CONCENTRATIVE MEDITATION

If we review the extraordinary diversity of the techniques of concentrative meditation in different cultures at different times, one general similarity seems to come through. No matter the form or technique, the essence of meditation seems to consist in an attempt to restrict awareness to a single, unchanging source of stimulation for a definite period of time. In many traditions, the successful achievement of this is termed "one-pointedness of mind."

If the exercise involves vision, the meditator gazes at the object of meditation continuously. If the meditation is auditory, the sound, chant, or prayer is repeated over and over again, either aloud or silently. If the meditation consists in physical movement, the movement is repeated again and again. In all cases, awareness is focused completely on the movement, the visual object, or the sound.

Buddhist Meditation

In Zen, as a first exercise, the student is instructed to count his breaths from one to ten, and repeat. When the count is lost, as it will be by beginners, the instructions are that "the count should be returned to one and begun again." After he is able to concentrate completely on his breaths, the student then begins a more advanced exercise and focuses attention on the *process* of breathing itself. He thinks about nothing but the movement of the air within himself, the air reaching his nose, going down into the lungs, remaining in the lungs, and finally going out again. This is a convenient way to begin meditating, since breathing is a repetitious, rhythmic activity, which continues whether we will it or not.

In *What the Buddha Taught*, Walpola Ruhula gives these instructions:

> You breathe in and out all day and night, but you are never mindful of it, you never for a second concentrate your mind on it. Now you are going to do just this. Breathe in and out as usual, without any effort or strain. Now, bring your mind to concentrate on your breathing-in and breathing-out, let your mind watch and observe your breathing in and out; let your mind be aware and vigilant of your breathing in and out. When you breathe, you sometimes take deep breaths, sometimes not. This does not matter at all. Breathe normally and naturally. The only thing is that when you take deep breaths you should be aware of its movements and changes. Forget all other things, your surroundings, your environment; do not raise your eyes and look at anything. Try to do this for five or ten minutes.
>
> At the beginning, you will find it extremely difficult to bring your mind to concentrate on your breathing. You will be astonished how your mind runs away. It does not stay. You begin to think of various things. You hear sounds outside. Your mind is disturbed and distracted. You may be dismayed and disappointed. But if you continue to practice this exercise twice a day, morning and evening, for about five or ten minutes at a time, you will gradually, by and by, begin to concentrate your mind on your breathing. After a certain period you will experience just that split second when your mind is fully concentrated on your breathing, when you will not hear even sounds nearby, when no external world exists for you.[5]

As the student of Rinzai Zen progresses, he learns to keep himself motionless, and to sit in the lotus position. As he learns to maintain awareness of his breath successfully, he is given a more advanced meditation exercise: a riddle or a paradox, called a koan, to meditate on. To many commentators, at least to those who try to fit it into a linear framework, the koan has been the subject of much misunderstanding and confusion. The question-and-answer routine has seemed to be one for the Marx Brothers. The "question" may be, "Show me your face before your mother and father met." The "answer" may be the student's slapping the questioner in the face. The master asks the student, "Move that boat on the lake right now with your mind!" and the student stands up, runs over and hits his head against the gong, turns a somersault, and lands in front of the master, "fully enlightened." Since the student "answered" successfully, it is quite clear that the "answers" to the koan are not to be considered logically, as set answers to a rational problem that can be solved by the usual manner of thinking through various rational alternatives and choosing one. In fact, the lack of a rational solution is intended to demonstrate to the practitioner that the solutions in this new mode of experience are not those of the intellect.

We might instead consider the koan exercise in the terms of the psychology of consciousness. In these terms, the koan is an extreme and compelling method of forcing intense concentration on one single thought. This is an early koan exercise:

> In all seriousness, a monk asked Joshu, "Has the dog Buddha nature or not?"
> Joshu retorted, "Mu!"

This koan is to be taken not verbally and logically, not as something to be worked through like a problem, but as an extreme exercise in concentration. This is confirmed in instructions given in the lectures of a contemporary Zen master, Yasutani Roshi:

> You must concentrate day and night, questioning yourself about Mu through every one of your 360 bones and 84,000

pores . . . what this refers to is your entire being. Let all of you become one mass of doubt and questioning. Concentrate on and penetrate fully into Mu. To penetrate into Mu means to achieve absolute unity with it. How can you achieve this unity? By holding to Mu tenaciously day and night! Do not separate yourself from it under any circumstances! Focus your mind on it constantly. "Do not construe Mu as nothingness and do not conceive it in terms of existence or nonexistence." You must not, in other words, think of Mu as a problem involving the existence or nonexistence of Buddha-nature. Then what do you do? You stop speculating and concentrate wholly on Mu—just Mu! [6]

Later koan exercises involve other unanswerable questions, such as "What is the sound of one hand clapping?" and "What is the size of the real you?" A contemporary Los Angeles Zen master gives "How can I attain enlightenment by driving on the freeway?" Because no verbal-logical answer to the question can be found, the koan becomes a useful and demanding focus of attention over a very long period of time. The koan becomes a meditation object, day and night, a constant and compelling focusing of awareness on a single source. The lack of a rational, logical solution forces the student to go through and to discard all verbal associations, all thoughts, all solutions—the "left hemisphere" activity usually evoked by a question. He is then forced by the nature of the question itself to approach the condition known as "one-pointedness"—concentrating solely on one thing: the unanswerable koan. It is an attempt actively to destructure the ordinarily lineal mode of consciousness.

Focusing attention is helped by the social demands put on the student, by the pressures he imposes upon himself to achieve a breakthrough (to solve the koan), by the attitude of his fellow students, and by his interviews *(dokusan)* with the Zen master. In the interviews, the Zen student is often asked to demonstrate his level of understanding by giving an "answer" to the koan. Obviously, the desired answer is not verbal or logical; ideally, it should be nonverbal, nonlineal communication of a new level of awareness brought about by the *process* of concentrating on the koan. The "correct" answer, which may be only one of many possible ones, seems strange only in terms of logic; it is intended to communicate to the "other" side.

The use of the koan is strongest in the Rinzai school of Zen, which emphasizes sudden alterations of awareness (satori) brought about by this extreme concentration on one point over a long period of time under stress.

Yoga

The practices of Yoga are much more varied than those of Zen. Concentrative meditation in Yoga is only one part of a totality of activity, each part of which contributes to alterations of consciousness. Many Yoga practitioners devote their effort to attempts to alter basic "involuntary" physiological processes—blood flow, heart rate, digestive activity, muscular activity, breathing, etc. There are many popular and semi-scientific reports of Yoga masters being buried alive for long periods of time, of stopping their blood flow, of walking barefoot on hot coals. In a laboratory study, Anand and his associates have found that some yogis can reduce oxygen consumption to levels far below normal.[7]

A common form of yogic meditation practice involves the use of mantras. Mantras are often words of significance, such as names of the deity, but for the psychology of consciousness the important element is that the technique uses a word as the focus of awareness, just as the first Zen exercises make use of breathing. The instructions are to repeat the mantra over and over again, either aloud or silently. The mantra is to be kept in awareness to the exclusion of all else; just as in the first Zen exercise, when awareness lapses from the breathing, the attention is to be returned to it. Mantras are sonorous, flowing words that repeat easily. An example is *Om.* This mantra is chanted aloud in groups or used individually in silent or voiced meditation. Another mantra is *Om mani padme hum,* a smooth mellifluous chant. Similar mantras have analogous sounds such as *Ayn* or *Hum,* somewhat similar in sound to *Mu* in the first Zen koan.

Quite recently, a form of Mantram Yoga, "Transcendental Meditation," has become fairly well-known in the West, especially in the United States. In this form of meditation, too, the practitioner is given a specific mantra and repeats it silently over and over for about half an hour twice a day, once in the morning and again in the evening. No special posture is required for the exercise; rather, one is instructed to assume a comfortable posture, such as sitting erect in a chair. The thoughts that arise during the meditation are considered to be of no significance, and as soon as one is aware that one is no longer focused on the mantra, attention is to be returned to it.

The specific mantras used in "Transcendental Meditation" are not given publicly, since the devotees of this technique claim that there are special effects of each word, in addition to the general effects of the concentration. But it can be noted here that these mantras are also mellifluous and smooth, including many M's, Y's, and vowels, similar to *Om* or the sound of *Mu* in Zen. The devotees of "Transcendental Meditation" also claim that this technique presents the essence of meditation in a form suitable for Westerners.[8]

There is no doubt that Mantram Yoga, including "Transcendental Meditation," is a very convenient form of meditation. As in the breathing exercises, it is quite easy to produce and attend to a silent word, anywhere, at any time. Since no special posture is required, the arduous training for sitting in a lotus position is unnecessary. If the essential component of meditation involves concentration on an unchanging stimulus, then "Transcendental Meditation," as well as other forms of Mantram Yoga, can be said to possess this essence.

Other forms of Yoga practice make use of visual meditation techniques. The yogi generally sits in a lotus position and views a specially constructed visual image, a mandala. Mandalas take many forms: they may be very simple, like a circle, or extremely complicated, like the Yantra of Tantric practice.[9]

Mandalas are used much like mantras. The practitioner focuses his gaze on the mandala, and restricts his awareness to the visual input. Any stray thought or association or feeling that arises is ignored; attention is withheld from the stray thought or association and returned to the mandala. Simple mandalas often employ a circular motif, in which awareness is drawn to the center as one continues to contemplate, fixing one's gaze more and more closely on the center.

Another visual meditation technique in Yoga involves a "steady gaze" *(tratakam)* on external objects. External objects are used in meditation to provide a focus for a fixed point of concentration, rather than for their physical characteristics; so one can use a stone, a vase, a light, a candle, etc. Rammurti Mishra, a teacher of one sect of Yoga, in his manual *Fundamentals of Yoga*, gives instructions for this practice:

> *Tratakam* on external objects: Select a picture of a perfect Yogi or respected teacher; or you can select some small, round object on the wall of your room if you do not know any liberated soul: a round object, a miniature, a small round point, or zero. Think of the thing selected, that is, the symbolic nature, and by gazing at the symbol you are gazing at supreme consciousness and supreme nature. . . . Look at this object steadily, practice constantly and regularly, never gaze long enough to tire your eyes, close your eyes and meditate when you feel strained. After a few months of constant and regular practice, you will increase your power to stare at this object almost indefinitely without strain, fatigue, and blinking.[10]

The repetitive processes of the body, such as breathing and heartbeats, can serve as similar foci for concentration in Yoga. These techniques are described in Mishra's manual and in many others. Internally generated sounds *(nadam)* can also be foci for meditation. The sounds used in meditation can be internal, imaginary, or natural. Often the yogi sits near a source of repetitive sound, such as a waterfall, wind source, or beehive, and simply listens and concentrates. When these repetitious, monotonous sounds are imagined, the technique becomes quite similar to the silent repetition of a mantra. The creation of a meditation image can extend to visual meditation as well. Frederic Spiegelberg, in *Spiritual Practices of India*, describes the dharana, or fixation of consciousness procedures, in the *kasina* exercises:

> The point of primary importance is that one should really create such a meditation image to accompany him continuously; only as a secondary consideration does it matter what this particular image may be, that is, through which one of the Kasina exercises it has been produced. Instead of contemplating a disc of earth, for example, one can meditate on an evenly ploughed field seen from a distance. In the water Kasina, the yogi concentrates either on the circular surface of water in a jar, or on a lake seen from a mountain. So, too, the fire on the hearth, the flame of a candle, the wind that sways the crests of the trees may also be used as Kasina. The exercise of Color Kasina makes use of round colored discs, and even of bright-colored flags and flowers. In Space Kasina one meditates on a circular window opening, the attention in this case being directed primarily to the dimensional proportions of the opening.
>
> Every image that remains permanently in one's consciousness and every enduring mood can be a help to this fixation of one's consciousness. As a matter of fact, every hallucination, every unappeasable hatred, every amorous attachment provides a certain power of concentration to him who cherishes it, and helps him direct the forces of his being towards a single goal. This is of course more the case with the man who has achieved self-control and freedom from his passions, and who after having mastered his sense impulses succeeds in giving to his consciousness a definite turn of his own choosing. . . . Every activity is of equal value as a basis for a Dharana exercise.[11]

Mudra, another variety of yogic meditation practice, consists of repetitive physical movements, usually of the arms, legs, or fingers. In these exercises, the specified movement of the limbs is repeated over and over in the same way as a mantra. Awareness is continually directed toward the process of making the movements. Mudras vary in complexity; a simple one may be touching the thumb to the other four fingers in order, and repeating this procedure. The mudra may be combined with the mantra. For instance, this fourfold repetitive mudra is often combined with the mantra *Om mani padme hum,* each word corresponding to the thumb's movement to a finger.

The Sufis

Manuals for Sufic practice are not readily available, whereas ones are for Yoga and Zen. The Sufis hold that techniques must be administered with the time, place, and state of the student taken into account, and that publication of the details of their practices may lead to faulty application of the exercises. They say, for instance, that a technique such as meditation is useful at a specific stage of development, and persistence in any technique after the appropriate period would be a waste of time or might even be harmful.

However, there are fragmentary reports of some Sufic meditation exercises which, although they are intended to be used in a Moslem culture, can be summarized here. Of all the Sufi sects, the Maulavi (whirling) dervishes are perhaps the most familiar to the West. They perform a dance involving spinning and repetition of phrases. George Gurdjieff, who was trained by dervishes, explains the dance of the dervishes as an exercise for the brain based on repetition. Idries Shah writes of these orders: "The so-called dancing dervishes accomplish trance and ecstatic phenomena through monotonous, repetitious circumambulations, and this is marked in the Maulavi order, most popular in Turkey." [12]

The dance of the dervishes involves the repetition of physical movements and, concurrently, sounds. One of the few available first-person descriptions of this dance is found in Roy Weaver Davidson's valuable symposium, *Documents on Contemporary Dervish Communities.* It is an account by Omar Michael Berg, who traveled to a dervish assembly in Tunisia and participated in a dervish dance.

Explanation of the Zikr (repetition). The Dhikr, it was explained to me, is a dance; or, more properly, a performance of a series of exercises in unison. The objective is to produce a state of ritual ecstasy and to accelerate the contact of the Sufi's mind with the world mind, of which he considers himself to be a part. . . . The dance is defined by them as bodily movements linked to a thought and a sound or a series of sounds. The movements develop the body; the thought focuses the mind and the sound fuses the two and orientates them toward a consciousness of divine contact, which is called *Hal*, meaning "state" or "condition."

Description of the *Zikr* at *Nefta*. A double circle is formed in the center of the hall. Dervishes stand while the sheik intones, the opening part of this and every similar ceremony—the calling down of the blessing upon the congregation upon the Masters, "past, present, and future." Outside the circle stand the sheik, drummer, and flute player, together with two "callers," men who call the rhythm of the dance. The drum begins to beat, the caller begins to call a high-pitched flamenco-type air, and slowly the concentric circles begin to revolve in opposite directions. Then the sheik calls out, *"Ya Haadi!"* (O Guide!) and the participants start to repeat this word. They concentrate on it, saying it at first slowly, then faster and faster. Their movements match the repetitions.

I noticed that the eyes of some of the dervishes took on a far-away look, and they started to move jerkily as if they were puppets. The circles moved faster and faster until I (moving in the outer circle) saw only a whirl of robes and lost count of time. Now and then, with a grunt or a sharp cry, one of the dervishes would drop out of the circle and would be led away by an assistant, to lie on the ground in what seemed to be an hypnotic state. I began to be affected and found that, although I was not dizzy, my mind was functioning in a very strange and unfamiliar way. The sensation is difficult to describe and is probably a complex one. One feeling was that of a lightening; as if I had no anxieties, no problems. Another was that I was a part of this moving circle and that my individuality was gone; I was delightfully merged in something larger.

[He leaves the dance, and later] I went out into the courtyard to assess my feelings; something *had* happened. In the first place, the moon seemed immensely bright, and the little glowing lamps seemed surrounded by a whole spectrum of colors.[13]

The Sufis use other forms of concentrative meditation, some of which appear rather similar to those of Zen and Yoga. The first line of the Koran is quite often used for verbal repetition.

> Having prepared a room which is empty, dark, and clean, in which he will, for preference, burn some sweet-scented incense, let him sit there, cross-legged, facing the *qibla* (direction of Mecca). Laying his hands on his thighs, let him stir up his heart to wakefulness, keeping a guard on his eyes. Then with profound veneration he should say aloud: *"La ilaha illa'llah."* The *"La ilaha"* should be fetched from the roots of the navel, and the *"illa'llah"* drawn into the heart, so that the powerful effects of the *Zikr (dhikr)* may make themselves felt in all the limbs and organs. But let him not raise his voice too loud. He should strive, as far as possible, to damp and lower it according to the words "Invoke thy Lord in thyself humbly and with compunction, without publicity of speech." . . .
>
> After this fashion, then, he will utter the *Zikr* frequently and intently, thinking in his heart on the meaning of it and banishing every distraction. When he thinks of *"La ilaha,"* he should tell himself: I want nothing, seek nothing, love nothing *"illa'llah"*—but God. Thus, with *"La ilaha"* he denies and excludes all competing objects, and with *"illa'llah"* he affirms and posits the divine Majesty as his sole object loved, sought and aimed at.
>
> In each *Zikr* his heart should be aware and present *(hazir)* from start to finish, with denial and affirmation. If he finds in his heart something to which he is attached, let him not regard it but give his attention to the divine Majesty, seeking the grace of help from the holy patronage of his spiritual Father. With the negation *"La ilaha"* let him wipe out that attachment, uprooting the love of that thing from his heart, and with *"illa'llah"* let him set up in its place the love of Truth (God).[14]

There exist fragmentary descriptions of other exercises used by the Sufis and some of their followers. A student of George

Gurdjieff writes of meditating on a series of dots on a piece of paper. The dervishes repeat the phrase "Ya hu" like a Yoga mantram or the Zen koan *Mu* and also repeat stories over and over in their minds, as Zen Buddhists do with the koan.

Western Meditation

Similar forms of meditative practices exist in familiar Western religions, as well as in sects less known than Yoga, Zen, and Sufism. In Christianity, for example, the exercise of contemplation performed a function similar to that of meditation in Zen, Yoga, and Sufism. Jakob Böhme, the Christian mystic, practiced fixing his gaze on a spot of sunlight on his cobbler's crystal as his object of contemplation throughout the entire day. He then carried this image with him all the time, in the same way, perhaps, that the yogi can construct a yantra at will and observe it. Deikman comments that the Christian mystics Walter Hilton and St. John of the Cross gave instructions for contemplation exercises that were strikingly similar to those of Patanjali, the author of the Yoga sutras.

> In Hilton one reads, "Therefore if you desire to discover your soul, withdraw your thoughts from outward and material things, forgetting, if possible, your own body and its five senses." St. John calls for the explicit banishment of memory. "Of all these forms and manners of knowledge the soul must strip and void itself and it must strive to lose the imaginary apprehension of them, so that there may be left in it no kind of impression of knowledge, nor trace of thought whatsoever, but rather the soul must remain barren and bare, as if these forms had never passed through it, and in total oblivion and suspension. This cannot happen unless the memory can be annihilated of all its forms, if it is to be united with God. . . ." Patanjali comments, "Binding the mindstuff to a place is fixed attention, focusing the presented idea on that place is contemplation." [15]

Some current practices in the Christian church and in Judaism have some similarities to, and even perhaps their origins in, the practices of meditation. Prayer, in general, is a practice most similar to concentrative meditation. St. John Climacus said: "If many words are used in prayer, all sorts of distracting pictures hover in the mind but worship is lost. If little is said or only a single word pronounced, the mind remains concentrated." The "Russian Pilgrim" said: "If thou wilt that thy prayer be pure, made up of good and lovely things, thou must choose a short one consisting of a few powerful words and repeat it many times."

Many prayers are monotonous, repetitive chants. Judaism makes use of ritual nodding movements and intoned prayers. Hasidism and the Cabalistic tradition contain many elements similar to Zen, Yoga, and Sufism, and, similarly, the cross and the Star of David appear as contemplation objects in traditions other than the Jewish and Christian; some of the yantras in *Tantra Art*, for instance, contain many six-pointed stars.

Perhaps one reason for today's decline of interest in these more-organized religions is that their original emphasis on direct experiential knowledge has largely been muted. Although the techniques for altering consciousness still persist, they have often become "automatic," part of a set ritual, something lacking their original purpose. The "Prayer of the Heart" in the Greek Orthodox tradition, however, is much less removed from the meditative traditions.

> The mind should be in the heart—a distinctive feature of the method of prayer. It should guard the heart while it prays, revolve, remaining always within, and thence, from the depths of the heart, offer up prayers to God. (Everything is in this; work in this way until you are given to taste the Lord.) . . .
> As to other results which usually come from this work, with God's help, you will learn them from your own experience, by keeping your mind attentive and in your heart to holding Jesus, that is, His prayer—Lord Jesus Christ, have mercy upon me! One of the holy fathers said: "Sit in your cell and this prayer will teach you everything."

A Christian breathing exercise is also described.

> You know, brother, how do we breathe: we breathe the air in and out. On this is based the life of the body, and on this depends its warmth. So, sitting down in your cell, collect

your mind, lead it into the path of the breath, along which the air enters in, constrain it to enter the heart together with the inhaled air, and keep it there. Keep it there, but do not leave it silent and idle; instead give it the following prayer: "Lord, Jesus Christ, Son of God, have mercy upon me." Let this be its constant occupation, never to be abandoned. For this work, by keeping the mind free from dreaming, renders it unassailable to suggestions of the enemy and leads it to Divine desire and love.[16]

A similar focusing of awareness is also part of Taoist meditation. Instructions are given to sit quietly and focus awareness on the center of the body, on one point, on the abdomen. The medieval alchemists described long and repetitive exercises—the continual redistillation of water, the prolonged grinding exercises—which were written down allegedly for the "distillation" of base metal in order to transmute it into gold, but which can also be considered symbolically as descriptions of attempts to alter man's awareness from his ordinary "base" level to a higher one, symbolized by the gold.

Peter Freuchen, in his *Book of the Eskimos*, describes a technique for meditation in which the Eskimo sits facing a large soft stone; he takes a small hard stone and begins to carve a circle in the larger one by moving the small stone continuously around and around the larger surface. This practice, similar to the creation of a mandala, often lasts for several days at a time and is designed to produce a trance state.[17] Many primitive peoples, such as the Bushmen of the Kalahari Desert, dance in a circle facing a fire, staring at the fire, and repetitiously chanting. Some gaze continuously at the full moon, the sun, or at a candle.

This has been a fairly quick, selective review of some of the major forms of concentrative meditation. Each of the major Eastern traditions—Buddhism, Yoga, Sufism—uses exercises involving different sensory modalities. A chant is repeated in the various traditions: a word, koan, mantra, prayer, or dervish call. Concentration is focused on the breath, on the heart beat, on the short prayer, on a longer prayer, on a story, or on natural sounds, such as a waterfall or the humming of bees, or on vibration. Symbols or pictures of gurus are gazed at steadily, and images are created in the mind's eye of the practitioner. Sufi dervishes dance in a repetitive whirl; Indian yogis make continuous movements with their limbs; Taoists concentrate on their abdomen. The early Christian Fathers contemplated an object or the cross. These are all externally different forms of the same type of meditation.

The common element in these diverse practices seems to be the active restriction of awareness to one single, unchanging process, and the withdrawal of attention from ordinary thought. It does not seem to matter which actual physical practice is followed; whether one symbol or another is employed; whether the visual system is used or body movements repeated; whether awareness is focused on a limb or on a sound or on a word or on a prayer. This process might be considered, in psychological terms, as an attempt to recycle the same subroutine over and over again in the nervous system. The instructions for meditation are consistent with this surmise: one is instructed always to rid awareness of any thought save the object of meditation, to shut oneself off from the main flow of ongoing external activity, and to pay attention only to the object or process of meditation. Almost any process or object seems usable and has probably been used. The specific object used for meditation is much less important than the maintaining of the object as the single focus of awareness during a long period of time, as in the story which begins this chapter. It seems that the sensory mode of meditation, too, makes little difference. The important effect is the state evoked by the process of repetition.

In terms of consciousness, the effect of concentrative meditation is to lead to a "one-pointedness" or to a "clear" state. The state is generally described as "dark," or in Indian terminology, "the void," or "emptiness." It is a withdrawal of the senses, a "turning off" of perception of the external world in order to enter the receptive, "night" consciousness, *The Darkness*. In yogic practice this withdrawal is most explicitly sought. In Buddhism, recall that Rahula says, in describing the breathing meditation, that "after a certain period you will have experienced just that split second when your mind is fully concentrated on your breathing, when you will not even hear sounds nearby, when no external world exists for you." Augustine Poulain describes it as "a mysterious darkness wherein is contained the limitless Good, a void, other than solitude." St. John of the Cross describes it as the "annihilation of memory."

These techniques have persisted for centuries. Many sensory modalities have been employed, and many different symbols or objects within any one sensory modality have been used. This may indicate that one primary effect of the concentrative meditation exercises is the state of emptiness, the nonresponsiveness to the external world, evoked in the central nervous system by the continuous subroutine called up by the exercise, regardless of what the specific input is or what sensory modality is employed. Since we, the Bushmen, the Eskimos, the monks of Tibet, the Zen masters, the Yoga adepts, and the dervishes all have the same kind of nervous system, it is not so surprising that similarities in techniques should have evolved.

Some Psychological Research
Related to Concentrative Meditation

There is research which casts some light on *how* the meditation exercises affect consciousness: a body of work on the psychological and physiological effects of restricting awareness to an unchanging stimulus. We can examine meditation techniques in these psychological terms. For instance, one variety of concentrative meditation uses a "steady gaze" on either a natural object or a specially constructed one, a mandala. A very similar situation would arise if input to the eye were always the same, no matter how one moved one's eyes.

Normally, as we look at the world, our eyes move around and fixate at various points in large movements which are called "saccades." We hardly ever gaze steadily at any one object for a prolonged period of time. Even when we try to fix vision on a single object, very small involuntary movements of the eye occur, called "optical nystagmus." The image on the retina is kept in constant motion by both types of eye movements, and different cells are stimulated from moment to moment.

A group of physiological psychologists has succeeded in devising a system that will keep a visual image perfectly stable on the retina, even though the eyes are in constant motion. One apparatus for producing this "stabilized" image consists of an extremely small projector mounted on a contact lens worn by the subject. The contact lens moves with every movement of the eyeball, and so does the projector. The projector faces the eyeball, and no matter how the eye is moved, the same image always falls on the retina.[18]

This study of stabilized images was undertaken in psychology primarily to investigate a theory of Donald Hebb, according to which continuous change in input is needed to maintain normal awareness. It was felt that "stabilizing" the image would eliminate the continuous changes in input that normally occur as we move our eyes. The subjects, looking at the stabilized images, reported that the images disappeared.

Lehmann, Beeler, and Fender attempted to investigate the brain state evoked by the stabilized image.[19] The electroencephalogram (EEG), recorded at the scalp, consists of the tiny electrical potentials that emanate from the brain. These potentials, which are about 5 to 50 millionths of a volt as recorded at the scalp, are amplified and written out on paper by the electroencephalograph. The first brain rhythm was discovered by Hans Berger in 1924, and was termed the "alpha" rhythm; it consists of rhythmic activity between 8 and 12 Hertz (cycles per second). Since Berger, other rhythms have been classified: beta, defined as 12 cycles and above; theta, 4–7 Hz; and delta, 1–4 Hz. The alpha rhythm in the occipital cortex is usually thought to represent a state of decreased visual attention to the external environment. It almost always increases when the eyes are closed, or when the eyes are rolled up into the head, cutting off vision.

These investigators recorded the EEG from the occipital cortex of the brain while their observer was viewing the stabilized image. They asked their observer to press a button when the stabilized image disappeared, and they attempted to correlate the subjective experience of the disappearance of the image with the concurrent brain state. They found that the alpha rhythm was likely to appear at the time when the subject reported the disappearance of the image.

Another way to supply the observer with uniform visual input is to have him observe a completely patternless visual field, called a "ganzfeld." This field can be produced in many ways. A white-washed surface can serve as a ganzfeld, as can two halved ping-pong balls placed over the eyes.[20]

In viewing the ganzfeld, some observers reported an absence of any visual experience—which they called "blank-out." This was not merely the experience of seeing nothing, but one of not seeing, a complete disappearance of the sense of vision for short periods of time, as Cohen put it. The experience of not seeing at all usually occurred after about twenty minutes of exposure to the ganzfeld. During "blank-out" the observers did not know, for instance, whether their eyes were open or not, and they could not even control their eye movements. Cohen's suggestion was that this continuous uniform stimulation resulted in the failure of any kind of image to be produced in consciousness. He also found that the periods of blank-out were associated with bursts of alpha rhythm. He suggested that the appearance of alpha during these continuous stimulation periods indicated a functional similarity between continuous stimulation and no stimulation at all. He also found that individuals with high-alpha EEG's were more susceptible to the blank-out phenomenon.

Tepas performed a study on the ganzfeld similar to that of Lehmann, Beeler, and Fender on the stabilized image. His observers watched the ganzfeld for five-minute periods while EEG's were recorded. When the observer experienced the blank-out, he was asked to press a microswitch that marked the EEG record. Tepas found that the alpha activity of the brain increased during the period of blank-out.[21]

Both the situation and the effects of the stabilized image

and of the ganzfeld are similar to those of concentrative meditation. Consider the activity of the observer in meditation and in the two precisely regulated input situations: in both an attempt is made to provide unchanging input. And the subjective experience is analogous in these situations: there is a loss of contact with the external world. In both situations, EEG monitoring of the brain's activity reveals an increase in alpha rhythm. The electrophysiological studies of meditation by Bagchi and Wenger, those by Anand and others in India on Yoga meditation, and those by Kasamatsu and Hirai, and by Akishige in Japan, on Zen meditation, and by Wallace in the United States on Transcendental Meditation, indicate that meditation also is a high-alpha state.[22] The more precisely controlled situations seem to produce, both psychologically and physiologically, effects similar to those of concentrative meditation.

One consequence of the way our central nervous system is structured seems to be that, if awareness is restricted to one unchanging source of stimulation, a "turning off" of consciousness of the external world follows. The common instructions for concentrative meditation all underscore this; one is advised to be constantly aware of the object of meditation and nothing else, to continuously recycle the same input over and over. Stabilizing a visual image or homogenizing visual input results in the same experience. A set of instructions from the English mystical tradition given by Knowles indicates that this blanking-out is a desired function of meditation that can be produced by restriction of awareness.

> Forget all creatures that God ever made, and the works of them so that thy thought or thy desire not be directed or stretched to any of them, neither in general nor in special. . . . At the first time when thou dost it, thou findest but a darkness and as it were a kind of unknowing, thou knowest not what, saving that thou feelest in thy will a naked intent unto God.[23]

The interpretations of this experience of "darkness," of "blank-out," of the "void," of the disappearance of an image in the subject of a scientific experiment, would certainly differ: the subject of a physiological experiment would have extremely different expectations and ideas about his experience than a man who has sought to reach such experience by subjecting himself to an esoteric discipline. But the experiences themselves have essential similarities and are produced through quite similar procedures.

"OPENING-UP" MEDITATION EXERCISES

The second form of meditation exercises is much more closely related to daily activity. These exercises do not attempt to isolate the person from ordinary life processes; rather, they attempt to use these processes in the training of consciousness. An example is found in the Zen tradition; in the more advanced forms of Zen (in the Soto sect), once the concentrative exercise of breath-counting is mastered, the second form of meditation exercises, *shikan-taza*, is practiced—"just sitting." The Zen master Yasutani Roshi describes this exercise as follows:

> *Shikan* means "nothing but" or "just," while *ta* means "to hit" and *za* "to sit." Hence *shikan-taza* is a practice in which the mind is intensely involved in just sitting. In this type of Za-Zen it is all too easy for the mind, which is not supported by such aids as counting the breath or by a koan, to become distracted. The correct temper of mind therefore becomes doubly important. Now, in *shikan-taza* the mind must be unhurried yet at the same time firmly planted or massively composed, like Mount Fuji, let us say. But it also must be alert, stretched, like a taut bowstring. So *shikan-taza* is a heightened state of concentrated awareness wherein one is neither tense nor hurried, and certainly never slack. It is the mind of somebody facing death. Let us imagine that you are engaged in a duel of swordsmanship of the kind that used to take place in ancient Japan. As you face your opponent, you are unceasingly watchful, set, ready. Were you to relax your vigilance even momentarily, you would be cut down instantly. A crowd gathers to see

the fight. Since you are not blind you see them from the corner of your eye, and since you are not deaf you hear them. But not for an instant is your mind captured by these sense impressions.

This state cannot be maintained for long—in fact, you ought not to do *shikan-taza* for more than half an hour at a sitting.[24]

We can, then, consider *two basic types of meditation exercises*— both concerned with a common effect—those which "turn off" input processing for a period of time to achieve an aftereffect of "opening up" of awareness, and those which consist in the active practice of "opening up" during the period of the exercise.

Active practice in opening up awareness is practiced generally in the esoteric traditions, but in Zen it is a specific meditation exercise. A less demanding Buddhist practice stems from one component of the Buddha's Eightfold Path, and is usually termed "right-mindedness." It requires that one be "conscious" of each action, develop a present-centered consciousness, "open up" awareness of daily activities *while* engaged in them. Rahula says:

Another very important, practical, and useful form of "meditation" (mental development) is to be aware and mindful of whatever you do, physically or verbally, during the daily routine of work in your life, private, public, or professional. Whether you walk, stand, sit, lie down, or sleep, whether you stretch or bend your limbs, whether you look around, whether you put on your clothes, whether you talk or keep silent, whether you eat or drink—even whether you answer the calls of nature—in these and other activities you should be fully aware and mindful of the act performed at the moment. That is to say, that you should live in the present moment, in the present action. This does not mean that you should not think of them in relation to the present moment, to the present action, when and where this is relevant.

People do not generally live in their actions in the

present moment. They live in the past or in the future. Though they seem to be doing something now here, they live somewhere else in their thoughts, in their problems and worries, usually in the memories of the past or in desires and speculations about the future. Therefore, they do not live in nor do they enjoy what they do at the moment; so they are unhappy and discontented with the present moment with the work at hand. Naturally, they cannot give themselves fully to what they appear to be doing.[25]

In Yoga, a form of self-observation is called "the Witness." Here the attempt is to observe oneself as if one were another person. One tries to notice exactly what one is doing—to invest ordinary activity with attention. The Witness does not judge action nor does it initiate action. The Witness simply observes.

This practice is highly developed in Zen. Right-mindedness, or attention to what one is doing, can be a part of any activity that one performs, no matter how base. There is no action that cannot be used to develop one's consciousness. One simply need be "mindful" of present actions. One can be performing actions that are quite degrading to a Buddhist, such as butchering an animal, but simply by paying close attention to what one is doing, one's awareness can be developed.

In Sufism, at least in the version that is attributed to Gurdjieff, there are similar practices, one of which is called "self-remembering." As in Zen, no special constraints are put on action. There are no prohibitions about what can be eaten, nor do general rules of conduct exist. The attempt is simply to be aware of oneself. Gurdjieff's students are constantly instructed to "remember themselves" wherever they are, remember that they are present, and to notice what they do. When one is "remembering oneself," in Gurdjieff's terms, one is considered to be "awake."

A similar exercise attributed to Gurdjieff consists simply in maintaining continuous awareness of a part of one's body— an elbow, hand, leg. Another exercise of this tradition is to perform ordinary habitual actions slightly differently, such as putting shoes on in the opposite order, shaving the other side of the face first, eating with the left hand (if one is right-handed). These exercises can be seen as attempts to return habitual, "automatic" actions to full awareness.

Recall the phenomenon of habituation.* A slight change in input is enough to "dishabituate" and to return the stimulus to awareness. Similarly, slightly altering our usual "automatic" behavior, such as tying shoes, driving cars, shaving, can return the process to awareness.

Similarly, in the tradition of *Karma Yoga*, the intent is to treat everyday activities as a "sacrament"—to give them full attention. This exercise performs a function similar to "right-mindedness" and "self-remembering," and is a less extreme version of *shikan-taza*.

Many schools within these traditions combine the two major types of awareness exercises, devoting half an hour or so twice a day to the "shutting down" form of meditation and as much as possible of the remainder of the day to a form of self-observation.

DISHABITUATION RESEARCH

There have been some psychological and physiological studies of the state of awareness of practitioners in and after meditation. These studies have used the EEG to measure the response of the brain of meditators to external stimulation.

When we enter a room and hear a clock ticking, we ordinarily learn to tune it out fairly quickly. Physiologically, the normal "orienting response" to new stimulation begins to disappear after a few moments and does not reappear. On the psychological level, this pattern could be described as the construction of an internal model of the clock which then allows us to ignore it. But if consciousness were like a mirror, then each time the clock ticked it would be "reflected."

The Indian psychologists' studies on Yoga meditation showed this result. By recording the yogi's EEG while

* See pages 45–47.

introducing external stimuli, they confirmed this analysis of the effects and aftereffects of meditation. During the meditation and during the withdrawal, there was no interruption in the alpha rhythm of the yogi's brain because of the external stimuli. However, when the yogi was not meditating, repetition of an external stimulus showed none of the habituation that presumably would have occurred in other subjects.[26]

The Japanese neuropsychiatrists Kasamatsu and Hirai studied the habituation of the orienting response to a repeating click, both in ordinary people and in Zen masters. The subjects in this experiment sat in a sound-proof room and listened to a click repeated each fifteen seconds while an EEG was being taken. The normal subjects showed the customary phenomenon of habituation. The response of the brain's electrical activity to the clicks began to decrease after the third or fourth click. After habituation, each time the click occurred there was no response in the brain of the subject: the click had been tuned out of awareness. When the Zen masters were meditating and were exposed to this same repetitive click over a period of five minutes, they did not show the customary habituation; they responded to the last click just as strongly as they did to the first. They did not seem to make a "model" of the repetitive stimulation and so tune it out.[27]

It seems, therefore, that there is dishabituation *during* the advanced form of Zen meditation—that is, a consistent response to a stimulus which continues. There is a "shutting down" of awareness of external stimuli during Yoga meditation, but when the yogi is not in meditation, we might expect no habituation to a repetitive stimulus (if he is advanced enough in his practice).

DEAUTOMATIZATION

In general, the esoteric traditions characterize consciousness in terms similar to those of modern psychology. The Sufis' conceptions are clear precursors of those of modern psychology. Sufi teaching stories frequently focus on men who are too preoccupied to hear what is being said, or who misinterpret instructions because of their expectations, or who do not see what is in front of them because of the limitations of their constructs. The Sufis emphasize the constantly changing biases that constitute our normal awareness. "What a piece of bread looks like depends on whether you are hungry." The Sufis quite explicitly consider the effects of our limited category system on consciousness. Many of their descriptions of consciousness could have been a statement of Bruner's about category systems, or a summary by Lettvin of his research on the frog, e.g., "Offer a donkey a salad, and he will ask what kind of thistle it is." They emphasize that we, like the rugseller, can only be aware of what our conceptions will allow, and of what our senses will transmit to us.

The Sufi and other traditions contend that our selective and restricted ordinary consciousness is to be overcome by the process of meditation, among many other possible exercises and techniques. One specific aim in these traditions is to dismantle the automaticity and selectivity of ordinary awareness. The Sufis characterize ordinary consciousness as a state of "deep sleep" or "blindness"—an overconcern with the irrelevant dimensions of the world. Gurdjieff's image is that man places shock absorbers between himself and the world. "We must destroy our buffers; children have none; therefore we must become like little children." In Indian thought, personal consciousness is compared to a "drunken monkey" living solely in his constructs—the world of "illusion." This same thought is a metaphorical meaning of the "fall" of man in the Christian tradition. These metaphors, without their derogatory connotations, can be understood in terms of modern psychology as depicting our selective, constructed awareness, our model-building, automaticity, and limited category systems.

One aim of the esoteric disciplines is to remove "blindness" or the "illusion," to "awaken" a "fresh" perception. "Enlightenment" or "illumination" are words often used for progress in these disciplines, for a breakthrough in the level of awareness—flooding a dark spot with light. The Indian tradition speaks of opening the third eye, of seeing more and from a new vantage point. Satori, in Zen, is considered an intuitive "awakening." The Sufis speak of the development of a "new organ" of perception.

Reports of the experiences of those who practice the meditative disciplines indicate that a primary *aftereffect* of the concentrative meditation exercises is an opening up of awareness, a "deautomatization," as Deikman calls it, which might be a reduction of the normal selectivity of input. Deikman's own subjects in experimental meditation, who gazed at a blue vase for half an hour at a time for several sessions, reported that the vase appeared "more vivid" and "more luminous." [28] Deikman quotes Augustine Poulain, who emphasized that concentrative meditation is a temporary process of withdrawal, similar to the blank-out of consciousness, but here with the intent to become deautomatized.

> It is the mysterious darkness wherein is contained the limitless Good. To such an extent are we admitted and absorbed into something that is one, simple, divine, and illuminable that we seem no longer distinguishable from it. . . . In this unity the feeling of multiplicity disappears. When afterwards these persons come to themselves again, they find themselves possessed of a more distinct knowledge of things, some luminous and more perfect than that of others.[29]

Some speak of seeing things "freshly" or as if for the first time. To William Blake, it is a "cleansing of the doors of perception." Others, like Gurdjieff, compare their experiences to that of a child, who presumably has not yet developed many automatic ways of tuning out the world. In Zen, one speaks similarly of seeing something the five-hundredth time in the same way that one saw it the first time.

These descriptions are understandable and translatable into contemporary psychological terms—as the process of building a model of the environment, and testing and selecting input against the model. When we see something for the five-hundredth time, we have developed a model for it and tune out the input.

These characterizations of consciousness represent a meeting point between scientific psychological research and the metaphors of the esoteric psychologists. Contemporary psychologists speak of the brain's controlling input, building models, responding "automatically" to the external environment. The esoteric traditions refer to this process as man's lacking full awareness of his surroundings, and consider this "blindness" the barrier to his development. The practice of meditation, then, can be considered as one attempt to turn off linear, verbal activity temporarily, and to shut off all input processing for a period of time.

A result of this "turning off" of the input selection systems seems to be that, when the same sensory input is later introduced, we see it differently, "anew." When we leave our normal surroundings and go on vacation, we usually return to find ourselves much "more aware" of the immediate environment. We play many of our old records, which we haven't "heard" in a while. We look anew at the plants in our garden, the painting on our walls, our friends. Getting away and returning seem to have the same effect on awareness as presenting new stimuli.*

We can consider the process of concentrative meditation as similar to that of taking a vacation—leaving the situation, "turning off" our routine way of dealing with the external world for a period, later returning to find it "fresh," "new," "different," our awareness "deautomatized."

We easily adapt to almost any new input. A new technology, a new person, a change in our immediate environment, quickly become an integral part of our lives, part of our model of the external world. This model-building process is specifically what is to be dismantled by the practice of meditation. In Zen, one is invited to stop conceptualizing while remaining fully awake. In Yoga, the aim is to leave the "illusion"—to cease identifying the external world with our constructed models of it. The esoteric traditions thus speak of developing a

---

* Compare the phenomenon of "spontaneous recovery" in habituation.

consciousness that allows every stimulus to enter into consciousness, devoid of normal input selection, model-building, and category systems.

A mirror metaphor is used in many traditions to describe the desired mode of consciousness. The Sufi poet Omar Khayyám says: "I am a mirror, and who looks at me, whatever good or bad he speaks, he speaks of himself." The contemporary Zen master Suzuki Roshi says, "The perfect man employs his mind as a mirror, it grasps nothing, it refuses nothing, it receives but does not keep." Christ said in prayer, "A mirror I am to thee that perceivest me." The metaphor of consciousness as a mirror fits well with some of the psychologists' own metaphors. A mirror allows every input to enter equally, reflects each equally, and cannot be tuned to receive a special kind of input. It does not add anything to the input, and does not turn off repetitive stimuli; it does not focus on any particular aspect of input and retune back and forth, but continuously admits all inputs equally.

"Direct" Perception

The metaphor of a mirror leads to another consideration. Many of the traditions claim to allow men to experience the world *directly*. The Sufis speak of attaining an "objective consciousness," others of "cosmic consciousness." The statement is often made that one can have *direct* perception of reality. Whether one can perceive "reality" directly is not yet a question for science, but some comment within the terms of psychology might be made. The ability to "mirror," to be free of the normal restrictions—of the tuning, biasing, and filtering processes of consciousness—may be a part of what is meant by "direct" perception.

This state can perhaps be considered in psychological terms as a diminution of the interactive nature of awareness: a state in which we do not select, or "bet" on the nature of the world, or sort into restrictive categories; rather, a state in which all possible categories are held at once. It has also been described as a state of living totally in the present, of not thinking about the future or the past; a state in which everything that is happening in the present moment enters into awareness.

MEDITATION, DEAUTOMATIZATION, AND THE "MYSTIC EXPERIENCE"

The two major forms of meditation exercises, the concentrative and the "opening up" forms, are intended to cause a shift in the mode of consciousness of the practitioner. The concentrative form turns off the normal mode of operation and allows a sensitivity to subtle stimuli which often go unnoticed in the normal mode, as the stars remain unseen in the light of day. It also produces an *aftereffect* of "fresh" perception when the practitioner returns to his usual surroundings, as a vacation allows us to "see" our environment anew.

Concentrative meditation, coupled with dishabituation exercises, undoes the normal construction of consciousness. When the normal mode is temporarily dismantled, the other major mode can emerge—that of the "night," the receptive, the often misunderstood and devalued mode of intuition.

In many traditions, a full emergence of this mode has come to be known as a "mystic" experience. The word "mystic" may be unfortunate, since many confuse it with "mystical," and with occultism and "mystery." We should not be surprised that the very name given to this experience implies incomprehensibility, since the experience is not within the province of the linear, verbal mode of consciousness. One part of us may simply be incapable of fully understanding the experience of the other part, and may give it a name which reflects this lack of comprehension.

This mode of consciousness, though, is to some degree a part of the daily experience of each of us. Its full development can result from a life crisis, by accident, or sometimes "spontaneously." It may be occasioned by many methods other than meditation—by fasting, by ritual dance, by the ingestion of certain psychoactive drugs, all of which upset the normal lineal construction of consciousness. The work of the esoteric psychologies is toward extending normal linear consciousness to include such experience.

The "mystic" consciousness is described by many, in almost every esoteric tradition, from the ancient Hindu to the contemporary European. It is described in the Bible, in the Koran, in Whitman, in James's *The Varieties of Religious Experience*. It is the "mysterious darkness" of Augustine Poulain, a mode in which ordinary consciousness of a "multiplicity" of people and objects disappears, to be replaced by the awareness of "unity."

The consciousness of "unity," or "oneness" as it is sometimes called, is perhaps the most fully developed form of this mode of experience. In terms of the story of the blind men and the elephant, the mystic experience involves a shift in consciousness from the analytic, individual, piecemeal approach to knowledge, to a more receptive, holistic mode, one which can encompass the entire elephant as a whole.[30]

A second characteristic of these experiences, as described both by William James and by Arthur Deikman, is their sense of "realness"; they involve reliance on a type of verification that is more intuitive than our usual linear and inferential one.[31]

This mode of consciousness is admittedly quite unusual in its most-developed form, in which the "vividness" and "richness" of normal consciousness is greatly enhanced, in which linear time, as we know it, has no meaning. Deikman attributes the "vividness" and "richness" to a "deautomatization" of consciousness. To repeat William Blake: "If the doors of perception were cleansed, man would see everything as it is, infinite."

The contents of this experience are often said to be "ineffable," incapable of being fully communicated by words or by reference to similar experiences in ordinary life. One person echoes this feeling, wishing that he had some competence in the more ordinary aspects of the holistic mode of consciousness, so that he might communicate it more clearly.

What is a "transcendent dimension of being"? Such words on paper are little more than metaphysical poetry. Somehow I feel I could better communicate my experience by composing a symphony or by molding a twisted piece of contemporary sculpture, had I the talents required for either form of artistic expression. In no sense have I an urge to formulate philosophical or theological dogmas about my experience. Only my silence can retain its purity and genuineness.[32]

The essence of this mode is experiential, and the insights available in this mode cannot always be translated into sequential terms. As Arthur Deikman says, "Ordinary language is structured to follow the logical development of one idea at a time, and it might be quite inadequate to express an experience encompassing a large number of concepts simultaneously." [33]

So the practices of meditation—whirling, chanting, concentrating on a nonsensical question, repeating a "sacred" prayer over and over, visualizing a cross, gazing at a vase—are not quite so exotic as those who deliberately seek the esoteric might wish; but neither are they exercises in reason or problem-solving. They are exercises in attentional deployment, both those which focus on one stimulus and those which are intended to actively deautomatize ordinary consciousness.

The "mystic" experience—brought about by concentrative meditation, deautomatization exercises, and other techniques intended to alter ordinary, linear consciousness—is, then, a shift from that normal, analytic world containing separate, discrete objects and persons to a second mode, an experience of "unity," a mode of intuition. This experience is outside the province of language and rationality, being a mode of simultaneity, a dimension of consciousness complementary to the ordered sequence of normal thought.

But why have people sought to develop this mode, and what value is there in a "mystic" experience? The answers to these questions are not easy. Many of the traditional replies are well-known; yet some brief interpretation and comment can usefully be made.

First, the analytic, linear mode of consciousness cannot encompass many aspects of life which many people want to experience and understand. That these phenomena have been "ruled out" of much of Western scientific inquiry does not lessen the need that many now feel to explore these areas personally. Meditation is an attempt to alter consciousness in such a way that other aspects of reality can become accessible to the practitioner, who can add personal knowledge to intellectual.

Second, the analytic mode, in which there is separation of objects, of the self from others (I-it relationship), has proved useful in individual biological survival; yet this mode apparently evolved to fit the conditions of life many thousands of years ago. The evolution of culture proceeds much more quickly than biological evolution; so the analytic mode may not be as all-important a criterion for our contemporary Western society as it once was. The awareness of separation was a great advantage when survival threatened an individual's existence; for instance, one could isolate an enemy animal, kill it, and use it for food. However, this basic need, for individual survival, is no longer quite so basic for many in the West. After all, most of us now buy our food; we do not need to hunt for it. Few readers of this book are in any danger of imminent starvation. Instead, the survival problems now facing us are collective rather than individual: problems of how to prevent a large nuclear war, pollution of the earth, overpopulation. And notice that in these examples, a focus on individual consciousness, individual survival, works against, not for, a solution. A shift toward a consciousness of the interconnectedness of life, toward a relinquishing of the "every man for himself" attitude inherent in our ordinary construction of consciousness, might enable us to take those "selfless" steps that could begin to solve our collective problems. Certainly our culture has too severely emphasized the development of only one way of organizing reality. Perhaps at this point in time we can begin to see that the complementary mode can have survival value for our culture as a whole. (In a very minor way, some recent cultural events can be seen in this light: I refer to the increasing awareness of the earth as one system that is part of the ecology movement, and to the increasing development of interdisciplinary training and systems analysis within science.)

Additionally, Keith Wallace and Herbert Benson, among others, point out that the change in our culture to a predominantly technological, scientific one during the last few centuries has caused a radical increase in the environmental stresses placed on each person. Many diseases, such as the increased incidence of hypertension, can in some part be linked to these radical changes in our environment. Wallace and Benson suggest that the development of increased self-knowledge and quiescence through meditation may be a way in which we could learn to cope with the stress, since the demands placed on us by our society are unlikely to diminish greatly.[34] But most importantly, it is the shift from an individual and analytic consciousness to the attainment of an overall perspective of "unity," of "humanity as one organism," which is the purpose of the esoteric traditions and the aim of these meditation exercises. We shall have more to discuss on this in the next chapter.

For further reading

Philip Kapleau. *The Three Pillars of Zen.* Boston: Beacon Press, 1967.

Walpola Rahula. *What the Buddha Taught.* New York: Grove Press, 1959.

Frederic Spiegelberg. *Spiritual Practices of India.* New York: Citadel Press, 1962.

Robert Keith Wallace and Herbert Benson. "The Physiology of Meditation." *Scientific American* (Feb. 1972), pp. 84–90.

Arthur Deikman. "Deautomatization and the Mystic Experience." *Psychiatry*, 29 (1966), 329–343.

The above are reprinted, in whole or in part, in Robert Ornstein, ed., *The Nature of Human Consciousness.* San Francisco: W. H. Freeman and Co. New York: The Viking Press. 1973.

Claudio Naranjo and Robert Ornstein. *On the Psychology of Meditation.* New York: The Viking Press, 1971. London: George Allen & Unwin, 1973.

Chogyam Trungpa. *Meditation in Action.* Berkeley, Ca.: Shambala, 1970.

A. Kasamatsu and T. Hirai. "An Electroencephalographic Study on Zen Meditation (Zazen)." Reprinted in Charles T. Tart, ed., *Altered States of Consciousness.* New York: John Wiley & Sons, 1969.

Shunryu Suzuki. *Zen Mind, Beginner's Mind.* New York and Tokyo: Weatherhill, 1973.

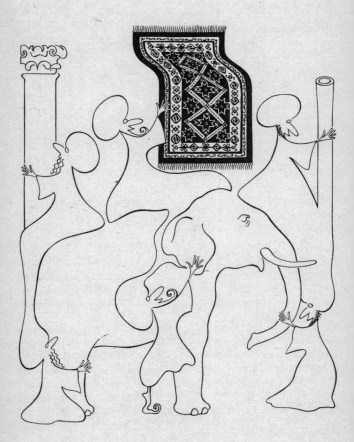

Chapter 7

The Education
of the Intuitive Mode

The Blind Men and the Elephant

*Beyond Ghor there was a city. All its inhabitants were blind. A king
with his entourage arrived nearby; he brought his army and camped in the
desert. He had a mighty elephant, which he used in attack and to increase
the people's awe.*

*The populace became anxious to learn about the elephant, and some
sightless from among this blind community ran like fools to find it. Since
they did not know even the form or shape of the elephant, they groped
sightlessly, gathering information by touching some part of it. Each
thought that he knew something, because he could feel a part.*

*When they returned to their fellow-citizens, eager groups clustered
around them, anxious, misguidedly, to learn the truth from those who
were themselves astray. They asked about the form, the shape, of the
elephant, and they listened to all they were told.*

*The man whose hand had reached an ear said: "It is a large, rough
thing, wide and broad, like a rug."*

*One who had felt the trunk said: "I have the real facts about it. It is
like a straight and hollow pipe, awful and destructive."*

*One who had felt its feet and legs said: "It is mighty and firm, like a
pillar."*

161

Each had felt one part out of many. Each had perceived it wrongly. No mind knew all: knowledge is not the companion of the blind. All imagined something, something incorrect. The created is not informed about divinity. There is no Way in this science by means of the ordinary intellect.[1]

The "ordinary intellect" works analytically, piecing together elements of a large puzzle. If the complementary mode is developed, consciousness becomes more complete, according to the traditional esoteric psychologies. The story of the blind men and the elephant is often used to convey this.

A complementary working of intellect and intuition is hardly restricted to the procedures of the esoteric traditions, although these specialize in cultivating such a working. The physicist Robert Oppenheimer contrasted the two modes:

These two ways of thinking, the way of time and history, and the way of eternity and timelessness, are both part of man's efforts to comprehend the world in which he lives. Neither is comprehended in the other nor reducible to it . . . each supplementing the other—neither telling the whole story.[2]

I have been using the distinction between the light of daytime and the darkness of night to describe the essential difference between these two types of psychology. The traditional esoteric psychologists are the specialists of the "night," having developed procedures for contacting and mastering subtle phenomena that are masked by the brilliance of the day. The paradigm of contemporary psychology could well be expanded to include the recognition that, under certain conditions, man is potentially sensitive and permeable to very weak, and often unnoticed, energy sources which exist within himself and on earth. A fuller treatment of this possible shift in emphasis is given in Chapter 9, on biofeedback training, and in Chapter 10, on biological rhythms, gravity, and "paranormal" communication.

Sometimes the metaphorical distinction between the light and the darkness can become quite literal. Carlos Castaneda, an American anthropology student, spent several years with an Indian shaman living in northern Mexico. In two extraordinary books, *The Teachings of Don Juan* and *A Separate Reality*, Castaneda records the conflict he experienced between the two major modes of consciousness: his own, highly verbal and analytical nature found it very difficult to comprehend the intuitive mode, which I think Don Juan refers to as "seeing."

> I told Don Juan how much I enjoyed the exquisite sensation of talking in the dark. He said that my statement was consistent with my talkative nature; that it was easy for me to like chatting in the darkness because talking was the only thing I could do at that time, while sitting around. I argued that it was more than the mere act of talking that I enjoyed. I said that I relished the soothing warmth of the darkness around us. He asked me what I did at home when it was dark. I said that invariably I would turn on the lights or I would go out into the lighted streets until it was time to go to sleep.
>
> "Oh!" he said incredulously. "I thought you had learned to use the darkness."
>
> "What can you use it for?" I asked.
>
> He said the darkness—and he called it the "darkness of the day"—was the best time to "see." He stressed the word "see" with a peculiar inflection. I wanted to know what he meant by that, but he said it was too late to go into it then.[3]

Since Western education is heavily dominated by the verbal-analytical mode, the procedures of the traditional esoteric psychologies may seem a bit strange at first. Their function, however, is to open up the other mode of knowledge, the complement to the normal one. They are primarily concerned with questions that are usually left out of or ignored within the Western tradition, questions considered unanswerable within purely linear and scientific terms. These include such deep, "nighttime" wonderings as "What is the meaning of life?" and "What is Man?" and "What is the nature of consciousness?" and "Is consciousness individual or cosmic?" Indeed, to the strict logical positivist, these questions would have no possible answer, since they cannot be tested experimentally.

These questions may be posed simply and reasonably. But, say the esoteric psychologists, they can unfortunately not be answered fully in a verbal-intellectual manner. That is, the procedures of the esoteric psychologies are incomprehensible only when we are restricted to the mode of verbal logic. These exercises and techniques are, then, attempts to answer the questions left out of science and logical inquiry, attempts carried out intuitively and personally rather than in formal, intellectual terms.

This point is made in a story of the Sufi tradition. A group of conventional wisemen came to visit Nasrudin's village, and prepared to address the townspeople. As they arrived on stage, Nasrudin—a scruffy figure—clambered up on stage to join them. "Why are you up on stage, Nasrudin?" they asked, somewhat askance at the inelegant figure. "I am here to answer some of the questions that you cannot. Shall we begin with some which baffle *you*, gentlemen?"

The techniques of the esoteric psychologists are intended to augment our normal mode of information-gathering. They attempt to provide a tacit knowledge of one's own self, of one's place in the world. These psychologies aim beyond technique, beyond "states," toward a personal knowledge that can answer the primary questions of psychology and philosophy.

THE TRADITIONAL ESOTERIC PSYCHOLOGIES: SOME GENERAL REMARKS

Any linear, written account of these psychologies is limited by its very linearity; yet we *can* learn from such an account, while granting that it may not be complete, just as a written description of ski lifts, bindings, equipment, and intermediate ski techniques does not substitute for the experience of skiing down the slope.

One distinguishing feature of the traditional psychologies is that they are very practical, are almost what we would term "Applied Psychology." These disciplines cover many aspects of life which our Western educational process often omits— *how to* breathe, *how to* care for the body, *how to* master bodily functions usually considered "involuntary." These esoteric traditions approach psychology purely as a practical, personal discipline, and emphasize techniques which effect certain alterations in body states and in consciousness, for the purpose of gaining knowledge that is other than, but additional to, the intellectual.

Compared with that of Western psychology, the perspective in these traditions is considerably wider. Man is considered as one part of a larger organism, reciprocally influencing and being influenced by the "environment," as in the story "Moment in Time" (which begins Chapter 4). The concept of the environment in these esoteric psychologies is also much more inclusive than the Western one. It includes the importance of subtle geophysical forces, such as the rhythmic changes which daily occur on Earth, the light-dark cycle, internal and external biological rhythms, and the effects of certain microclimactic conditions, such as the ionization of the air. These forces have not, until quite recently, been included within the Western scientific worldview.

However, before we are carried away in this new and exciting area of research and personal experience, we should once again note the very grave problems which the esoteric psychologies have encountered in their own social and cultural areas. The sources of their problems, and of those in contemporary Western psychology, have been quite similar. Each system tends to cling to specific techniques whose original purpose has been forgotten. For instance, in the traditional esoteric psychologies, a balanced development of intellectuality and intuition is usually sought. Since most who become interested in these traditions are well-developed intellectually, the exercises usually stress the development of the receptive, holistic mode. The specific techniques employed for this purpose sometimes come to be considered all-important. Then the intellect becomes devalued, cast aside, ignored, in favor of an unbalanced overreaction. This may happen with an individual, and even within an entire discipline, leading to an "official" devaluation of the intellect and the preaching of incomprehensible doctrine. A similar process, although entirely reversed in content, has occurred within contemporary science, and has led to an unbalanced development of an "objective" approach. The original aim may become forgotten, but the techniques of study persist.

Let us consider an example of this tendency in esoteric tradition. In some esoteric practices, it is found useful for *certain people* at *certain periods* of their study to renounce all sexual practice, largely to remove the biasing effects of desires on consciousness (although other functions of this technique are often mentioned). But such renunciation has often been extended far beyond these bounds, leading in the Hindu tradition, for instance, to people who withdraw entirely from sexuality and who consequently devalue the opposite sex as "Temptation."

A comic instance of such distortion occurred recently, when an Indian "holy man" visited San Francisco. Upon his arrival at the airport, he had to be shielded by his aides, for even seeing a woman was "forbidden" by his religious practices; he had remained shielded from women for his entire life in India. The television newsreels showed various "women's liberation" demonstrations, women attempting to crash through the barricade and stand in front of this exponent of "higher consciousness." Even when the rejection of normal sexuality is not so extreme, many lesser distortions filter through as a result of such an attempt to withdraw from life.

Similarly, the achievement of a state of receptivity and quiescence through meditation may lure the practitioner into withdrawing completely from the continuing life of his culture, leading him to ignore serious personal and societal problems as "illusory." Although the corrective to such a withdrawal is often applied within these traditions, it is not often heard. Ustad Hilmi writes: "Traditions about monasticism and isolation are reflections of short-term processes of training or development, monstrously misunderstood and grotesquely elaborated by those who want to stay asleep." [4]

Many other difficulties exist. The virtue of, say, humility is often taken as the end point in the esoteric traditions, and may even become a moral imperative. But this personal characteristic is to be taken not as an end in itself, but as a *technique.* "It enables a person to function in a certain manner." Similarly, diets that have been developed for a community at one stage may become promulgated across cultures and epochs—the style may remain (e.g., not eating meat, or eating only a certain type of meat or a certain type of vegetable), but the original context is lost, and the diet is left as an empty ritual. Dress and other exercises can also follow this process.

If we can keep a wary eye on the excesses of both types of psychology, we may be able to rid each of imbalance, and achieve a synthesis of the highest elements in both types, rather than of their excesses. Two main sections follow: The first opens up for consideration some areas that are not well-represented in Western thought, such as the nature of subtle body energies, the concept of nonattachment, and death as it relates to psychology. The second attempts to conceptualize many of the esoteric rituals in terms of how they train intuition; it is similar in intent to the meditation chapter, in that it stresses communality within diversity.

THE ESOTERIC TRADITIONS: PRACTICES AND CONCEPTS

1. Physiological Self-Mastery

For many years reports have come in from India that Yoga adepts can control the "involuntary" functions of the body. Since our dominant Western paradigm has ruled out the possibility that we can contact these faint internal signals, we have tended to ignore these reports. As we begin to credit, even as a working hypothesis, that such things may be possible, we can examine the evidence more dispassionately. A new branch of research has appeared, which uses contemporary psychophysiological methods in the study of yogic self-regulation.

In a study conducted at the Menninger Foundation by Elmer Green, a Yoga master demonstrated his ability to raise the temperature at one point in his hand while simultaneously lowering it at another. At the end of the experiment, the two points of the hand were 11 degrees apart in temperature. Other recent reports document that yogis can control their blood flow and blood pressure and can lower their basal metabolic rate by more than 15 per cent for hours on end. One yogic exercise, the *Shavasana* (dead man's pose), has been shown to be effective in lowering blood pressure; obviously, this exercise might be very useful in treating hypertension. These experiments, together with the new technology of biofeedback training, indicate that our Western scientific tradition may have grossly underestimated our own capabilities for self-regulation.[5] "Self-knowledge" has been stated by many teachers to be the aim of the esoteric traditions, but in Yoga it takes on a most intimate, physiological meaning. The instances cited here hardly begin to indicate how great the potential of self-regulation may be for the control of internal states, both the psychological and physiological.

2. The Influence of Body States on Consciousness

Many of the esoteric traditions emphasize practice in cultivating certain body postures and exercises. More consideration is given within these traditions to the interrelatedness of consciousness and "the body" than is usual in Western psychology. In Yoga a series of postures (asanas) is often included as part of the practice. Breathing exercises are performed both in Yoga and in the Sufi tradition. Fasting is a technique often used to so upset the balance of ordinary awareness that another mode can develop. Ritual movements and dances are performed, such as *Tai-chi Ch'uan* and the dance of the dervishes.

3. The Esoteric Concept of Subtle Body Energies

In a realm even further from the usual Western scientific concept is the esoteric concept of subtle "body energies." Most of these esoteric concepts may be merely convenient fictions, metaphors that were found to be useful as images, which unfortunately have become hardened and concrete with time. However, similar concepts were common in Western science until about the turn of this century. They included the "vital principle" of Hans Driesch and the "élan vital" of Henri Bergson. These ideas, such as "vitalism" in biology, did not prove very useful and were completely discarded. In everyday discourse, we use these concepts quite loosely. One might say, "I don't have much energy today," using "energy" in the sense of "life-force." The esoteric traditions, practical psychologies that they are, have worked on this everyday concept, have refined and perfected the use of these "energies." Consider the following example from the Japanese discipline of aikido.

Ask a friend to lift you three times. Without saying anything to him, do not do anything out of the ordinary the first time. On the second, think "up." Imagine your "energy" focused just above your head. Actively imagine it flowing upward through your head. On the third lift, think "down." Visualize your legs as part of the earth, and imagine your "energy" as flowing downward through the soles of your feet. Do *not* tense your muscles, or make any other attempt to help or hinder the lift. Then reverse roles. Lift your friend, but ask him to mix up the order of the three procedures (and not to inform you, of course). You will easily be able to feel the results of his "convenient visualization," and he of yours.

This is a very simple demonstration: no one has yet tried to find out whether any measurable process has actually been altered at some biological level, but something has been changed in the body, something beyond our usual concepts of how our "energy" can operate.

In aikido this "energy form" is named *Ki;* in Chinese it is called *Chi.* It forms the basis of the *Tai-chi Ch'uan* exercise, a rhythmic series of movements intended to balance the "flow of *Chi* energy" throughout the body. A similar attempt at "energy direction" underlies the oriental martial arts, the Japanese karate and judo and the Chinese kung fu.

The concept of "*Chi* energy" also partially underlies the Chinese technique of acupuncture. The practitioner of this discipline is taught to recognize the points in the body through which the "*Chi* energy" flows. In some cases, needles are inserted in these strategic "centers" to reopen a blocked energy flow. This "energy," which is held to be the body's healing force, can also be used to immobilize or anesthetize segments of the body. The metaphor of the "energy form" may prove incorrect, but the phenomenon may remain valid: witness the recent experience of travelers and physicians in Chinese hospitals. Now that China is beginning to become more accessible to Western scientific observers, perhaps these techniques can be more fully explored.

The very diverse and sometimes abstruse Indian traditions postulate several types of body energies. Prana is closest to our ordinary concept of "energy." It is held to be the "life-force," the living element in all organic existence. Many of the special yogic breathing exercises *(pranayama)* are said to accumulate this "energy form."

A much more extraordinary form of energy in the yogic tradition is named *Kundalini.* This form of Yoga postulates seven centers *(chakras)* in the body, distributed from the root of the spine to the top of the head. In *Kundalini* Yoga the aspirant attempts to concentrate on these "centers" and to raise the "*Kundalini* energy" through them. This is held to be an exceedingly powerful and potentially destructive experience, and many have afterward found it almost impossible to regain normal consciousness. The Arabic fairy tales of a powerful "genie" locked in a bottle are warnings within these esoteric traditions about an unprepared opening up of energy or capacity.[6]

These *chakras*, or centers in the body, may actually be constructive visualizations or metaphors which have been taken somewhat too literally by some adherents. Considering them to be physical centers may be an instance of intuitive knowledge that has gone unchecked by intellect. On the other side of the coin, an attempt to identify the *chakras* with physical points of the body's anatomy, such as endocrine glands or autonomic ganglia, may be a very unfortunate confusion of metaphor with physical fact. A similar situation once held in psychoanalysis, when some looked to brain structures for the site of the id, ego, and superego. Idries Shah thus writes on the *lataif*, the Sufic system of body centers:

> The activation of the special Organs of Perception *(lataif)* is part of Sufi methodology analogous to, and often confused with, the *chakra* system of the Yogis. There are important differences. In Yoga, the *chakras* or *padmas* are conceived as physically located centers in the body, linked by invisible nerves or channels. Yogis generally do not know that these centers are merely concentration points, convenient formulations whose activation is part of a theoretical working hypothesis.[7]

Baraka is the name given to a special energy form within Sufism. The word is sometimes translated as "blessing" or "impalpable grace." The Jewish tradition involves a very similar concept, that of *Baruch* or "blessing." The Sufi conception differs from many others, in that baraka is held to be transmitted from individual to individual, generally from teacher to student, if the student is sufficiently advanced in his practice to receive it. On this concept is based the medieval tradition, still current in the Middle East, of the master and his apprentices, who learn from the master in the ordinary way and are also said to pick up "something else" from his presence.

These ideas on "subtle body energies" seem to border on the archaic to the Western sensibility. We relegate such ideas to the realm of magic and superstition, where the vast majority of them may well belong, given the continual tendency toward misinformation and degeneration in the esoteric traditions. But that such concepts may *almost* always be safely considered credulous and naive does not necessarily mean that *all* of them can be. Here one of Gurdjieff's teachers discourses on breathing exercises to a Western student:

"I taught Gurdjieff to breathe. I say this and you burst into a flood of hows, whys, and ifs and buts and can I teach you? The answer is, 'I can but I will not.' "

"May I ask, Sheikh, why only breathing?"

"Only! Only! Stupid question! More stupid than to have asked why or how. Do you think that to learn to breathe correctly is easy? Does your shallow panting do more than supply your blood with the minimum amount of oxygen needed to keep that portion of your brain that you use alive? One of the functions of correct breathing is to carry the baraka to the farthest recesses of the deep consciousness. Undeveloped men try to use thought or random action to affect the consciousness. Neither of these works, as the dose and the direction and the intensity are not known to them. Only to breathe! Do you know how long it takes before you can be trained to take your first *real* breath? Months, even years, and then only when you *know* what you are aiming for.

"Gurdjieff came to me with a capacity to breathe, and I taught him how to do it and how to breathe with his system, his consciousness, and his entire being. You breathe to sustain your level of existence. Higher man breathes to maintain the breakthrough that he has made into a superior realm of being. Your ignorance, while not surprising, terrifies me. Gurdjieff stayed with me for twenty years. Yes, twenty years! Five months in Erzurum and the remainder of the time in rapport with me wherever he was learning to use his breath. Do you know what can be carried into your consciousness by your breath? Do you know why a Sheikh will breathe on a disciple? Do you know why a Sheikh breathes into the ear of a newly born child? Of course you do not! You put it down to magic, primitive symbols representing life, but the practical reasons, the deadly serious business of nourishing the inner consciousness, passes you by." [8]

And, although this is frankly quite a conceptual leap, we should at least hold open the possibility that Western science has overlooked a subtle source of internal body energies, as the stars may be missed in the brilliance of the daylight. We may in fact be at a state of knowledge about these energies similar to that of physics just before electricity was discovered, made explicit, and harnessed. At the very least, the esoteric traditions offer a set of useful metaphors for the body, which may enable us to function in a more integrated manner and may perhaps open up new areas of research, such as acupuncture. The possibility that such energies exist opens up new ways of considering the body in physiology and in medicine. Idries Shah has given this subject some thought. Concerning Indian magicians, he writes in *Oriental Magic*:

> In common with several Western investigators, I have been forced to the conclusion that we must conceive of the existence of some principle, whose harnessing becomes a possibility through the disciplines of the Indian priest-magicians. Occult it may be—since anything which is not understood may be termed occult: it is much more likely that there are forces—perhaps akin to magnetism or electricity, or forms of these—whose functions we do not as yet understand. After all, we know very little of the *nature* of electricity or magnetism, even today. We know how to *use* these forces, and we know what they can do. Yet they were known for centuries before they were harnessed. What places this "occult force" in a slightly different category is the apparent fact of its use through mind control.
>
> On the other hand, it may well be that one day machines will be developed which can control this strange power or force. From personal observation of the trance-like condition of the practitioners, my own feeling is that the greatest barrier preventing the objective study of this power is the lack of scientists prepared to undergo the rigorous training necessary to become adepts.[9]

4. The Ignoring of Thought

In many writings, the traditional psychologists stress that thoughts, the "mind" in the restricted "left-hemisphere" sense, are the barrier to entering the other mode of consciousness.

Patanjali, the author of the *Yoga Sutras*, defined his discipline: "Yoga is the inhibition of the modifications of the mind." In Zen the intent is to "stop conceptualizing while remaining fully awake." Our thoughts and expectations construct and maintain our personal consciousness as it is. To alter the construction, say the esoteric psychologists, ordinary thoughts must be placed in abeyance for a while. Thus a function of concentrative meditation is to "turn off" that active verbal mode, and especially, to avoid thinking. Some monks even take "vows" of silence, to further restrict the province of the verbal-intellectual mode. Certain highly developed and seemingly bizarre exercises are performed to rid the practitioner of a strict reliance on verbal intellectuality. These often involve *questions* which can have no possible verbal-rational solution: the koan exercise of the Zen tradition is one example. In one koan, the Zen master brandishes a stick over the pupil's head, and says fiercely, "If you say this stick is not real, I will strike you with it. If you say this stick is real, I will strike you with it. If you don't say anything, I will strike you with it."

What can you *say?*

The anthropologist Castaneda complains to his teacher, Don Juan:

"For years I have truly tried to live in accordance with your teachings," I said. "Obviously I have not done well. How can I do better now?"

"You think and talk too much. You must stop talking to yourself."

"What do you mean?"

"You talk to yourself too much. You're not unique at that. Every one of us does that. We carry on an internal talk. Think about it. Whenever you are alone, what do you do?"

"I talk to myself."

"What do you talk to yourself about?"

"I don't know; anything, I suppose."

"I'll tell you what we talk to ourselves about. We talk about our world. In fact we maintain our world with our internal talk."

"How do we do that?"

"Whenever we finish talking to ourselves the world is always as it should be. We renew it, we kindle it with life, we uphold it with our internal talk. Not only that, but we also choose our paths as we talk to ourselves. Thus we repeat the same choices over and over until the day we die, because we keep on repeating the same internal talk over and over until the day we die.

"A warrior is aware of this and strives to stop his talking. This is the last point you have to know if you want to live like a warrior."

"How can I stop talking to myself?"

"First of all you must use your ears to take some of the burden from your eyes. We have been using our eyes to judge the world since the time we were born. We talk to others and to ourselves mainly about what we see. A warrior is aware of that and listens to the world; he listens to the sounds of the world." [10]

5. Nonattachment

We create our personal world by thought and expectation, and it is desire, the esoteric psychologists hold, that gives rise to our thoughts. Just as some students in these traditions work on the suspension of thought by meditation, others work on the suspension of desire.

Needs, hopes, and wants are strong biasing factors in personal consciousness. When hungry, we are likely to search out food or even to create food images and smells. Since we continuously "tune out" the portions of the environment which do not suit our needs, we can ignore much when in severe need. If hungry, we might not notice the river flowing by, or the people speaking to us, or our reading. At these moments, we are almost totally concerned with food and construct our world around food.

An attempt at nonattachment to objects and to sense pleasures is another exercise designed to destructure normal consciousness. There are several different types of such practices, involving either prohibitions on behavior or the cultivation of a psychological state that combines renunciation and nonattachment. In the Judeo-Christian tradition, these practices usually involve behavioral restrictions. For example, some churchgoers are required to abstain from eating meat during Lent. The usual result of this kind of practice is that awareness is focused on the forbidden object. Most people find themselves craving meat, thinking about it, devising substitutes (vegetarian imitations of meat, for instance), waiting until the period of prohibition is over.

But the practice of renunciation, according to the various esoteric traditions, is intended to create a psychological state of *cessation,* not enhancement, of desire, and such cessation is not necessarily tied to any change in external behavior. Most of the traditions emphasize that merely abstaining in practice, but still desiring, fantasizing about, or planning to consume the object, is worthless—perhaps worse than not giving it up at all.

Renunciation is the process, it is said, of conquering desire, of not requiring or needing anything. The Hindu practices emphasize the cultivation of a psychological state of nonattachment, as well as prohibitions on actual behavior. Many yogis are vegetarian and chaste and live in poverty. Often yogis withdraw from society and its "temptations" into an ashram, in which one lives as a monk on a simple diet. Christian monasteries often emphasize psychological nonattachment, as well as actual cessation of certain "impure" behavior—the vows of poverty, chastity, solitude—a separation from the culture in order to "purify" oneself.

In the Zen and Sufi traditions, the emphasis is solely on the psychological state of nonattachment, and not on prohibitions in actual practice. Both Zen and Sufism emphasize, as they do in the exercise of self-awareness, that one can do whatever one wishes as long as one is not attached to it.

The difference between this aspect of Sufism and Zen on the one hand, and much of the yogic and Christian tradition on the other, is illustrated in some advice given to Rafael Lefort, who traveled to the Mideast in search of the teachers of Gurdjieff—the Sufis—and was asked:

> "Are you prepared to leave the world as you know it and live in a mountain retreat on a very basic diet?" I signified that I was.
>
> "You see," he nodded his head regretfully, "you still feel that to find knowledge you must seek a solitary life away from impure things. This is a primitive attitude and one satisfactory for savages. . . . Can you comprehend the uselessness of abandoning the world for the sake of your selfish development?
>
> "You may need a course," he went on, "at a Sarmoun Center, but that will not mean total abandonment of your mundane worldly activity provided you do not allow it, nay invite it, to corrupt you. If you have enough skill you can actually harness the negative forces to serve you . . . but you must have enough skill." [11]

Zen masters also point out that "worldly" activity can be a perfect vehicle for development, as long as one is free from attachment. Pleasures are legitimate in Zen, as long as one is not in their service. The Sufi admonition is, similarly, "Be *in* the world, but not *of* the world." The attempt here is to dissociate the important aspect of renunciation, the psychological state of nonattachment, from the external behavior. This is illustrated by a student's experience with Gurdjieff, when she felt that she was unduly bound to her habit of cigarette smoking. Gurdjieff, who stressed that people are often the "slaves" of their habits, instructed her to give up smoking. On returning to him a year later, she told Gurdjieff triumphantly that she had given up smoking and was no longer a slave to her cigarette habit. Gurdjieff smiled and offered her a very expensive Turkish cigarette, indicating it was not the specific behavior but the fact that she had been a slave to her cigarette habit that was important. Only when she no longer needed to smoke was it permissible to smoke again. Gurdjieff himself kept a quite well-known larder stocked with delicacies from all parts of the world.[12]

But why is nonattachment to "worldly" pleasures a major part of the meditative disciplines? One answer can be given in terms of our analysis of ordinary consciousness. Recall that normal consciousness is constructed in light of our past experience, our expectations, and our needs. The esoteric traditions consider that one major barrier to the development of an extended consciousness is that we continuously tune out those portions of the external environment which do not suit our needs at the moment. A Sufi tale illustrates this general point.

> Two men were sitting in a cafe, and a camel walked past.
> "What does that make you think of?" said one.
> "Food," said the other.
> "Since when are camels used for food?" said the first.
> "No, you see, everything makes me think of food." [13]

In its effect on awareness, the practice of nonattachment can be considered an additional way to remove the normal restrictions on input. If there are no desires, there is less bias at any one moment toward specific "tuning" of perception. Our awareness of the external environment becomes less restricted, less of an interaction, less a function of our desire at the moment, and more like a mirror.

There is another function of nonattachment. If, for instance, one *needs* nothing from another person or from the external environment—prestige, sex, food, love—one can exist "for them" as a mirror, like Omar Khayyám, Suzuki Roshi, or Christ. We sometimes reach this state when our needs are satisfied. Many have observed that the world appears different when we are in love or are a success. It is also commonplace to observe, however, that the sensualist is often the one who becomes the renunciant, a "worldly" man who gives up all for his religion—a Thomas à Becket.

But nonattachment is not a *de*tachment from life, as many have assumed. That some have regressed into such a withdrawal from life does not imply that such was the original purpose of this exercise. It *is,* rather, an attempt at a total present-centeredness, an acceptance of sensual pleasure as it comes, without "clinging" to it, as is said in Zen. A dervish saying echoes this point: "When it is time for stillness, stillness; in the time of companionship, companionship; at the place of effort, effort. In the time and place of anything, anything." [14]

6. Death

Many persons deliberately confront death in their lives. We may drive a car quickly, race on skis, climb mountains, all for the purpose of returning full awareness to the immediate moment, where a false move may kill. It is another means by which we try to destructure our usual mode of consciousness. There is no time for our usual internal talk or for any fantasies about the future or regrets about the past when one is in danger.

Since death is inevitable in each person's life, it forms a part of the traditional psychologies. The awareness of one's own death is employed in these traditions in a manner like that of the motorcyclist or the driver of a racing car. This awareness can remove some of the transitory bias from normal consciousness. Many actions, disagreements, petty jealousies, begin to seem trivial and hardly worth pursuing in the face of a personal death. Our own death is something which we usually ignore; yet, the writers of the traditional psychologies suggest, its lesson can be taken while we are still alive. Uwais, a contemporary of Mohammed, was asked,

> "How do you feel?"
> He said, "Like one who has risen in the morning and does not know whether he will be dead in the evening."
> The other man said, "But this is the situation of all men."
> Uwais said, "Yes. But how many of them *feel* it?" [15]

Within these traditions, the death of an individual is regarded as much less final than is usual within Western society. Here is the poet Rumi:

What Shall I Be?

Again and again I have grown like grass;
I have experienced seven hundred seventy molds.
I died from minerality and became vegetable.
I died from vegetableness and became animal.
I died from animality and became man.
Then why fear disappearance through death?
Next time I shall die
Bringing forth wings and feathers like angels:
After soaring higher than angels—
What you cannot imagine. I shall be that.[16]

THE EDUCATION OF INTUITION

Western educational systems largely concentrate on the verbal and intellectual. We do not possess a large-scale training system for the other side, but it is just this training that is the specialty of the esoteric psychologies. They form a complement to most of modern Western education. If we examine some of the techniques and exercises of the esoteric traditions, we find that they generally seem to work in the tacit language of the receptive mode.

In the Chinese *I Ching*, this mode is even named *K'un*—the receptive. In Sufism it is variously called "deep understanding," intuition, or direct perception. Don Juan apparently calls it "seeing." In Zen, the word *kensho,* a word for the enlightenment experience, also means "to enter inside," the same meaning as intuition, which is from *in* and *tueri* in Latin. Satori in Zen is often pictured as a flash of intuition illuminating a dark area.

There are two major ways, then, in which men have approached knowledge about themselves and the nature of life. One, the scientific and logical, employs the steady input and accumulation of information; the other, the intuitive, attempts the development of another "organ of perception," as the Sufis call it.

Even given all we have considered in this book, this practice may still be difficult for many to grasp fully. Perhaps an analogy can help a bit. Suppose we say to a group of pretechnological people: "There is information available 'in the air,' so to speak, which you normally cannot receive. It is present in this room, on the floor, in the walls, above the ceiling. It exists where you walk, where you sleep, where you sit; but you do not yet possess the receptive capabilities to make use of it. If you work with us, you may be able to construct a piece of specially tuned apparatus, and you may then be able to receive these ever-present, subtle, ordinarily unseen signals. Among other things, there is music, special instruction, and diversion available to you on this new avenue of sensation. You will be able to perceive events in the past and events taking place at this moment at great distance. You can receive this information almost whenever you wish, if you possess the proper sort of receptive capabilities."

Now, this sounds like obvious nonsense to most of these people, but to us it is simply a description of television. The TV signals are carried by high-frequency electromagnetic radiation; at all moments such radiation is present, in the room in which you read, outside "in the air." Without a proper receiver *it might as well not be present,* for our normal sensory systems cannot receive high-frequency electromagnetic energy directly. But if the proper technology is developed, we can tap into a dimension of knowledge which is almost always available and which is *already developed*.

We can then begin to comprehend the statement of the traditional psychologists that their teaching is "not for the intellect" and "not for the rational mind." This training is for the tacit, "intuitive" side of ourselves. The techniques of the traditions work in the tacit language of that mode, including body movement, music, spatial forms, sounds, crafts, dreams, and stories which function as word-pictures.

1. Geometric Forms

The employment of spatial form, the special province of the right hemisphere, plays a large role in esoteric psychology. Often a room or an entire structure will be built in order to affect that mode of consciousness directly in a certain manner.

One surviving example is the Alhambra, the Moorish temple, in Spain. It is intended to have an effect that is spatial, experiential, and difficult to encompass linearly. More familiarly, we can note the perceptual effects of Gothic cathedrals and churches, and of certain rooms whose structural pattern produces an effect on us.

The student of esoteric psychology is often invited to contemplate specially constructed, two-dimensional geometric patterns, in the Middle Eastern "magic carpets" or in yogic mandalas. They may serve as the focus of concentrative meditation. Often an apparently simple form will contain many different levels of organization within it. The student may also attempt to see as many of these levels of organization as he can at once. One from the Sufi tradition is reproduced in Figure 7.1.

Figure 7.1
A Sufi contemplation object.

2. Crafts

Our usual Western concept of "metaphysical" or "spiritual" training involves abstruse ideas and ritual, including secret initiatory rites and occult symbols. In fact, however, the education of these adepts has been far more concerned with such things as movement in space, visualization, and especially crafts, all in the province of the right hemisphere of the brain.

A student of George Gurdjieff traveled to the Middle East to study the methods by which this teacher was trained. He found that Gurdjieff studied "mundane" activities, crafts for the most part, in addition to his breathing exercises and reading. He was taught to weave carpets, to do calligraphy, to hammer copper—all activities that we would not normally associate with "mysticism," until we can consider that these activities each call on that tacit, spatial, intuitive mode.[17]

3. Dreams

The way of the esoteric traditions involves mastery over the "involuntary" physiology, as well as over the "unconscious." Each night we dream, but we dream unaware. If we do become aware of a dream, it may be only as a passive bystander watching events take place. Rarely do we discuss remembered versions of a dream with a friend, or with a therapist. We do not usually consider the third of our life spent asleep as an opportunity for self-discovery. If we do return from our dreams with an image or a thought, it is personal, shared only once in a very great while with others. We have no psychological or cultural mechanism for allowing the dream consciousness to enrich the remainder of life.

In other cultures, however, techniques have been developed for actively entering the world of the dream. The Senoi, a culture of the Malay Peninsula, are reported to work with dream consciousness, taming it and interweaving it with the fabric of their social life. The interpretation of dreams is a feature of child education and is part of the shared knowledge of the Senoi tribe. It is practiced by the ordinary Senoi citizen as a feature of his daily life. The breakfast in the Senoi house is like a dream clinic, in the words of Kilton Stewart, with the elder males hearing and analyzing the dreams of their children.[18]

The most intriguing aspect of the Senoi dream work is their technique for actively entering and reshaping the dream while it is still in progress. This technique is taught at the group meetings. If a child dreams of falling, for instance, and is terrorized, the elder may answer with enthusiasm, "This is wonderful. It is one of the best kinds of dreams. Now, where did you fall and what did you discover?" The child may respond that it did not seem so wonderful to him, that he was frightened. The adult informs him that every aspect of the dream world has a purpose, beyond his understanding while he is asleep. The child is taught to relax and enjoy himself while dreaming, and remember that the dream is "the quickest way to get in contact with the powers of the spirit world." A frightful falling dream, then, can be transformed into a flying dream, for instance. The flying is encouraged until the dreamer can return with something of value to the society.

Kilton Stewart reports that the Senoi believe and teach that the dreamer is always in control of the dream, and that he should always advance and attack in the teeth of danger. The student is taught that the dream is his own property, that he creates his own images. Bad or evil characters in the dream are bad only if one is afraid and retreating from them. They continue to seem fearful as long as the dreamer refuses to come to grips with them. A tiger is often a frightening image to these jungle children, but the authorities tell them, "That tiger is *your* tiger; you can make friends with him in the dream. He can teach you his dances or his games. Play with him until you learn something."

Our information on this technique is currently limited to Stewart's account. He is extremely enthusiastic about the effects of the self-mastery of dreams in the Senoi culture, and perhaps overly optimistic. The technique may never serve the same function in our culture that it does for the Senoi. Even so, the cultivation and mastery of dream consciousness is a possibility which has yet to be fully explored in contemporary psychology. Stewart concludes that some difficulties in modern civilization may have arisen because people in our culture have failed to develop "half their power to think. *Perhaps their most important half*" (italics mine). He reports that the Senoi seem to suffer little in an intellectual comparison with Westerners, although how he determined this is not clear. However, our capacity to solve problems in dreams is certainly undeveloped compared with theirs.

4. Music and "Magic" Words

Western music is primarily melodic, consisting of temporal patterns of tonal organization. Many Westerners find Indian or Arabic music boring and monotonous. But according to the traditional psychologists, music can be used for special purposes, to communicate in an unusual manner. The contemporary Indian musician Ali Akbar Khan says, "Real music is not for the mind or for the body, but for the spirit which exists independently of each."

In the music of the Middle and Far East, melody plays a small role. Rather, it is the very *sound* of the music itself, the tonal quality, which is important. (It is this component of music which is associated with the right hemisphere of the brain.[19]) In these esoteric traditions, tonal vibrations of certain frequencies are held to stimulate parts of the mind which normally go untouched. The mantra of Yoga, the dervish call, are "magic" words. It is often thought that the "special" properties of these words lie in their *meaning*. Actually, the "magic" lies in the *sound* of the words, which are designed to have a certain effect on consciousness. Idries Shah comments on the derivation of the very word "Sufi":

> But acquaintance with Sufis, let alone almost any degree of access to their practices and moral traditions, could easily have resolved any seeming contradiction between the existence of a word and its having no ready etymological derivation. The answer is that the Sufis regard *sounds* of the letters S, U, F (in Arabic, the signs for *soad, wao, fa*) as significant in the same order of use in their effect on human mentation.[20]

Benjamin Whorf, one of our deepest analysts of language, considers the use of the mantra in Yoga:

Speech is the best show man puts on. It is his own "act" on the stage of evolution, in which he comes before the cosmic backdrop and really "does his stuff." But we suspect the watching Gods perceive that the order in which his amazing set of tricks build up to a great climax has been stolen—from the Universe!

The idea, entirely unfamiliar to the modern world, that nature and language are inwardly akin, was for ages well-known to various high cultures whose historical continuity on the earth has been enormously longer than that of Western European culture. In India, one aspect of it has been the idea of the *mantram* and of a *mantric art*. On the simplest cultural level, a mantram is merely an incantation of primitive magic, such as the crudest cultures have. In the high culture it may have a different, a very intellectual meaning, dealing with the inner affinity of language and the cosmic order. At a still higher level, it becomes "Mantra Yoga." Therein the mantram becomes a manifold of conscious patterns, contrived to assist the consciousness into the noumenal-pattern world—whereupon it is "in the driver's seat." It can then *set* the human organism to transmit, control, and amplify a thousandfold forces which that organism normally transmits only at unobservably low intensities.

Somewhat analogously, the mathematical formula that enables a physicist to adjust some coils of wire, tinfoil plates, diaphragms, and other quite inert and innocent gadgets into a configuration in which they can project music to a far country puts the physicist's consciousness on a level strange to the untrained man, and makes feasible an adjustment of matter to a very strategic configuration, one which makes possible an unusual manifestation of force. Other formulas make possible the strategic arrangement of magnets and wires in the powerhouse so that, when the magnets (or rather the field of subtle forces, in and around the magnets) are set in motion, force is manifested in the way we call an electric current. We do not think of the designing of a radio station or a power plant as a linguistic process, but it is one nonetheless. The necessary mathematics is a linguistic apparatus, and, without its correct specification of essential patterning, the assembled gadgets would be out of proportion and adjustment, and would remain inert. But the mathematics used in such a case is a *specialized* formula-language, contrived for making available a specialized type of force manifestation through metallic bodies only, namely, *electricity* as we today define what we call by that name. The mantric formula-language is specialized in a different way, in order to make available a different type of force manifestation, by repatterning states in the nervous system and glands—or again rather in the subtle "electronic" or "etheric" forces in and around those physical bodies. Those parts of the organism, until such strategic patterning has been effected, are merely "innocent gadgets," as incapable of dynamic power as loose magnets and loose wires, but *in the proper pattern* they are something else again—not to be understood from the properties of the unpatterned parts, and able to amplify and activate latent forces.[21]

5. Language

The function of language in these disciplines is manifold. First, paradoxically, books are written which announce that this type of teaching is "not to be found completely in books"; this either allows our verbal intellect to relax a bit or completely puts off a person who is unwilling even to consider that some mode of consciousness other than the linear and rational could exist. Second, language describes conditions under which certain experiences can take place. For example, in reading a book on sailing, we might obtain a clear idea of the effects of wind currents and angles on hull speed, and perhaps where dangerous parts of the coastline are hidden from view, but no one would claim to be an expert sailor who had never been out on the water.

In some very special instances, *language itself* can be the vehicle. Just as the very sound of language can be a primary aspect of communication in mantras and in dervish calls, so specially designed situations can contain elements, useful for the silent side, encoded in language. Atula Quarmani, one of the teachers of Gurdjieff, comments on this use of language:

"How were the texts studied?"
"By constant reading so that the different levels of meaning should be absorbed gradually. They were not read

to be 'understood' as you understand the term, but to be absorbed into the very texture of your conscious being and your inner self. In the West the intellectual teaches that you must understand a thing to profit from it. Sufi lore places no reliance upon such a clumsy thing as your superficial ability. The baraka seeps in, often despite you, rather than being forced to wait upon the doorstep until your 'intellect' permits it to filter through in an attenuated form." [22]

6. Oral Literature

In some cultures, especially those of the Middle East, stories or "fairy tales" have several functions. They can both entertain, and give pleasure to young children. Often they may contain a useful "moralistic" parable and help to form a common cultural heritage—a shared universe of discourse. They also provide the basis for more advanced instruction later in life.

The logic of these stories is not ordinary: it is more like that of the dream. In the stories, linear time, for instance, has little value. In fairy tales, events occur in, around, before, during, and after each other. Indeed, "magic carpets" exist here, which can transcend time. Many symbols in fairy tales, if looked at in terms of the psychology of consciousness, may take on a new meaning. I invite you to reflect for a moment on these: a genie locked up in a bottle, whose release may mean destruction; a beautiful and almost unattainable princess imprisoned in a tower; a dragon guarding a precious jewel.

Many books of quite innocent-appearing stories were written to provide a vehicle for the traditional esoteric psychology. Often they have been mistaken for either literal history or trivia. They include Aesop's *Fables*, the Greek myths, *The Arabian Nights, Don Quixote*, among very many others.

These stories have recently been given the name "teaching stories," since their effect is not only to provide pleasure or a useful parable but also to connect "with a part of the individual which cannot be reached by any other convention," and establish "in him or in her, a means of communication with a nonverbalized truth beyond the customary limitations of our familiar dimensions." [23]

How can these stories work on consciousness and communicate this way? Why are they to be read and reread constantly? To look at it loosely, consider that we recognize only the familiar. We can hear our name quickly, at lower intensity than most other words. We can recognize an English word more quickly than a random sequence of letters. We see red sixes of hearts much more quickly than red sixes of spades.

The aim, of course, in esoteric tradition is to receive unfamiliar information. Teaching stories purposely contain certain specially chosen patterns of events. The repeated reading of the story allows these patterns to become strengthened in the mind of the person reading them. Since many of the events are improbable and unusual, the reading of the stories begins to create new constructs, or new "organs of perception," so to speak. The stories take the mind along unfamiliar and nonlinear paths. It is not, then, necessary to "understand" the stories in the usual intellectual and rational mode. The constant rereading entices the consciousness into operating in an unusual manner; it creates patterns of operation or categories which are available when external events dictate them. This practice may allow a person to perceive aspects of reality which are so uncommon and unusual that he would not otherwise possess the needed constructs, or "receptive organ." As Eliot says, "Only by the form, the pattern, can words or music reach the stillness." It is the genius of this form of literature that intellectual analysis still has a function, although such analysis does not exhaust the story. This literature works on both modes.

These stories are conveyed primarily by oral tradition. It is quite rare at this moment in our culture for one to sit down and listen to stories. Reflect on the obvious differences between reading a piece of literature in the usual way and listening to it. Reading aloud takes longer and allows the events more importance. Listening takes the burden off our eyes and our visual system and returns balance to the ears, as Don Juan put it. It allows us to "picture" the events as they occur in space. Some of these books, especially the fairy tales, are illustrated for this very purpose, as are many tales in this book. Finally, listening involves the *sound* of the language, which can communicate to the tonally sensitive areas of the brain through the inflections and higher harmonics of the voice.[24]

The storyteller himself is one of the most important elements in these traditions, in using language to make an "end run around the verbal intellect," to affect a mode of consciousness not reached by the normal verbal-intellectual apparatus.

These special stories exist in every culture, but, like many other esoteric psychological techniques, without some supervision they become altered and degenerate. Sometimes people come to believe that the stories relate literal history; so they must be reformulated for each cultural age, by a person or a school sensitive to the many functions which a story can perform. It has currently become the work of Idries Shah to reintroduce this material to contemporary Western culture. Shah traveled for many years on several continents, collecting and comparing traditional teaching stories.

These stories can be employed in many ways. For instance, they can serve as reflection points. "Reflection" can mean both "to think about" and "to mirror." Often an action caught in a story forms a pattern which is also present on another level of consciousness, as when an electron-microscopic photograph contains the pattern which can be seen in a photograph of a river taken from an airplane, or in a picture of the earth seen from a satellite. This is a meaning of the esoteric saying, "As above, so below."

Some stories can serve as templates for consciousness, patterns frozen so that we can observe ourselves. In one, Nasrudin is interested in learning to play the lute. He searches out the lute master, and asks, "How much do you charge for lessons?" The lute master replies, "Ten gold pieces for the first month, one gold piece for the succeeding months." "Excellent," says Nasrudin. "I shall begin with the second month." [25]

Some quite brief and improbable situations can be simultaneously considered in different ways.

Nasrudin was walking on the main street of a town, throwing out bread crumbs. His neighbors asked, "What are you doing, Nasrudin?"

"Keeping the tigers away."

"There have not been tigers in these parts for hundreds of years."

"Exactly, effective, isn't it?" [26]

Here Nasrudin *at the same time* is the fool who performs a superstitious and useless action, and a teacher of the traditional psychology whose actions may be incomprehensible to the ordinary, linear consciousness.

In another story, Nasrudin is made a magistrate. During his first case the plaintiff argues so persuasively that he exclaims, "I believe you are right."

The clerk of the court begs him to restrain himself, for the defendant had not yet been heard.

Nasrudin is so carried away by the eloquence of the defendant that he cries out as soon as the man has finished his evidence, "I believe you are right."

The clerk of the court cannot allow this. "Your honor, they cannot both be right."

"I believe you are right," says Nasrudin.[27]

This story can be considered from several viewpoints simultaneously. First, Nasrudin is the part of us who latches on to any new idea or new technique, becomes excited, and maintains its worth to the exclusion of others. When we discover a new person in our lives, or a new writer, or a new movie star, it seems they can do no wrong. Our older friends and interests are forgotten. In school we may study Greek civilization and come to feel that the Greeks achieved the ideal way of life, and then we may study the Romans and then feel that *they* achieved the pinnacle of human development. This same tendency may exist in an entire discipline, such as psychology, where an idea, such as behaviorism, may come along, offering a new and useful technique, and we become totally focused on and committed to it, forgetting earlier commitments, interests, values.

Second, note that Nasrudin is a judge in this story. When we ourselves judge others, we usually are saying (in one form or another), "I believe that you are *wrong.*" This is evident in close personal relationships, as well as in scientific arguments. Two academics who may have extremely similar educations, ideas, and competences may spend years arguing over a small technical point and miss their numerous essential agreements. Two churches may exhibit the same tendency. Our education, too, is geared toward finding *differences* between things and trains us to analyze and separate different events as much as possible. "Compare and contrast . . . ." Here Nasrudin is opening up the alternative: to emphasize the agreement *first,* then, perhaps, consider the points of disagreement.

Third, and this recalls the story of the elephant, both the prosecution and the defense may be right *at the same time,* just as the man who says "It is cylindrical and solid," and the man who says "It is long and flexible and emits air," are both correct, when one looks at the entire elephant. *From such a higher perspective, many views that might otherwise seem opposite can be seen as complementary.* In psychology such views might be "consciousness is individual," "consciousness is cosmic," "we understand mediately, through language," "we understand immediately, through intuition." As our scientific and personal knowledge develop, we may gain a measure of perspective and be able to reconcile viewpoints that had once seemed to be opposites.

A very famous Nasrudin story (which we will use again in the next chapter) opens with a man looking at Nasrudin searching on the ground.

"What have you lost, Mulla?" the man asked.

"My key," said the Mulla.

So they both went down on their knees and looked for it. After a time the man asked, "Where exactly did you drop it?"

"In my own house."

"Then why are you looking here?"

"There is more light here than inside my own house." [28]

Although this story is funny (it has been performed on stage as such), it strikes an obvious superficial moral.

But we can work with the story a bit and open some of the deeper elements. I invite you to spend a little time with the story yourself, to read it over a few times. Then close your eyes and imagine yourself frantically searching for something.

What are you looking for?

Where are you looking?

Is there a "lot of light" there?

Now after you have done that, close your eyes once again and contemplate a key.

What is your key? (Take your time.)

What comes up?

After you have spent some time on the key, say to yourself, "I have lost my key," and see where this takes you.

Then spend some time on "My key is in my own house." Note where your thoughts go.

Then put the whole story together: "I am looking for my key—which I really know is in my own house—in places where I know the key is not, but where there is more light," and spend a little more time with the story. It is a good place to visit.

In addition to the personal associations called up by the story, I offer another, more directly related to the concerns of this book. Two areas of the mind are opposed, the light, or "day," and the dark, or "night." The key is inside the house, in the dark, unexplored area of our house, of the mind, of science. We are normally attracted and a bit dazzled by the light of the day, since it is generally easier to find objects in daylight. But *what are we looking for may simply not be there*, and often we may have to grope around somewhat inelegantly in the dark areas to find it. Once we find what we are looking for in the dark, we can then bring it into the light, and create a synthesis of both areas of the mind.

Not all the Sufi stories concern Nasrudin. This is "The Ants and the Pen."

An ant one day strayed across a piece of paper and saw a pen writing in fine, black strokes.

"How wonderful this is!" said the ant. "This remarkable thing, with a life of its own, makes squiggles on this beautiful surface, to such an extent and with such energy that it is equal to the efforts of all the ants in the world. And the squiggles which it makes! These resemble ants; not one, but millions, all run together."

He repeated his ideas to another ant, who was equally interested. He praised the powers of observation and reflection of the first ant.

But another ant said: "Profiting, it must be admitted, by your efforts, I have observed this strange object. But I have determined that it is not the master of this work. You failed to notice that this pen is attached to certain other objects, which surround it and drive it on its way. These should be considered as the moving factor, and given the credit." Thus were fingers discovered by the ants.

But another ant, after a long time, climbed over the fingers and realized that they made up a hand, which he thoroughly explored, after the manner of ants, by scrambling all over it.

He returned to his fellows: "Ants!" he cried, "I have news of importance for you. Those smaller objects are part of a large one. It is this which gives motion to them."

But then it was discovered that the hand was attached to an arm, and the arm to a body, and that there were feet which did no writing.

The investigations continue. Of the mechanics of the writing, the ants have a fair idea. Of the meaning and intention of the writing, and how it is ultimately controlled, they will not find out by their customary method of investigation. Because they are "literate." [29]

Here the linear, cumulative mode of gathering knowledge is again contrasted with a holistic and tacit mode which can appear only when consciousness is organized differently. This story emphasizes the strengths and limitations of the ordinary mode, and the necessity to operate in a mode appropriate to the kind of knowledge one is seeking. The ants, believing themselves already literate, effectively block themselves from any possible understanding of the meaning of the writing.

To relate this to scientific inquiry, we *could* attempt to determine, say, a person's voting patterns by examining each cell in his or her body, and totaling these chemical and electrophysiological observations in a strictly additive, cumulative manner. This would not only be tedious and expensive, but it would almost surely not yield an appropriate answer (certainly not before the next election). A more appropriate level of analysis for this situation would be the sociological, rather than the biological. We would then attempt to consider the whole person as he exists within the social context, and we would conveniently ignore, for the purposes of this analysis, that he or she is composed of billions of discrete individual cells.

In this higher level of analysis, we would consider factors which are more relevant to the question at hand, such as the income or family status of the person. We would never think of asking "What is the income of this cell?" In the story of the ants, in order for them to fully understand the nature and meaning of the writing, their *level of analysis itself would have to be expanded*. But, just as the biological and sociological levels of analysis can simultaneously coexist, so can the personal, individual consciousness coexist with another that is often called "objective" or "cosmic" consciousness. The esoteric practices attempt to suppress temporarily the individual, analytic (here represented as looking at each cell separately) consciousness and to allow the consciousness of the "whole organism" to emerge.

Many have become confused at this point, believing this to be an either-or question, believing in the unique existence of one mode or the other. However, the existence of an individual and separate consciousness does not rule out the possibility of the simultaneous coexistence of another level of organization. Just as the existence of society does not deny the existence of the individual, so the existence in the body of billions of individual cells, as separate, discrete, analyzable units, does not rule out the existence of an emergent, whole person, with properties not traceable to any linear combination of cells.

This "higher" level of consciousness is often referred to as the mystic experience, the perception of unity, of "We are all one." This statement does not mean that "We are all the *same thing* and exactly alike," as it is often interpreted. Rather, it means that people are all individual components in an emergent level of organization, and that this level, this organization, may become perceptible in the same way that the sum of cells in a body are individual, yet make up one person.

The shift from the individual, analytic consciousness to a holistic mode, brought about by training the intuitive side of ourselves, is often referred to by a term that translates as "ego death" in esoteric tradition. This shift consists of a breaking down of the constructs which maintain personal consciousness, and a transition from this analytic mode to the emergent, "gestalt" mode of consciousness.

A CONCLUSION

The traditional esoteric psychologies are, in their essence, neither deliberately exotic and incomprehensible nor irrelevant to our concerns. They constitute important new input for modern scientific psychology, about an area of inquiry and an area of the mind which has largely been ignored and forgotten in contemporary culture and psychology.

In one sense, both types of psychology begin from common ground, and then develop in complementary directions. Both characterize normal consciousness as selective and restrictive, as a personal construction. Modern psychology, then, proceeds to a quite fine analysis of the accomplishment of this construction. It considers, for instance, the physiology of the eye, and the characteristics of transmission of the central nervous system; and psychologists perform experiments which demonstrate the effect of our biases and conceptions on the contents of personal consciousness.

The traditional esoteric psychologists proceed in another direction, to practical techniques such as meditation, for circumventing the "reducing valve" of normal consciousness, techniques for suspending the normal, analytic, linear mode. More advanced techniques then tune the intuitive mode by working in its own tacit language.

The further development of a modern psychology of consciousness may in large part rest on the integration of this new input, the extended perspective and practical exercises of the traditional psychologies, with the technology of the modern, making contemporary psychology more complete once again.

For further reading

Rafael Lefort. *The Teachers of Gurdjieff.* London: Gollancz, 1968.

Carlos Castaneda. *The Teachings of Don Juan: A Yaqui Way of Knowledge.* New York: Simon & Schuster, 1973.

Carlos Castaneda. *A Separate Reality: Further Conversations with Don Juan.* New York: Simon & Schuster. London: The Bodley Head. 1971.

Carlos Castaneda. *Journey to Ixtlan.* New York: Simon & Schuster. London: The Bodley Head. 1973.

Michael Murphy. *Golf in the Kingdom.* New York: The Viking Press, 1972.

Baba Ram Das. *Be Here Now.* New York: Crown Publ., 1971.

These first six books represent personal encounters of Western students with teachers of the esoteric traditions.

Claudio Naranjo. *The One Quest.* New York: The Viking Press, 1972.

Jacob Needleman. *The New Religions.* New York: Doubleday, 1970.

Paul Reps. *Zen Flesh, Zen Bones.* New York: Doubleday, 1968.

Idries Shah. *The Sufis.* London: Jonathan Cape, 1969. New York: Doubleday, 1971.

Idries Shah. *Tales of the Dervishes.* London: Jonathan Cape, 1967. New York: E. P. Dutton, 1970.

Idries Shah. *The Pleasantries of the Incredible Mulla Nasrudin.* London: Jonathan Cape, 1968. New York: E. P. Dutton, 1971.

Idries Shah. *The Elephant in the Dark.* London: Octagon Press, 1974.

Idries Shah. *The Subtleties of the Inimitable Mulla Nasrudin.* London: Jonathan Cape, 1973. New York: E. P. Dutton.

Idries Shah. *The Sufis.* See selections in Robert Ornstein, ed.,

The Nature of Human Consciousness. San Francisco: W. H. Freeman and Co. New York: The Viking Press. 1973.

Shah has written several more works on Sufism, all now readily available in cloth and paper, some referenced at the end of Chapter 10.

Kilton Stewart, "Dream Theory in Malaya," in Charles T. Tart, ed., *Altered States of Consciousness*. New York: John Wiley & Sons, 1969.

John White, ed. *The Highest State of Consciousness*. New York: Doubleday, 1972.

Omar Michael Burke. *Among the Dervishes*. London: Octagon Press, 1974.

Sirdar Ikbal Ali Shah. *The Spirit of the East*. London: Octagon Press, 1974.

Sadi. *The Rose Garden*. London: Octagon Press, 1974.

See also the further readings recommended at the end of Chapter 6.

THE NEW SYNTHESIS

Chapter *8*

A Brief
Introduction

The ideas, exercises, and techniques of the esoteric traditions point toward a change of paradigm in modern psychology. When such a change takes place, the concept of "normal" and "paranormal" undergoes a redefinition. As with the four-minute mile, once the limits of possibility are broken, a new area opens up. Beyond their practical techniques, the major import of the traditional psychologies is to inform us that we have been far too low in our estimation of ourselves. We are quite close to the position of the rugseller, having limited ourselves personally, scientifically, and culturally by our conception of the possibilities.

Actually, we are a *little* better off than the rugseller. Suppose someone had answered the question, "Is there any number higher than 100?" with "Yes" and a scrap of paper with "147, 793, 960" written on it. We have some indication that higher numbers exist, but what is their relationship with the known numbers under 100? What are the new limits?

We know, for instance, that our "normal" consciousness is not complete, but is an exquisitely evolved, selective, personal construction whose primary purpose is to ensure biological survival. But this mode, although necessary for survival, is not necessarily the only one in which consciousness can operate. As the material success of our culture eases the task of survival, it provides a secure basis for the development of another mode of consciousness.

The essence of the active mode of survival is selection and limitation. If we were indiscriminately aware of each quantum of energy reaching us, we would likely be dead within a day. We must, then, "automatically" limit our perceptions. Our internal state, too, is automatized. We could not survive if we each had to beat our hearts voluntarily seventy times a minute. We screen internal constancies from consciousness, as we screen the constancies in the external environment.

However, although certain internal physiological processes are *almost always* "automatic," they are not forever beyond volition. For individual biological survival, these processes seem best automatized, but for the further extension of consciousness, it may be necessary to make the effort to deautomatize them.

This is an instance in which our dominant Western paradigm has prevented us from clearly seeing the scientific import of the esoteric traditions. For hundreds of years reports have reached the West of yogis who could stop their hearts and alter their glandular and metabolic activity. But since we considered such control impossible, we have almost completely ignored these fragmentary communications. Just as the esoteric traditions have developed exercises, such as meditation, which deautomatize ordinary, outward-oriented consciousness, so they have developed techniques for deautomatizing the internal states. Psychological studies of Yoga masters point to a possibility of self-mastery far beyond our current limits. The impetus given by this possibility feeds the new research in physiological feedback training, which combines a concept of increased self-mastery with modern technological methods.

The automatization of ordinary consciousness is a tradeoff: for the sake of survival, we lose much of the richness of experience. We tune out the constancies of the environment and discard many subtle or slow-changing phenomena. But if a person's consciousness is deautomatized, he may be able to notice factors which are always present but which he has ignored. If the person is a scientist, he could then turn his full intellect to the study of sources of influence on man too subtle and too constant to enter ordinary consciousness. These sources include the rotation of the earth, the influence of the atmosphere, and the gravitational field.

Most modern psychologists may think it quite strange to consider these subtle geophysical forces as part of the psychology of consciousness. It is, however, becoming clear that humans are not so closed a biological system as we once thought. Some recent research confirms the esoteric assertion that subtle environmental forces do influence us, although their influence is often obscured by more brilliant phenomena.

THE NEW SYNTHESIS

A deautomatization of consciousness is a key. It enables us personally to note factors that had previously escaped attention. It is here that the work of the esoteric traditions is most fruitfully incorporated into Western science. They offer exercises and techniques designed for deautomatization. Additionally, the writers of these traditions direct attention to areas of consciousness which are usually not considered in contemporary science.

Pointing, merely pointing, at a critical time is often all that is needed. If we merely tell a person that although a six of spades is usually black, it could be red, he may be able to see what was in front of him all along. This is part of the current import of the esoteric traditions for us.

The two modes of consciousness can function complementarily in this work. Gaining a personal knowledge may lead us into the new area of inquiry, but, once there, we can make full use of modern scientific techniques and instruments to explore and to map the territory. We can then "translate" the metaphors of the esoteric traditions into more modern scientific terms when appropriate, and combine our technology with the traditional perspective.

We are just at the first moments of this new synthesis, from which an extended concept of man is beginning to emerge. A few of the elements which will go into this synthesis can be briefly listed.

1. Two major modes of consciousness exist in man, and function in a complementary manner. Since the dominant mode in our culture is the verbal and rational, recognition of their existence involves us in a cultivation of the second mode, the intuitive and holistic. The first mode is active, associated with our biological survival, the *day* in our metaphor. The second mode is receptive,

and constitutes the dark, subtle area of consciousness, the *night*.

2. Our personal and scientific attention is being shifted inward, to the importance of consciousness itself as an object of inquiry, and to the self-control of internal states. Physiological feedback research thus involves a fundamental redirection of technology toward the internal rather than the external environment.

3. Man is not so closed a system as the Western scientific community once thought. We are sensitive and permeable to subtle sources of energy from geophysical and human forces which often lie unnoticed in the brilliance of the day.

4. The concepts of "normal" and "paranormal" are in process of change. It was, for instance, previously considered "paranormal" to claim self-control of the "autonomic" nervous system or to claim sensitivity to subtle geophysical stimuli.

These "elements" are merely a brief sketch; the synthesis has not even begun to take on any recognizable form. This is not the moment to delineate the final form of this new psychology, but a time, once again, to open the boundaries of inquiry in modern psychology and to explore the new field with freshly extended conceptions. The following two chapters, then, are the very beginnings of this exploration.

Chapter 9 is on biofeedback training, which combines the esoteric emphasis on self-mastery with modern technology. Biofeedback is no substitute for the esoteric practices, nor is it a perfect translation of them into modern language. Yet in its own limited way (compared with the esoteric traditions), it is a significant extension of contemporary science.

Chapter 10 is much looser, much more tentative and speculative. It deals with the beginnings of research on subtle environmental factors, techniques in body therapies, and psychotherapies which respond to this new input. It concludes with a consideration of a contemporary example of esoteric psychology.

Chapter 9

Techniques
of Self-Regulation

There Is More Light Here

A man saw Nasrudin searching for something on the ground. "What have you lost, Mulla?" he asked.

"My key," said the Mulla.

So the man went down on his knees too, and they both looked for it. After a time, the other man asked: "Where exactly did you drop it?"

"In my own house."

"Then why are you looking here?"

"There is more light here than inside my own house." [1]

Our ordinary consciousness is largely directed toward active manipulation of the external environment. For the most part we remain unaware of our internal physiological processes, those phenomena occurring "within our own house," in the dark. We each tune out subtle internal stimuli and direct attention outward, toward the external world, in order to survive. We would not be able to accomplish much if we had to "take time" to digest our food, to pump additional blood to an injury, or "consciously" to direct the operation of the kidneys. It is almost always more economical to place these processes "on automatic," out of direct awareness.

The split in personal consciousness between outward and inward has led to a paradigm in science which conceptually divides the nervous system in two. The central nervous system, which includes the brain and the nerves that direct skeletal muscle activity, is concerned with thought, voluntary action, and manipulation of the external environment through the limbs. The "autonomic" nervous system maintains the internal milieu—it controls the activity of the heart, the stomach, and the glands.

For the most part, this internal functioning is automatized, out of volitional control. Once again, that a process is almost always in a certain state does not mean it must remain so under all conditions. But the very labels affixed to this portion of ourselves have effectively "legislated" it beyond any possibility of self-regulation—in addition to "autonomic," it has at times been termed the "involuntary" (and even the "vegetative") nervous system.

We have here another example of how a concept of what is possible determines what is considered "normal" and "paranormal." The reports of yogic self-regulation were simply ignored as evidence, since they did not fit into the conventional paradigm of two nervous systems with fundamentally different natures, one "voluntary," one "autonomic."

In ordinary consciousness, the state of our internal physiology is usually irrelevant. Normally, we are little aware of the processes within our kidneys or of alterations in our blood-flow pattern, and, for the most part, we do not need to be more aware. Yet the esoteric traditions note the effect of controlled inner states on consciousness. In some of the exercises of the esoteric traditions, the priorities are reversed: ordinary, outward-directed consciousness is turned off by exercises, such as meditation, which produce a shift to an inward, receptive state. In this other mode, ordinary awareness is irrelevant, for its brilliance would overshadow the faint internal signals. And, when the proper exercises are performed, these normally invisible signals are brought into consciousness, and what was "autonomic" in ordinary awareness can be changed.

We can, then, extend our interpretation of the Nasrudin story that begins this chapter to the physiological level. Like many, Nasrudin is accustomed to look for the key outside of himself, in the light of the day. But it lies inside—symbolically, within his house, in the darkness.

YOGIC SELF-CONTROL

Of all the esoteric traditions, it is Yoga that places the most emphasis on physiological self-regulation. To take one example, Swami Rama, Elmer Green's subject at the Menninger Foundation, has demonstrated that he can voluntarily beat his heart 300 times per minute. He can alter his body and skin temperature and can also enter a state of "yogic sleep," in which he can remember all that takes place during a 25-minute interval, although he gives outward (and EEG) appearances of being sound asleep. These and other well-documented reports are only now becoming readily available. As the psychophysiological study of these adepts progresses, their capacities will be charted with increasing accuracy. Some very preliminary studies report yogis living on diets that seem impossible to Western science. Some have reported that Tibetan adepts can raise their body heat enough to melt ice on cold nights, high up in the mountains.[2] This mastery, in esoteric tradition, is considered technique—a means by which consciousness can be changed.

And yet, once our concept of the possible is even slightly extended, "paranormal" self-regulation seems much less spectacular and unusual. We may even note that many people possess such capacities in a rudimentary form. One person may know how to relax at will, another can slow the heart, another is able to hold his breath for long periods of time, etc.

Several exceptional individuals have developed these "paranormal" capacities to some extent. To take one instance, in *The Mind of a Mnemonist*, the Russian physiologist Luria describes a man who could perform fantastic memory feats and who could also raise the temperature in one of his hands while simultaneously lowering it in the other, simply by mental imagery.[3]

The famous escape artist Houdini learned some autonomic control in order to perform his "amazing" feats. In one of his tricks, his hands would be fastened in a set of handcuffs, and he would be placed in a locked trunk and thrown underwater. Yet he would escape. How? He held no key (he was searched often enough by reputable people who were sure of that), and the locks were burst-proof. Limited to an ordinary conception of man's capabilities, most people thought the task impossible. If that conception is slightly extended, the "amazing" feat becomes less amazing. As with Nasrudin, the key was inside. Houdini had swallowed the key (which unlocked both the handcuffs and the trunk) before the demonstration began, and, having learned control over his digestive system, he regurgitated the key once inside the box and opened the locks.

We could collect many other reports of individuals who have had more than a normal degree of self-mastery. The import of the esoteric traditions, practical psychologies that they are, lies in their development of procedures which allow the student to *train* himself in the deployment of these extra-ordinary capacities. More careful study of these adepts may enable us to find out just how much self-mastery and self-knowledge *each person* could achieve, given the development of a more modern method of training, although the applications of this self-control may well be different in the western context.

Our normal educational process is primarily directed toward the active mode—the verbal, intellectual, and manipulative processes. We learn to write, to play ball, or to play a musical instrument through a process of feedback. When we make a mistake in playing a note, or in penmanship, or mathematics, our teacher corrects us. But we do not have a similar tradition in our culture of learning about the internal environment. We learn little about our emotions, little about what happens in our bodies when we are angry or afraid. We learn little even about the nature, function, and placement of our internal organs. A recent English survey reports that most people do not know where their bladders, kidneys, or intestines are.[4] If our education could be refocused slightly, to include more attention to the inward spaces of our bodies, many might learn to play internal organs as they learn to manipulate external forces. The forces involved, however, are subtle, and are usually screened out of personal awareness.

RESEARCH ON PHYSIOLOGICAL SELF-CONTROL

If we look to modern science, there is a body of evidence consistent with the esoteric approach to the nervous system. A series of investigations that K. M. Bykov began in Russia in 1924 demonstrate that the autonomic nervous system is only *relatively* autonomic and is subject to voluntary control if the situation is set up appropriately. Bykov and his associates used Pavlov's method of the conditioned response. That a bell sounds means nothing in itself to a hungry dog; but if the sound of the bell always precedes feeding, the dog will begin to salivate each time the bell sounds. Bykov's studies indicated that if a process can be conditioned, then it is a modifiable process, and if autonomic processes can be conditioned, they are not really autonomic at all.[5]

Several investigators working in Bykov's laboratory demonstrated that many involuntary processes could be conditioned. Experimental animals could learn to increase or decrease their body heat, as well as to alter the heat in specific limbs by controlling the blood flow to those limbs. They could control their heart rhythms, and remove blocks in the electrocardiogram introduced by morphine. Pancreatic secretion could be affected, and the urine excretion of the kidneys could be increased or decreased. The volume of the blood in the spleen could be changed, or the secretion of bile altered, as could many other processes. These processes had previously been considered unalterable, part of the "automaton," the body.

The work of the Russians clearly indicates that there is far more modifiability of the heart, liver, spleen, kidneys, blood flow, etc., than we normally suppose. It also indicates that the division some have made between mind and body—the mind as a process of reason and will, the body as an automaton, à la Descartes—is unnecessarily limiting. As Bykov and Gantt put it, "The gap between the two disconnected worlds of *psyche* and *soma* is being bridged."

There have been many other sources of evidence on the possibility of internal self-regulation. The original explorations of Freud and Breuer on hysteria point in the same direction. One of their early patients was a woman whose hand was paralyzed. Her paralysis took the shape of a glove, which Freud considered "anatomical nonsense," since the muscles that would have been affected by a "real" paralysis did not stop at the line marked by the glove. Freud's brilliant insight was that this paralysis was under the voluntary, although in his terms "unconscious," control of the woman. From this woman's problem and from those of many other of Freud's patients, the concept of psychosomatic medicine was born—a discipline whose very name links the worlds of the mind and the body. Freud discovered that the woman's paralysis could be cured by bringing this "unconscious control" into her awareness.[6]

Psychosomatic medicine has so far limited itself to removing the misapplications of our self-regulation, as in Freud and Breuer's work. But there is an important theoretical point for our consideration here. The fact that one can voluntarily bring about paralysis in the shape of a glove makes it clear that one can achieve precise control of the blood flow and musculature in quite specific areas of the hand. The esoteric claim to control internal states seems much less fantastic when this evidence is considered. Since Yoga adepts spend many years attending to these processes with the intent to alter them, it seems reasonable that, in view of Bykov's work and that of psychosomatic medicine, these alterations can be accomplished.

Certainly the most sophisticated and the most theoretically relevant research in the voluntary alteration of physiological processes has been that of Neal Miller and Leo DiCara of Rockefeller University. Their research has been designed explicitly to investigate the possibility that learning may take place in the autonomic nervous system.[7] Bykov's work had been limited to classical (involuntary) conditioning, which learning theorists have considered inferior to voluntary learning (operant conditioning). Bykov's work, as he himself stated, was intended to show that the activity of the autonomic nervous system could always be modified by the central nervous system.

Miller and DiCara's work indicates that the alterations in blood flow, and in the activity of internal organs and of the glands, can be brought about voluntarily by the type of learning that psychologists consider to be "higher." Most important, their research demonstrates that learning can take place within the autonomic nervous system* seemingly without the involvement of the voluntary skeletal musculature. When the attempt is to chart the new possibilities of human self-regulation, these "academic" distinctions may not seem very important. Most often it will be of no practical concern whether an action, such as slowing the heart rate, may be accomplished with or without the involvement of the skeletal muscles. However, the distinctions are theoretically of great significance, because they rule out any possible conception of an "autonomic nervous system" existing alone.

---

* It is almost impossible to rule out central nervous activity *completely* even in these quite careful experiments.

Miller, DiCara, and their associates studied experimental animals (rats, mostly) in which they could implant electrodes, thermistors, or photocells at specific sites in the stomach and kidneys, in the cardiovascular system, and in the brain. Information about the selected activity in these sites (for instance, blood flow) was converted into electrical stimulation to "rewarding" areas of the brain. (Stimulation of certain areas of the brain has been found to be a reward to most animals.) In order to increase the rate of the electrical brain stimulations, the animals had to alter that specific aspect of their autonomic activity—in this example, blood flow. Miller and DiCara eliminated the influence of the skeletal muscles in this autonomic learning by administering the drug curare, which selectively paralyzes the skeletal musculature and allows no central nervous system commands to reach the muscles.

With sensors implanted in specific sites to pick up the signal, and with the information given to the brain in terms of direct brain reward, the animals could quickly learn to alter blood flow, blood pressure, stomach acidity, kidney functioning, and the electrical activity of the brain. Miller and DiCara required that differential control over each process be demonstrated—for instance, both the raising and the lowering of blood flow, both the increase and the decrease of the kidney functions. Once the information is made directly available, many "involuntary" processes seem quite modifiable. The processes controlled can be surprisingly specific. In one experiment, sensors were implanted in both ears of a rat, and reward was given only when there was a difference between the blood flows in the two ears. In this situation, the rat could not produce the desired results by altering a *general* process, such as an increase in blood flow or an alteration in heart rate. The rat learned to control its blood flow to each ear *differentially,* raising it first in one and then in the other.

Another result of the studies of Miller and DiCara relates directly to meditation as a process of turning off competing activity, or metaphorically of turning off the light of day. When Miller first administered curare to his animals, he feared it might slow down their rate of learning to control physiological processes. The reverse turned out to be true. The animals that were paralyzed by curare could learn much more quickly to alter their heart rate, blood flow, kidney functions, etc. Curare is a drug that halts all ordinary movements and the proprioceptive impulses that would normally enter awareness. It may be, then, that curare in these experimental animals performs a function similar to that of meditation in people. Both are means of reducing irrelevant activity, and both may make the detection of faint internal signals much more possible.

There have been several other studies of the training of cardiovascular functioning. Peter Lang has extended this research work to man, allowing people to learn to "drive" their heartbeat in a narrow range, using a feedback system similar to an amusement park game of keeping a car on a small track.[8] At Harvard, David Shapiro and his associates have been able to train their undergraduate volunteers to alter their heart rate and blood pressure in a single half-hour session of feedback training.[9]

THE PROCESS OF INTERNAL CONTROL

There are, now, two major procedures available for contacting the weak signals within. In the esoteric traditions, one tries to turn off the competing activity, to turn day into night, so that the subtle signals are perceptible. In the newly developed feedback system, the "stars" are brought to consciousness by another method. The faint signals *themselves* are amplified, to make them perceptible even in the brilliance of the daylight. In the esoteric traditions, the "noise" is lessened; in biofeedback research, the "signal" is strengthened. In both cases, when these normally unconscious processes enter consciousness, we can receive this subtle information and can learn to control what was previously an "unconscious" or "autonomic" process.

Biofeedback Experiments with Humans

The basic feedback experiment is quite simple in concept, yet it rests on quite complex technological achievements. In research on "brain waves," for instance, electrodes are placed on the scalp at several points. If the experiment is "alpha feedback," the entire EEG is filtered, leaving only the 8 to 12 Hz alpha band. Then the filtered EEG is converted into a tone or a light which signals the presence or absence of alpha to the subject. Ordinarily, we remain unaware of the transitory alterations of our brain, but with sensitive equipment to detect, amplify, and feed back these weak internal signals, we are placed in a new and intimate relationship with ourselves.

As we listen to the tone varying in loudness, we can gradually come to discriminate internal states, and eventually to discover which internal manipulations produce the desired changes in the brain. After control is learned, the feedback apparatus may no longer be as necessary, since we may possibly reproduce the desired internal state without the feedback apparatus.[10]

A similar research procedure is usually followed in the experiments on self-control of heart activity and the tension of the muscles. The physiological monitoring machinery may be expensive and complex, but the entire process is quite simple. From one viewpoint, this research may be electronic Yoga, from another, physiological cybernetics, and from another, it is purely behaviorism (operant conditioning).

However, contrary to what has been claimed in the popular press, physiological feedback research is in the earliest of stages. Although some writers have given the impression that Electric Zen is just around the corner for all, this prophecy will be fulfilled only (if at all) after years of research. The current developments in feedback training are hardly in the same league with the procedures of the esoteric traditions. But although research speculation has often seemed fact, what *has* already been discovered is enough to break the old concept in the scientific community, of our inability to self-regulate the brain, heart, and muscular activity. In the esoteric traditions,

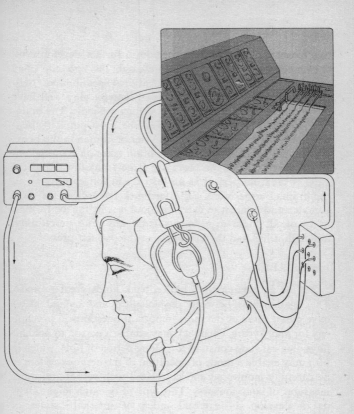

Figure 9.1
A schematic drawing of a biofeedback experiment. Here the EEG is recorded from the scalp, displayed on the polygraph, then filtered and converted into a tone, which is fed back to the subject through the earphones.

this mastery is often only a prelude to further development.

In modern science and clinical research, this "prelude" may open up new medical and educational possibilities. Self-control of muscle tension and heart activity may well have direct therapeutic applications for ordinary people. The brain-control work has certainly received the most popular attention, since the brain is the most mysterious organ in the body, and anything which relates to the brain takes on a special air. But the workings of the brain are largely unknown, and the EEG is far from perfect as an instrument for learning about the brain. Furthermore, EEG feedback research is the most complex and difficult to carry out, and it is by far the furthest away of all these experiments from any true practicality, although it has had the most play in the popular press.

RESEARCH

Yet, as a research tool, biofeedback holds great promise. The relationships between physiological and mental states have posed some of the most important questions in psychology for many years. Feedback may enable a person to hold his physiological state constant for a long period of time, which in turn may enable a mode of operation of the nervous system to be carefully monitored and correlated with verbal and other measures of consciousness. This type of research might allow us to develop an external index of internal "states of consciousness," so that experimenters may be able to train the occurrence of desired nervous system conditions. A similar development occurred some time ago in dream research, when it was discovered that people moved their eyes rapidly while they were in the process of dreaming. These Rapid Eye Movement (REM) periods then enabled the scientific study of the dream state. For example, researchers could predict the appearance of dreams and awaken subjects after REM periods for dream recall.

As it relates to the understanding of consciousness, biofeedback training may allow us to renew the exploration of introspection, which has been dormant since Titchener, since reports of self-observation may now be correlated with an objective physiological index, such as the EEG. A major research problem is that the EEG is a somewhat poor instrument for studying the most complex organ in the world.

At first it was thought sufficient to monitor alpha from an arbitrarily selected area on the scalp. This approach was given some support by the finding that many subjects seemed to report a common experience during alpha control. They described the "high alpha" state as "relaxed," "dark," "back of the head," especially when alpha from the occipital area was being trained. But these communalities are no longer overwhelmingly impressive. A much more precise and complex configuration of electroencephalographic activity must be specified in order to study the relation of brain events to subjective events.

After all, the areas of the brain are specialized for different kinds of information-processing. Brain injury to one hemisphere or the other produces different effects on the verbal and spatial modes, for instance. The appearance of a certain brain rhythm indicates a different mode of information-processing, *depending on the area from which it is recorded*. To speak, for instance, of a "high alpha" state without describing both where it is recorded from and the concurrent activity throughout the brain is an incomplete and almost useless statement.

The alpha rhythm does seem, though, to indicate a diminution of information-processing activity in a given area of the brain. For instance, when the eyes are closed, alpha in the occipital (visual) cortex is increased, and during the "turning off" form of meditation, alpha is generally enhanced.

David Galin and I have recently compared the EEG activity of the two sides of the brain during the performance of tasks designed to engage predominantly one or the other cerebral hemisphere. An increase in alpha rhythm tends to appear in the hemisphere less involved in the task. There is more alpha in the left hemisphere during spatial information-processing than during verbal thought. This reverses for the right hemisphere: there is more alpha in the right side during verbal information-processing than spatial. The brain seems to "turn off" the area not involved in the situation. This research may lead to a more functionally relevant form of EEG feedback, one which takes the lateral specialization of the brain into account. With the development of this technique, students, for instance, may be able to learn to place themselves in the "correct" brain state for different kinds of information-processing situations, one for making ceramics, the other for reading.[11]

MEDICINE

Our medical endeavor is primarily directed toward the treatment of diseases, not toward individual responsibility for health. We attempt to control bodily problems from the "outside" with drugs, rather than attempting to employ the individual's built-in capacity for self-regulation. The disease of hypertension, for instance, is most often controlled by a multitude of drugs, some of which must be used to balance the effects of others. As each new drug is developed, as each new surgical procedure is perfected, less and less responsibility for the cure is delegated to the patient himself. Although we have achieved an extraordinary amount of sophistication in drug and surgical therapy in Western medicine, this development has been a bit unbalanced. We have almost forgotten that it is possible for the "patients" *themselves* to learn directly to lower their blood pressure, to slow or speed their heart, to relax at will.

Perhaps we might begin the long process of returning at least some responsibility to the patient, of allowing him a much more active role in his own healing. The current developments in self-regulation research may, in time, enable a physician to "prescribe" specific kinds of training for certain disorders instead of drugs. Some possible uses of feedback in medicine might include reduction of hypertension, the control of gastrointestinal disorders, the lessening of tension headaches, the regulation of cardiac arrhythmia. In a few years, inexpensive trainers might possibly be developed to allow the patient to monitor and to control his disorder, and once the control is learned, to aid in preventing the recurrence of the disorder. Little is known about the eventual applications of feedback training at present. The limits of our voluntary alteration, as well as the aftereffects, are still items for speculation and for further empirical research. However, it is known that, in addition to the brain and heart rhythms, blood flow, the galvanic skin response, the muscular tension of certain groups (the frontalis muscles on the forehead), and skin temperature are alterable in people. Johann Stoyva and Thomas Budzynski at the University of Colorado Medical Center have been investigating the possibility of "deconditioning" or "desensitizing" by feedback. In behavioral psychotherapy many psychological problems—such as phobias, headaches, and anxiety—are thought of simply as faulty learning.[12]

According to this view, a neurotic person is simply responding in an inappropriate manner, becoming anxious and increasing muscle tension in a situation that does not call for it. The therapy consists in training a person to relax, instead of tensing, in response to the "threatening" stimulus. Stoyva and Budzynski have used the electromyogram (EMG), which measures muscular tension, as an indication of relaxation in response to previously threatening stimuli. Their preliminary findings indicate that the process of learning to relax in a situation that previously had elicited anxiety can be greatly speeded up by the use of physiological feedback techniques. If a person can "hear" his own muscle tension and his brain's electrical activity, he can monitor them continuously and keep them more precisely in the desired state. These examples, built around current research, are an exciting and useful development of science's new view of the nervous system, although to the esoteric traditions they are just the beginnings of the possibilities.

EDUCATION

In education the uses of self-regulation training may be dual. First, it might increase the efficiency of ordinary education, by training attentional deployment, using physiological indicators, so that information can be more efficiently received. Second, feedback may extend our concept of education itself, to include teaching students, in the most intimate manner, to contact their own internal states.

On the first possibility, the great increase in the number of students results in less and less individual attention for each student. Computer-assisted instruction is often held to be the answer to this problem, but this technique does not consider the individual student, save perhaps in taking his pace and level into account. The application of computing machines to teaching has primarily been directed toward the development of very fast drill and practice machines. This type of instruction has never tried to take the "state" of the learner into account.

While reading, for instance, we all have experienced those times when our attention lapsed and we were "looking" at the pages, yet nothing was registering in our awareness. At other times, we may have been too tense or too preoccupied to "pay attention" to what was presented to us.

Physiological feedback training may be of aid here. Suppose that research could delineate certain physiological processes that are associated with, say, efficient verbal information-processing. We would then connect the student's nervous system, as well as his hands and eyes, to the computer teacher, which would present information only if there were an appropriate pattern of physiological activity. In order to see the text, the student would need to produce a physiological state in which he could read efficiently. If his attention lapsed (and if we could find a pattern of physiological activity that correlated with this), the material would disappear from view and the student would be made immediately aware that he needed to change his mode of information-processing.

We do not really know now whether we will actually be able to find patterns of physiological activity which unequivocally indicate efficient attention and memory, but this general aim is certainly worth investigating. We have little firm evidence to go on as yet, save for the one obvious step of working with students who are motivated to learn, but who are so tense they cannot. These students might be trained to produce low levels of muscular tension before they can see the information presented. Allowing a computer-tutor to monitor the physiology of the learner could be one of the possible solutions, and an extremely valuable one to the existing problem of overcrowded schools. It may be possible to train different modes of awareness—verbal, logical, spatial, etc.—based on different patterns of brain activity, taking the brain's lateral specialization of function into account.

In all this, the larger import of the newer view of our voluntary capabilities is that the definition of education itself may be broadened. We distinguish two types of knowing; one concerned with the reception of information, one concerned with direct experience. We shy away from the experiential mode in education, for it is not "objective," not easily monitorable. But if the proper feedback devices are developed, we could include in each person's basic learning experience a training in his or her own capacities of self-regulation. We could teach relaxation to students just as we teach baseball. The concept of "physical education" could be expanded to include the mastery of internal states. We could allow people to be more sensitive to the state of their own bodies, and, more in keeping with the intent of the esoteric psychologies, to "Know thyself" in a most intimate way, to master the self, to make oneself more often and more consistently what one wishes.

In the past, these capacities have been trained only by those who could learn the esoteric procedures of the traditional psychologies. With sensitive technological devices to bring the very faint and subtle signals into ordinary consciousness, this general form of self-mastery may be the province of many, in schools, in hospitals, in clinics, in educational resource centers.

Physiological feedback represents a high point of synthesis within modern science, yet it too is at its inception. It combines a traditional knowledge of the possibilities of human self-mastery and the most sophisticated tools of modern science and technology. The new synthesis may well extend the personal capacities of many in this culture in a readily assimilable way.

The research so far in biofeedback marks the merest beginnings of a new attempt to turn the direction of modern technology itself inward, away from the control and manipulation of the external environment. Just as technology has often limited man's personal capacities, so it can also extend them. Technology *itself* is neutral, and can be employed to make man less or more human. In the feedback paradigm, technology has been refocused toward an extension of our own personal capacities, rather than a diminution of them. This is a new development, man using his own technology to discover himself, personally, and at the same time observe himself in an objective, scientific manner. Rarely have the two forms of knowledge been combined so clearly in a single situation.

For further reading

Leo V. DiCara. "Learning in the Autonomic Nervous System." *Scientific American* (Jan. 1970), pp. 30–39. Offprint no. 525 (available in the U.K. from W. H. Freeman and Co., Reading).

Ralph Ezios. "Implications of Physiological Feedback Training."

The above two articles are reprinted in Robert Ornstein, ed., *The Nature of Human Consciousness.* San Francisco: W. H. Freeman and Co. New York: The Viking Press. 1973.

Theodore Barber, *et al.,* eds. *Biofeedback and Self-Control Reader.* Chicago: Aldine-Atherton, 1971.

Theodore Barber, *et al.,* eds. *Biofeedback and Self-Control, 1970.* Chicago: Aldine-Atherton, 1971.

Wolfgang Luthe. "Autogenic Training: Method, Research and Application in Medicine." In Charles T. Tart, ed., *Altered States of Consciousness.* New York: John Wiley & Sons, 1969.

See also the *Biofeedback and Self-Control* Annuals published yearly by Atherton. These are available in the U.K. through University bookshops.

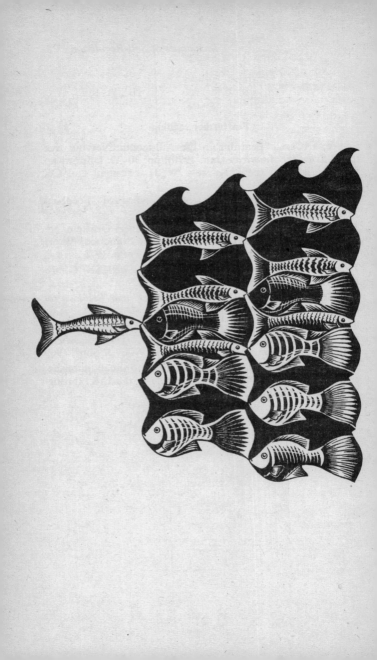

Chapter 10

An Extended Concept of Man

Fishes and Water

Fishes, asking what water was, went to a wise fish. He told them that it was all around them, yet they still thought that they were thirsty.[1]

Although it is quite tenuous and undeveloped, biofeedback research is one clear example of a new synthesis, of an extended concept of what is possible and of contemporary methodology. In terms of scientific knowledge, other aspects of this synthesis, and most of the systems and techniques concerned with them, have hardly begun to be developed; so much of this chapter must be theoretical, and speculative, and can attempt merely to point to what might be studied rather than to what is known. But the new synthesis does include a new awareness that humans are sensitive to the geophysical environment in ways not taken into account in modern science; that body states may link the geophysical surround to consciousness; that the intentions of many forms of psychotherapy may have been unduly restricted; that man is potentially sensitive to subtle "paranormal" communications from other people. These are a very few of the possible new directions of scientific inquiry, as I see them. The chapter ends by pointing to a complementary new synthesis, a fresh attempt at a contemporary projection of the esoteric traditions.

THE GEOPHYSICAL ENVIRONMENT

Like fish, we live in an unnoticed ocean, one of air, light, and gravity. We inhale and exhale 10,000 liters of air each day. Light energy constantly impinges upon us. Gravity is always present, wherever we are on earth. Our sense organs, by their very physiological design, detect only a small fraction of the available energy, and of the energy to which we are sensitive, it is primarily *changes* in the input that are transmitted to the brain. Any process beyond the "ordinary" sense range, as well as any constant process within our normal sense range, usually escapes our consciousness. We are aware of the quickly changing shapes of light images, but the light-dark rhythms of the earth move too slowly for our notice. We are aware of the air only when it is polluted. Gravity has shaped even the most intimate details of our structure, but since it is so constant and so slow to change, like water to the fish, gravity is easy to ignore.

The physiological and psychological effects of these subtle geophysical factors are difficult to conceptualize. It is like trying to imagine what a fish's physiology would be like without water. The contents of contemporary psychology (among many other academic disciplines) reflect our personal lack of awareness of the geophysical surrounding. Psychologists have devoted thousands of experiments, for example, to exploring how lists of nonsense syllables are learned, and yet we have performed almost no research on the effects of the air, of light per se, or gravity on man. Not only do individual people tend to screen out the subtle constancies of the environment, the scientific community does the same.

Yet these factors are constant and are important in behavior and psychology. The seasons come and go; the moon rises and sets; the earth turns continually. But people in our culture now live most of their lives indoors, perceptually isolated from these geophysical changes. For instance, living in a city may cause a person to miss seeing the moon for months on end. We remain unaware of the shortening and lengthening of the days; we allow our artificial environment to dissociate us from the geophysical nature of our world. Once again, let us return to the metaphor of stars and daylight; forces that are subtle and constant are difficult to perceive in the brilliance of daily life. Ordinary personal consciousness usually places these forces "on automatic," as it does the weak internal signals of the "autonomic" nervous system. It is beyond the norm to sense these weak energies, and generally we do not.

And yet, the esoteric traditional psychologies have emphasized that, under certain conditions, man can engage in a "paranormal" and subtle communication with the geophysical surroundings and with other people. Biofeedback training is beginning to synthesize the two kinds of psychologies; the current interest in biological rhythms, in the effects of the air, light, and gravity on man, as well as in "extrasensory" perception, may represent some future elements of this new synthesis.

1. Biological Rhythms

Ordinarily, we consider ourselves stable beings, with enduring personal characteristics. This consideration extends to our perception of other people as well. We may categorize one person as "aggressive" or "smart" or "moody," and file our memories of him in this category. The stability of an individual's personality is in large part a construction of ordinary consciousness. The idea of a person's stability seems to be a simplifying assumption, just as our ordinary, immediate assumption of the rectangularity of rooms is a simplifying assumption.

The everyday assumption of stability, whether it is about personality or about biology, does not seem to withstand a more rigorous empirical analysis. A new field of research challenges this assumption even in terms of biology. The earth is in constant movement, constant change. The sun rises and sets each day, yet the days slowly, imperceptibly lengthen and wane throughout the cycle of the year. There are well-known seasonal cycles of nesting, growth, migrating, etc.—and others that are less clearly demarcated and less well-known. There exist cycles in our daily lives as there are cycles in the earth. We are, for example, more sensitive to respiratory diseases at night than during the day. One drug study found that a fixed dosage of amphetamines would kill 77 per cent of the rats at one point in their activity cycle, yet only 8 per cent at another.[2]

The light-dark cycle of the earth is perpetually in a process of gradual alteration, and the growing and flowering of plants are in phase with this rhythm. Mating among animals is most prevalent during springtime. From research already done, we know there is a rhythmic structure in our bodies, in the action of the liver, in the sugar level of the blood, in our brain waves, all somewhat linked to the cycle of the day. But even these daily changes are so subtle and slow that they are not noticed by personal consciousness and are largely ignored by the scientific community.

The internal biological rhythms are subtle, and most are not marked by an obvious external signal, such as the full moon. One of the few rhythms in humans which does manifest as a readily observable event is the woman's menstrual cycle. "Premenstrual tension" is experienced by many women in the three to four days preceding the onset of the menses. Gay Luce writes, "An estimated 60 per cent of women suffer some palpable change at this time, perhaps just mild irritation, depression, headache, or decline in attention or vision." Body temperature undergoes daily rhythmic changes in both men and women. According to Luce, a person whose temperature peaks in the morning usually finds his or her highest periods of intellectual functioning during those morning hours, whereas a temperature peak in the late evening usually signifies a "night person."

The lack of awareness of our rhythmic structure may cause grave mistakes both in psychological research and in our personal assessments of others. To take one example, if a psychotherapist or physician sees a patient only early in the morning, he may be seeing a person whose activity, internal physiology, and mood differ radically during the remainder of the day.

These rhythmic variations in a person's state can sometimes become quite extreme. Gay Luce reports that one salesman was subject to periodic psychoses every four days. If he attempted to work on his bad days, he found himself completely unable to do anything but sit tense in his car all day. He finally became aware of the rhythmic nature of his illness, and remained home each fourth day, so he could work normally during the other three. Most biological rhythms are more subtle than periodic psychoses, but many intellectual and personal capacities may undergo such variations.

Passengers on east-west airplanes often report feeling "out of sorts" for a few days after the trip. This feeling is apparently caused by the inability of our internal rhythms to adjust quickly to time changes. The discomfort cannot be attributed to the length of the air ride itself, for travelers on north-south routes of equal length do not experience similar problems in adjustment. Most people are not yet conscious enough of their rhythmic structure to plan around these factors. Nevertheless, some account is beginning to be taken of biological rhythms. For instance, many companies and governments are sending executives to meetings three or four days early, so that their efficiency will not be disturbed by the alterations in time zones.

To take another example, the light-dark cycle of the earth varies daily. Our visual system is, of course, responsive to changes in light, but we are rarely aware of how the presence of light energy itself is important in the maintenance of many life processes. Alterations in the light-dark cycle affect the periods of the blossoming of flowers. The biologist Karl Linnaeus once constructed a "flower clock" which "kept time" by the opening and closing of different flowers during the day. In the spring, the exposure to increasing amounts of light sets off a chain reaction in the brains of many mammals. This reaction involves the pituitary gland, and results in an increase in sexual hormones. In experimental tests, optic fibers have been implanted in the pituitary gland, and the artificial introduction of light energy has resulted in a stimulation of sexual activity. The precise function of the pituitary and even the pineal glands in man remains unclear, but Von Bount, Ganong, and their associates have found that light energy does enter the brains of mammals directly, not only through the visual system.[3] The direct presence of light inside the brain may provide a mechanism that can explain how we are sensitive to factors of which our "ordinary consciousness" remains ignorant, e.g., alterations in the absolute amount of light present during a season. But how, and where this process might occur, if it does occur, is completely unknown. Some preliminary reports indicate that light may possibly regulate the menstrual cycle. A group of women whose menses were irregular were asked to sleep in lighted rooms during the fourteenth, fifteenth, and sixteenth nights of their cycle (i.e., the normal ovulation time of regular cycles). Gay Luce reports that for many of them the menses became regular.

In brief, many personal and biological cycles remain unnoticed. Daily cycles as well as monthly cycles are difficult to perceive, unless there is a physical event, such as menses or the new moon, to mark them. A yearly cycle is even more difficult, and one of ten years still more so. In addition, the scientific study of biological rhythms is extremely laborious and technically arduous. Such a study may require daily, or even hourly, records to be kept over many years. Then complex computer analysis may be required in order for any subtle rhythms in the data to emerge. This field clearly involves exacting and tedious research, but, in the words of Gay Luce, "Not knowing about our rhythmic structure is like not knowing that one has a heart or lungs."

2. The Air

We are continually in a process of exchange with the air, a fact so obvious and constant that it is largely taken for granted, much as water is by the fish in our story. Deprived of air for ten minutes, we would die.

Subtle alterations in the quality of the air do, in fact, affect us. When depressed indoors, we may open the windows to get "fresh" air. With more leisure and means, we might travel to a resort in the high mountains or to one by the sea. In many different countries, certain "winds of ill-repute," such as the Khamsin, the Mistral, the Santa Ana, the Foehn, are reported to affect the health and moods of many. In the seasons when these winds blow, admissions to mental hospitals, crimes of violence, and certain illnesses are reported to increase. Similarly, at these times, judges are said to exhibit greater leniency than usual.

The traditional esoteric psychologists have noticed the effects of variations in air quality on man. George Gurdjieff, for instance, emphasized that "nutrition" exists on many levels. In certain places, he held, the air contains a form of this human "nutrition." In considering the esoteric conception of energy forms, we earlier discussed the yogic concept of prana. The Yogi Vishnudevananda says of it, "Prana is in the air [but] . . . not in any of its chemical constituents. Animal and plant life breathe this energy." [4] Another book on Yoga is more explicit about the mechanism. It suggests, "Take every opportunity to spend time in rural surroundings, especially in large open areas, such as deserts, meadows, sea shores, or lakes. Atmospheric ions, which are minute charges in air molecules, are negative in large open spaces of this kind." [5]

The presence of the minutely charged atmospheric ions may constitute a physical analog of the esoteric "energy form" of prana. In the Hindu tradition prana is held to be the "life-force" from which health and creativity flow, the force that aids in physical as well as psychological growth. At this point, we cannot measure precisely how much overlap there is between negative air ions and the concept of prana, but some interesting similarities do exist. The esoteric traditions have long taken advantage of favorable microclimatic conditions for their students. Esoteric psychological schools have often been located on mountain tops, near waterfalls, near the ocean. Some recent biological studies have determined that the ionization of the air in these places is predominantly negative.

Many aspects of esoteric tradition stress that when breathing exercises are performed, "time and place" must be taken into account. The "time" is the acknowledgment of the rhythmic structure of man. The "place" may refer, in part, to the presence of the favorable microclimate—negative ionization. The relationship between breathing and consciousness has been little explored by contemporary psychology, but has been stressed in esoteric tradition. As it does for "body energies," our colloquial language preserves some of the dimensions of this relationship. To note one instance, "inspiration" refers to both creativity and the process of breathing.

On somewhat more conventionally empiric grounds, research is just beginning on the effects of atmospheric ionization on human (and plant and animal) physiology and consciousness. In one study, the "stuffy" feeling in rooms is reported to disappear when negative ionization is introduced, and the mood of those present is also reported to be altered.[6] The "winds of ill-repute" have been measured as carrying an unusually high amount of positive ions.[7]

In smog, as well as in certain wind patterns, positive ions have been linked to health disturbances. Some recent research has suggested that changes in air ions can even alter resistance to infectious diseases. An experiment by A. P. Krueger of the University of California at Berkeley indicates that mice who are deliberately exposed to an infectious disease die more quickly in a positively ionized atmosphere than in ordinary room air. For this study, Krueger and his associates observed mice living in chambers in which the air-ion content was rigidly controlled. Measured amounts of arithrospores carrying coccidioidomycosis (an infectious lung disease) were introduced into the noses of the rats. By the thirtieth day, 55 per cent of the mice who were breathing positively ionized air were dead, compared with 30 per cent of those breathing laboratory air.[8] In other studies, an increase in negative ionization seems to speed up tissue growth.[9] The increase of positive ions is reported to slow down the growth of certain plants.[10]

Some less well-controlled research suggests that negative ionization aids in healing, especially in recovery from burns.[11] A Russian report contends that, deprived of negative ions in the air, animals die within a month.[12] Although not all these reports have been fully confirmed, and few are directly on humans, it is now clear that atmospheric ions, present as subtle quantities in the air, do affect man, other animals, and plants.[13]

Research into the effects of ionization is now in its beginning stages. Many of the important questions have not yet even been asked. For instance, how much ionization is needed to cause significant effects in man? Does negatively ionized air alter mood systematically? Could the introduction of negatively ionized air produce results similar to those achieved by difficult and esoteric breath manipulations? Can healing be aided significantly by the introduction of post-injury or post-operative doses of negative ionization? Photochemical smog strips ions from the air, leaving a balance of positively charged ones. Could some of the deleterious effects of polluted air be countered by the artificial generation of negative ions? We need more carefully controlled studies (such as those performed by Krueger) to give us systematic answers to these and other questions, since our ordinary consciousness is inadequate to perceive the subtle effects of the air's ionization.

3. Gravity and Structural Integration

One of the forces ignored in personal consciousness is gravity, since we have no specific organ, no "eye," that could "see" it. Because gravity is perpetually present and virtually unchanging in its effects, those effects are imperceptible to us. But just as the structure of fishes has evolved to suit the medium of water, so our structure has been shaped by the gravitational field.

One recent approach to the study of man does take the gravitational field into account, the technique of Structural Integration developed by Ida Rolf.[14] This is a body-centered technique and gives due weight to the esoteric consideration that body states and subtle "body energies" can affect consciousness. The disciplines of aikido, *Tai-chi Ch'uan*, kung fu, karate, and hatha-yoga, among many others, followed a line of development similar to that of Structural Integration. The interrelatedness of body states and awareness is a part of ordinary experience as well, but has not been much explored by contemporary scientific psychology. To take an obvious example, pain is a dimension of consciousness associated with damage to the body, and when we are in pain, our awareness is radically different than in times of well-being.

Many of the contemporary scientific approaches to consciousness are purely "mentalistic," as if the brain were really a disembodied computer. It has, however, been noted by many theorists that the primary job of the brain is to control the body, and the body is one which has evolved to function within the gravitational field.

Just as biofeedback training may be a more modern approach to self-regulation than is hatha-yoga, and negative-ion generators might translate a traditional conception of "energy" into a modern form, so Structural Integration may constitute a more modern approach to some of the difficult body-alignment exercises.

The techniques of Structural Integration combine the traditional esoteric psychologist's emphasis on the interrelatedness of body states and consciousness with a much more modern knowledge of anatomy and physiology. This practice is a craft, in which the skilled hands of the practitioner align the body as a whole in a new relationship with the gravitational field. Working on somewhat similar assumptions, the yogic tradition has emphasized that the body is not fixed in structure, but is plastic, and can be altered through a series of postures (asanas).

Structural Integration extends the concept of the body's plasticity; the practitioner attempts to quicken this process of alignment by active manipulation. Whereas biofeedback techniques newly link the disconnected worlds of *psyche* and *soma,* Structural Integration works from the other end, manipulating the body structure to affect consciousness—a *somatopsychic* approach.

But could these bodily changes affect consciousness? Recent research on this point reveals a convergence of Structural Integration and some aspects of contemporary psychology. One major theoretical approach to consciousness in psychology holds that the contents of ordinary consciousness predominantly depend on the preparation for motor output. This theory has recently been set forth by Roger Sperry, and has been elaborated further by Leon Festinger and others.[15] This approach begins with the hypothesis that the major job of the brain is to run the body. This hypothesis implies that ordinary consciousness consists of an implicit preparation to respond to the external environment. This mode is active, obviously concerned with physical manipulation of the environment and the biological survival of the organism. The movements of the limbs and eyes, and the requirements of speech, involve large areas of the cerebral cortex. The most radical statement of this theory is that the "readiness" to issue a motor command which constitutes the brain's preparation for action *is* the contents of ordinary awareness.

In this theory, any alteration in body alignment, limb position, or responsivity to central commands would eventually alter the "readiness" of the brain, and consciousness will be changed. Through experimental tests of Structural Integration, we might be able to study these alterations in consciousness that are caused by changes in the patterns of muscle activity.

The technique of Structural Integration opens up many other possibilities for research, since it is directly manipulative and since the alterations in body structure are held to occur quickly and to be measurable. First, we will need some sound documentation of the actual changes which occur in the body as a result of Structural Integration. Additionally, we might ask *which* body changes can affect consciousness, whether memories might have some triggers in the body as well as in the brain, whether radical alterations in breathing patterns, for instance, can affect processes of awareness, and even whether orthodox medicine might benefit from a holistic approach to the body.

THE SEEDS OF SYNTHESIS:
OTHER CONTEMPORARY APPROACHES

1. Gestalt Therapy and Psychosynthesis

Two new forms of psychotherapy similarly contain the seeds of the new synthesis. The process of "Gestalt" therapy is an alternate route to the present-centeredness sought in meditation. In concentrative meditation, one is continuously instructed to discard thoughts. In Gestalt therapy, the thinking process is given the pejorative term "computing," and the participant in this technique is invited to concentrate more on the immediate situation, to "stay in the present continuum of awareness." In addition, this system strongly emphasizes that ordinary consciousness is a personal construction and that each person is capable, and even responsible for, changing the contents of his own consciousness.[16]

Gestalt therapy also recognizes the verbal-intuitive split in consciousness. Often we may utter an innocuous phrase, such as "I am very pleased with this," while our voice and gestures indicate just the opposite. The practitioners of Gestalt therapy invite the participants to become aware of their body language and therefore to bring their *whole** selves into consciousness. This is often done by constantly asking the participant, "What is your body telling you?" "What is your tone of voice saying?" "What is your hand saying?" In essence, these questions are—"What is happening within your nonverbal, 'right hemisphere' side? Bring it into consciousness."

Fritz Perls, the originator of the technique, comments on the two modes of consciousness:

> The right hand is usually the motoric, male, aggressive side that wants to control, to determine what is, to decide what is "right." The left side is the female side; it is usually poorly coordinated. *Left* means awkward in many languages: *gauche* in French, *linkisch* in German. When there is a conflict between emotional life and active life, there is neurosis. . . . But when both power and sensitivity are working in coordination, there is genius. . . . Ultimate awareness can only take place if the computer is gone, if the intuition, the awareness is so bright that one really comes to his senses. The empty mind in Eastern philosophy is worthy of highest praise. So lose your mind and come to your senses.[17]

The practice of Psychosynthesis similarly involves an attempt at a holistic working of the major modes of consciousness. The intent here is to balance the extremes, to develop the

* From which comes the word *Gestalt*, not to be confused with the Gestalt psychology of Wolfgang Kohler.

entire person. This system attempts to produce complementary functioning of intuition and intellect by means of specific practices (see pages 84–86). The techniques of Psychosynthesis are diverse, ideational, almost literary, often employing fantasy and guided daydreams. Its very name is intended to distinguish it from therapeutic approaches which emphasize the separateness of the various aspects of man, e.g., psychoanalysis.[18]

2. Research on "Paranormal" Phenomena

Contemporary science has rediscovered that man does possess many capacities beyond those usually considered normal. A few years ago it would have been considered "paranormal" to claim control over the blood pressure, but now a freshman in a psychological experiment can expect to learn some measure of blood-pressure control in half an hour. In most life situations, we are not very aware of the subtle signals of our internal physiology, but under certain conditions we can make contact with these phenomena that are usually obscured by our normal functioning.

To recapitulate briefly: The structure of our nervous system allows us only a limited selection from the available stimulation. Our eyes, ears, brain, each select, and we must then construct a stable personal consciousness from this limited input. Although we are usually insensitive to many aspects of the geophysical environment, we may, during special conditions or after special exercises, become sensitive to them. We do not possess a receptor for gravity; yet we have evolved to take advantage of this force. We are not normally aware of the light which enters our brain directly; yet it is there and may affect the pituitary. Our "autonomic nervous system" is usually screened from ordinary awareness; yet we may contact it, either by boosting the strength of the signal, as in biofeedback training, or by reducing the competing noise, as in the esoteric traditions.

The ordinary mode of consciousness can be characterized as analytic, sequential, and limited by the characteristics of our sense organs. A second major mode of consciousness is available to us; it may be characterized as receptive and holistic, one in which all action can be perceived simultaneously. For thousands of years the development of this mode has primarily been the province of the esoteric traditions. Within the writings of these traditions, many faculties considered "paranormal" are described, as symbolically portrayed in "The Man Who Walked on Water" at the beginning of Chapter 6. Meditation is reported to bring about a state of "darkness," a shift in the receptive characteristics of consciousness, so that sensitivity is increased to a new segment of the internal, personal, and geophysical environment.

The lineal sequence of events is our own personal, cultural, and scientific construction. It is certainly convenient, and is perhaps necessary for biological survival and the development of a complex, technological society—but it is only one of the many possible constructions of consciousness available to man. In the linear mode, we receive and process input primarily in sequence, one event following the other like the hours of the clock. If a second mode exists, in which the concepts of future and past are irrelevant, then many phenomena within that second mode will seem to "transcend" the ordinary notion of time—but only for those who attempt to account for *all* phenomena within the linear and sequential mode.

A shift, then, to the mode of the "night" may well enable an "extra-ordinary" communication. This "paranormal" communication can exist between different systems inside one person, or between individuals and the geophysical surround, or between two people.

The problem for a scientific inquiry into these phenomena is, of course, that science is restricted to the lineal and analytic. Each investigator would like "proof" of these phenomena within his own terms. However, just as an illiterate peasant must satisfy the requirements of technology in order to construct a spaceship, so Western scientists must be prepared to satisfy the conditions of these subtle phenomena in order to demonstrate their reality.

For instance, when we chart the fluctuations of biological activity over many days, an often-unnoticed rhythm emerges. When we measure the tiny electrical charges in the atmosphere before and during a certain wind, a subtle phenomenon emerges. When we build a machine to amplify the subtle internal signals of which we are usually unaware, they can come to consciousness.

Similarly, even to begin any scientific analysis of "paranormal" communication, certain relevant questions must be asked. "In what mode of consciousness do these communications occur?" "What is the nature of the information transmitted?"

Just as with biofeedback training and biological rhythms, some clues may be found in the writings of the traditional esoteric psychologists, the specialists in the intuitive mode. Their writings often report that at night, during sleep, when the normal, outward-oriented consciousness is turned off, when the "silent" side is dominant, some people can receive this unusual form of communication. The paranormal communications reported in esoteric tradition are often of great importance and of great emotional significance. It might be said that "emotion is the fuel of this manner of communication." [19]

In a scientific experiment, then, it might be difficult to observe such communication in a "neutral" laboratory, employing information of little import to the receiver. The obtained results may be only of statistical significance. The Hot Line between Washington and Moscow was not instituted to play cards.

If we take the mode and the nature of the communication into account, we may be able to determine the conditions under which these subtle phenomena occur. At the dream laboratory of Maimonides Hospital in New York, Stanley Krippner and Montague Ullman have begun to investigate paranormal communication in this manner.[20] Their study concerns "transmission" during sleep, using information of varying degrees of emotional significance. In these experiments, the "receiver" goes to sleep in a closed room and is monitored by the EEG. The physiological signs of dreaming include a change in the frequency characteristics of the EEG and the appearance of Rapid Eye Movements. These REM periods are used conventionally as an indicator of dreaming in the sleeping subject.

When the EEG of the "receiver" shows that he is dreaming, the "sender" in another room, physically isolated from his partner, opens one of twelve envelopes containing a painting. The reproduction might be Salvador Dali's *The Last Supper*, or a quiet scene at the beach. The "sender" concentrates on transmitting the scene to the "receiver."

At the end of a dream period, rapid eye movements stop. Using the EEG as an indicator, an experimenter in the control room near the "receiver" awakens the sleeper at the end of his REM period and tape-records the remembered contents of the dream. Of course, this experimenter does not know what was in the envelope. The sender then awaits the onset of the next REM period and resumes "transmission"; the receiver is again awakened after the dream. This process continues throughout the night.

Later, the transcripts of the records are sent to a panel of judges, who do not know which painting was "sent" during which dream. The judges attempt to match the transcripts of dreams and the set of twelve paintings. Each painting has, then, a chance probability of being judged the stimulus that was "sent." An increase in that probability beyond chance would presumably be due to the similarity of the dream and the painting. The matches for the paintings containing highly emotional situations were found to be much higher than chance.

These experiments are but one series which seem to indicate that emotionality has an effect on this mode of communication, but these reports will need confirmation by other investigators.[21] During normal, waking consciousness, the communication may be obscured by the brilliance of the active mode, and the information may not come to awareness. Some studies of paranormal communication have found, for instance, consistent changes in physiological reactions that the person is not aware of. If the subtle nature of the phenomenon is considered, if the nature of the information to be transmitted is considered, if the mode of consciousness of the participants is considered, these subtle, paranormal communications can be scientifically studied. But these communications are weak, and often go unnoticed in the light of the day.

3. Contemporary Sufism—The Work of Idries Shah

A new synthesis is in process within modern psychology. This synthesis combines the concerns of the esoteric traditions with the research methods and technology of modern science. In complement to this process, and feeding it, a truly contemporary approach to the problems of consciousness is arising from the esoteric traditions themselves.

When we refer to these traditions, we refer largely to teachers, exercises, and techniques of the past. The Buddha formulated his techniques especially for those in India 2,600 years ago. Mohammed's school and teaching were formulated for the Middle East 1,300 years ago. But Mohammed, although primarily speaking to those of his own time and place, made many statements which apply to many teachers of these traditions, independent of their situation. One which is relevant to this discussion was "Speak to those in accordance with their understanding."

Our cultures have changed drastically since the time of Mohammed, and any formulation of that tradition must undergo a fresh adaptation. Such a new formulation is currently being presented by Idries Shah. His work employs current technology when appropriate, and draws from contemporary research in psychology and philosophy. Sometimes it requires an extension of contemporary technology; for example, it involves the design and construction of a machine to produce negative ionization of the air. This modern technological work is coupled to the special form of literature which he has recently reintroduced to this culture, a contemporary version of an oral tradition, using material freshly translated into modern idiom. We have become familiar with these stories throughout this book, for they introduce the chapters and are discussed in a major section of Chapter 7. A review of these Sufi stories can also briefly summarize this book:

Our "ordinary" consciousness is selective and limited. Our concepts of what is possible limit our personal consciousness, our performance, and our scientific paradigm—we constantly ask ourselves questions such as "Is there any number higher than 100?" There are many ways in which we limit ourselves. Throughout much of each day, we act like the double-seeing son, and often confuse our own personal construction with external reality.

There is, however, a second mode of consciousness available to man. It exists on many levels, the cultural, the personal, and the physiological. On the physiological level, it has recently been shown that the two cerebral hemispheres of the cortex are specialized for different modes of information-processing. The left hemisphere operates primarily in a verbal-intellectual and sequential mode, the right hemisphere primarily in a spatial and simultaneous mode. The "right hemisphere" mode is often devalued by the dominant, verbal intellect. "Since you have not learned grammar, half your life has been wasted," said the pedagogue to the boatman. This second mode often appears inelegant, lacking the formal reasoning, linearity, and polish of the intellect. It is more involved in space than in time, more involved in intuition than in logic and language. It is a mode often forgotten and ignored, especially within the scientific community, but one which may prove important for science and even for our own survival. "Have you ever learned to swim?" asks the boatman of the pedagogue. Since it is nonlinear, this second mode is not involved in the "ordinary" realm of cause and effect which underlies so much of our personal and intellectual life. It is present-centered, a mode in which all occurrences are said to exist as a "patterned whole," as in the drawing which accompanies "Moment in Time."

The two major types of psychology have each predominantly investigated one mode of human consciousness. Modern science is primarily verbal-logical—the mode identified with the Day. The esoteric traditions have specialized in the tacit, receptive, holistic mode, the mode identified with the Night, one largely inaccessible to language and reason. The techniques of these esoteric traditions are often thought to involve a deliberately exotic and mysterious training, such as the use of special mysterious "magic words" in meditation. However, the essence of the often-misunderstood technique of meditation is the focusing of awareness on one single, unchanging source of stimulation. It is the attitude, not the specific form of meditation, which is primary. If the exercise is performed correctly, a new set of capacities may emerge, as symbolically portrayed in "The Man Who Walked on Water." The techniques of meditation, the dishabituation exercises, and other special exercises, such as crafts, music and dance, are in their totality designed to cause a shift from the ordinary analytic consciousness to the holistic. These two modes are portrayed in the story of the blind men and the elephant. One mode of consciousness approaches the elephant by piecemeal investigation; the other attempts to develop a perspective of the whole organism.

Like Mulla Nasrudin, we have been looking for the key to understanding ourselves in the brilliance of the day. But it may not be there. It lies within, in the dark side of ourselves, a side often forgotten, because "there is more light here." Once we can locate the key within the dark area, we may be able to bring it out into the light and to achieve a new synthesis of the two modes of investigation, as in the emerging technology of biofeedback training.

Since we construct our ordinary world around the limited input from our sensory systems, we remain largely unaware of much of our immediate environment, either because we lack the receptive organs, or because the phenomena change slowly. But although fishes are unaware of the medium in which they live, we need not remain unaware of our own geophysical ocean. Under certain conditions this "paranormal" awareness can be developed, leading to an extension of personal and intellectual knowledge.[22]

For further reading

Gay Luce. *Body Time*. New York: Pantheon, 1971. London: Paladin, 1973.

Claudio Naranjo. "Present-Centeredness: Technique, Prescription, and Ideal." In Joen Fagan and Irma Lee Shepherd, eds., *Gestalt Therapy Now*. New York: Harper & Row, 1970.

Roberto Assagioli. *Psychosynthesis*. New York: The Viking Press, 1971.

Lawrence Leshan. "What Is Important About the Paranormal?"

David S. Sobel. "Gravity and Structural Integration."

A. P. Krueger. "Preliminary Consideration of the Biological Significance of Air Ions."

The preceding, or selections from them, are reprinted in Robert Ornstein, ed., *The Nature of Human Consciousness*. San Francisco: W. H. Freeman and Co. New York: The Viking Press. 1973.

Idries Shah. *The Way of the Sufi*. London: Jonathan Cape, 1968. New York: E. P. Dutton, 1970.

Idries Shah. *Wisdom of the Idiots*. New York: E. P. Dutton, 1971.

Idries Shah. *The Dermis Probe*. London: Jonathan Cape, 1970. New York: E. P. Dutton, 1971.

Idries Shah. *Thinkers of the East*. London: Jonathan Cape, 1971. Baltimore: Penguin Books, 1972.

Idries Shah. *The Magic Monastery*. London: Jonathan Cape, 1972. New York: E. P. Dutton, 1972.

Charles T. Tart, ed. *Altered States of Consciousness*. New York: John Wiley & Sons, 1969.

A. P. Krueger. "Are Air Ions Good for You?" *New Scientist*, June 14, 1973, pp. 668–670.

Montague Ullman and Stanley Krippner, with Alan Vaughan. *Dream Telepathy: Experiments in Nocturnal ESP*. London: Turnstone Books, 1973. Baltimore: Penguin Books, 1974. An informal account of their research, brought up to date journalistically.

Frederick Perls, Ralph Hefferline and Paul Goodman. *Gestalt Therapy*. New York: Dell, 1965. Harmondsworth, England: Penguin Books, 1973.

Thomas S. Szasz. *The Manufacture of Madness: A Comparative Study of the Inquisition and the Mental Health Movement*. New York: Harper & Row, 1970. London: Paladin, 1973.

A Postscript

After all our talk of synthesis, new work, new understandings, there remains a word of caution, addressed especially to those who work in science. It would be the height of absurdity if we were to settle, now, for a strictly intellectual understanding of the existence of a second mode of consciousness. The possible danger here is of a newer and more elegant reductionism, of feeling we have tasted the implications of the esoteric traditions simply by calling them "intuitive education" or by some such term, of reducing them to words and logic once again.

The new possibility can go beyond this: to a confluence of the two streams of knowledge, the esoteric and the modern, in science and in each of us. This confluence cannot affect the contents of science unless enough scientists work in both areas of inquiry, both professionally and personally. We can achieve a more complete science of psychology, but only if enough people make the effort to train those aspects of themselves which are usually uncultivated in Western education. This book only begins to consider some of the very radical possibilities of the esoteric traditions. If it does anything, it will be to further an organic process of synthesis of the two traditions. By its very nature, such a synthesis must draw from the personal experiences, as well as the intellectual investigations of many. Otherwise, the limits of possibility may close on us once again; then someday someone will need to write a book which begins, "Is there any number higher than *1,000?*"

Notes

Preface

1. See also Roger Sperry, "A Modified Concept of Consciousness," *Psychological Review*, 76 (1969), 532–536.
2. This type of writing has been called "protopsychological" by Jerome Bruner. See *On Knowing: Essays for the Left Hand* (New York: Atheneum, 1965).

Chapter 1

1. This story is from a Central Asian oral tradition.
2. Jerome Bruner and Leo Postman, "On the Perception of Incongruity: A Paradigm," *Journal of Personality*, 18 (1949), 206–223.
3. The definitive work on paradigms is Thomas S. Kuhn, *The Structure of Scientific Revolutions* (Chicago: University of Chicago Press, 1962).
4. This point is made in Ernest R. Hilgard, "Altered States of Awareness," *The Journal of Nervous and Mental Disease*, 149 (1969), 68–79. Reprinted in *Biofeedback and Self-Control* (Chicago: Aldine-Atherton, 1971), pp. 763–774.
5. William James, *The Varieties of Religious Experience* (New York: New American Library, 1958).
6. Abraham Maslow, *The Psychology of Science: A Reconnaissance* (Chicago: Henry Regnery, 1969).
7. Jacob Needleman, *The New Religions* (New York: Doubleday, 1970; London: Allen Lane, The Penguin Press, 1971).

8. Thomas R. Blackburn, "Sensuous-Intellectual Complementarity in Science," *Science*, 172 (June 4, 1971), 1003–1007. Reprinted in Robert Ornstein, ed., *The Nature of Human Consciousness* (San Francisco, W. H. Freeman and Co.; New York, The Viking Press; 1973).

Chapter 2

1. This story is from Idries Shah, *Caravan of Dreams* (London: Octagon, 1968; Baltimore: Penguin, 1972), p. 172.

2. William James, *The Principles of Psychology* (New York: Dover Publications, 1950), I, 288–289. (Original copyright, 1890.)

3. Aldous Huxley, *The Doors of Perception* and *Heaven and Hell* (New York: Harper & Row, 1954, pp. 22–24; London: Chatto & Windus, 1954).

4. J. Y. Lettvin, H. R. Maturana, W. S. McCulloch, and W. H. Pitts, "What the Frog's Eye Tells the Frog's Brain," *Proceedings of the Institute of Radio Engineers*, 47 (1959), 140–151. Reprinted in Warren S. McCulloch, *Embodiments of Mind* (Cambridge, Mass.: The M.I.T. Press, 1965), pp. 230–255.

5. For an introductory review of this and other related research, see Julian Hochberg, *Perception* (Englewood Cliffs, N.J.: Prentice-Hall, 1964).

6. R. W. Sperry, "The Eye and the Brain," *Scientific American* (May 1956), pp. 48–52. Offprint no. 1090. NOTE: All *Scientific American* reprints are available in the U.K. from W. H. Freeman and Co., Reading.

7. Ivo Kohler, "Experiments with Goggles," *Scientific American* (May 1962), pp. 62–72. Offprint no. 465.

8. Ulric Neisser, "The Processes of Vision," *Scientific American* (Sept. 1968), pp. 204–214. Offprint no. 519.

9. Karl H. Pribram, "The Neurophysiology of Remembering," *Scientific American* (Jan. 1969), pp. 73–86. Offprint no. 520.

10. Charles Furst, "Automatizing of Visual Attention," *Perception and Psychophysics*, 10, no. 2 (1971), 65–69.

11. Jerome Bruner, "On Perceptual Readiness," *Psychological Review*, 64 (1957), pp. 123–152.

12. W. H. Ittelson and F. P. Kilpatrick, "Experiment in Perception," *Scientific American* (Aug. 1951), pp. 50–55. Offprint no. 405. Reprinted in Robert Ornstein, ed., *The Nature of Human Consciousness* (San Francisco, W. H. Freeman and Co.; New York, The Viking Press; 1973). See also note 17 below.

13. George Kelly, *The Psychology of Personal Constructs* (New York: Norton, 2 vols., 1955).

14. D. N. Spinelli and K. H. Pribram, "Changes in Visual Recovery Functions and Unit Activity Produced by Frontal and Temporal Cortex Stimulation," *Electroencephalography and Clinical Neurophysiology*, 22 (1967), 143–149.

15. This theoretical approach is sometimes difficult to follow. Roger Sperry, "Neurology and the Mind-Brain Problem," *American Scientist*, 40 (1951), 291–312, is quite a clear statement; and Leon Festinger, H. Ono, C. A. Burnham, and D. Bamber, "Efference and the Conscious Experience of Perception," *Journal of Experimental Psychology*, 74 (1967), 1–36, is clear and contains several interesting experiments.

16. Jerome Bruner and C. C. Goodman, "Value and Need as Organizing Factors in Perception," *Journal of Abnormal and Social Psychology*, 42 (1947), 33–44.

17. Albert Hastorf and Hadley Cantril, "They Saw a Game: A Case Study," *Journal of Abnormal and Social Psychology*, 49 (1954), 129–134. Reprinted in Ornstein, *The Nature of Human Consciousness*.

18. William James, *Principles of Psychology*, I, 239.

19. J. B. Carroll, ed., *Language, Thought, and Reality: Selected Writings of Benjamin Lee Whorf* (Cambridge, Mass.: The M.I.T. Press, 1951).

20. Dorothy Lee, "Codifications of Reality: Lineal and Nonlineal," *Psychosomatic Medicine*, vol. 12, no. 2 (March–April, 1950). Reprinted in Dorothy Lee, *Freedom and Culture* (Englewood Cliffs, N.J.: Prentice-Hall, 1959). Also reprinted in Ornstein, *The Nature of Human Consciousness*.

21. W. Penfield and L. Roberts, *Speech and Brain Mechanisms* (Princeton, N.J.: Princeton University Press, 1959).

22. A. N. Whitehead, quoted in J. De Marquette, *Introduction to Comparative Mysticism* (New York: Philosophical Library, 1949), p. 15.

23. William James, *The Varieties of Religious Experience* (New York: The New American Library, 1958), p. 298.

Chapter 3

1. From Idries Shah, *The Exploits of the Incomparable Mulla Nasrudin* (New York: E. P. Dutton, 1972, p. 18; London: Jonathan Cape, 1966).

2. G. William Domhoff, "But Why Did They Sit on the King's Right in the First Place?" *Psychoanalytic Review*, 56 (1969–70), 586–596.

3. Perhaps the best review of right-hemisphere functions is Joseph E. Bogen, "The Other Side of the Brain, I, II, III," *Bulletin of the Los Angeles Neurological Societies*, vol. 34, no. 3 (July 1969). Reprinted in part in Robert Ornstein, ed., *The Nature of Human Consciousness* (San Francisco, W. H. Freeman and Co.; New York, The Viking Press; 1973).

4. Brenda Milner, "Brain Mechanisms Suggested by Studies of Temporal Lobes" in F. L. Darley and C. H. Millikan, eds., *Brain Mechanisms Underlying Speech and Language* (New York: Grune & Stratton, 1965). Also Brenda Milner, "Interhemispheric Differences in the Localization of Psychological Processes in Man," *British Medical Bulletin*, 27, no. 3 (1971), 272–277.

5. A. R. Luria, *Higher Cortical Functions in Man* (New York: Basic Books, 1966).

6. R. W. Sperry, "The Great Cerebral Commissure," *Scientific American* (Jan. 1964), pp. 42–52. Offprint no. 174. Michael S. Gazzaniga, "The Split Brain in Man," *Scientific American* (Aug. 1967), pp. 24–29. Offprint no. 508.

7. *Ibid.*

8. Roger Sperry, "Problems Outstanding in the Evolution

of Brain Function," James Arthur Lecture, American Museum of Natural History, New York, 1964.

9. Margaret Durnford and Doreen Kimura, "Right-Hemisphere Specialization for Depth Perception Reflected in Visual Field Differences," *Nature*, 231 (June 11, 1971), 394–395.

10. R. A. Filbey and Michael Gazzaniga, "Splitting the Normal Brain with Reaction Time," *Psychonomic Science*, 17 (1969), 335–336.

11. Marcel Kinsbourne, unpublished manuscript, Duke University, 1971. Katherine Kocel, David Galin, Robert Ornstein, and Edward Merrin, "Lateral Eye Movements and Cognitive Mode," *Psychonomic Science* (1972), in press.

12. Marcel Kinsbourne and Jay Cook, "Generalized and Lateralized Effects of Concurrent Verbalization on a Unimanual Skill," *Quarterly Journal of Experimental Psychology*, 23 (1971), 341–345.

13. David Galin and Robert Ornstein, "Lateral Specialization of Cognitive Mode: An EEG Study," *Psychophysiology* (1972), in press.

14. J. Levy-Agresti and Roger Sperry, "Differential Perceptual Capacities in Major and Minor Hemispheres," *Proceedings of the National Academy of Sciences*, 61 (1968), 1151.

15. Josephine Semmes, "Hemispheric Specialization: A Possible Clue to Mechanism," *Neuropsychologia*, 6 (1968), 11–16.

16. Domhoff, *op. cit.*

17. M. E. Humphrey and O. L. Zangwill, "Cessation of Dreaming after Brain Injury," *Journal Neurol. Neurosurg. Psychiatry*, 14 (1951), 322–325. Bogen, "The Other Side of the Brain, II," *loc. cit.* M. D. Austin, "Dream Recall and the Bias of Intellectual Ability," *Nature*, 231 (May 7, 1971), 59.

18. R. Wilhelm, trans., and C. F. Baynes, ed., *I Ching* (Princeton, N.J.: Princeton University Press, 1950), pp. 3, 10–11.

19. W. I. B. Beveridge, *The Art of Scientific Investigation* (New York: Random House, 1950).

20. Roberto Assagioli, *Psychosynthesis* (New York: The Viking Press, 1971), pp. 217–224.

21. Jerome Bruner, *On Knowing: Essays for the Left Hand* (Cambridge, Mass.: Harvard University Press, 1962), pp. 2–5.

Chapter 4

1. From Idries Shah, *The Exploits of the Incomparable Mulla Nasrudin* (New York: E. P. Dutton, 1972, p. 112; London: Jonathan Cape, 1966).

2. A. V. Astin, "Standards of Measurement," *Scientific American* (1968), pp. 50–63.

3. J. B. Carroll, ed., *Language, Thought and Reality: Selected Writings of Benjamin Lee Whorf* (Cambridge, Mass.: The M.I.T. Press, 1951). See selection entitled "An American Indian Model of the Universe."

4. Joseph E. Bogen, "The Other Side of the Brain, I, II, III," *Bulletin of the Los Angeles Neurological Societies*, vol. 34, no. 3 (July 1969). Reprinted in part in Robert Ornstein, ed., *The Nature of Human Consciousness* (San Francisco, W. H. Freeman and Co.; New York, The Viking Press; 1973).

5. H. Nichols, "The Psychology of Time," *American Journal of Psychology*, 3 (1891), 453–529.

6. Lawrence Durrell, *Clea* (London, Faber; New York, E. P. Dutton; 1960). One novel of a set of four, concerned in large part with time.

7. J. A. Gunn, *The Problem of Time* (London: Allen and Unwin, 1929).

8. See George Miller, "The Magical Number 7 ± 2: Some Limits on Our Capacity for Processing Information," *Psychological Review*, 63 (1965), 81–97. L. R. Peterson and M. Y. Peterson, "Short-term Retention of Individual Verbal Items," *Journal of Experimental Psychology*, 58 (1959), 193–198.

9. Henri Bergson, *Duration and Simultaneity* (New York: Bobbs-Merrill, 1965).

10. My experiments, summarized in Robert Ornstein, *On*

the Experience of Time (Harmondsworth, England, and Baltimore, Md.: Penguin, 1969).

11. J. J. Harton, "An Investigation of the Influence of Success and Failure on the Estimation of Time," *Journal of General Psychology*, 21 (1939), 51–62.

12. There is a rich and diverse literature on these matters. Tart's volume is an attempt to begin a scientific consideration of drug-users' experiences. R. E. Masters and Jean Houston, *Varieties of Psychedelic Experience* (New York: Dell, 1966). Charles T. Tart, *On Being Stoned: A Psychological Study of Marijuana Intoxication* (Palo Alto, Calif.: Science and Behavior Books, 1971).

13. A. Carmon and I. Nachshon, "Effect of Unilateral Brain Damage on Perception of Temporal Order," *Cortex*, 7 (1971), 410–418.

14. T. S. Eliot, *Four Quartets* (New York: Harcourt, Brace & World, 1943, pp. 7–8; London: Faber, 1943).

15. Dogen, quoted in Alan Watts, *The Way of Zen* (New York: New American Library, 1957, p. 123; Harmondsworth, England: Penguin, 1970).

16. Dorothy Lee, "Codification of Reality: Lineal and Nonlineal," *Psychosomatic Medicine*, vol. 12, no. 2 (March–April 1950). Reprinted in Ornstein, *The Nature of Human Consciousness.*

Chapter 6

1. Adapted slightly from Idries Shah, *Tales of the Dervishes* (New York: E. P. Dutton, 1970, pp. 84–85; London: Jonathan Cape, 1967).

2. Two less positive views of these traditions are worth considering: Arthur Koestler, *The Lotus and the Robot* (New York: Harper & Row, 1960; London: Hutchinson, 1966), and A. Dalal and T. Barber, "Yoga, Yoga Feats, and Hypnosis in the Light of Empirical Research," *American Journal of Clinical Hypnosis*, 11 (1969), 155–166.

3. Philip Kapleau, ed., *The Three Pillars of Zen: Teaching, Practice and Enlightenment* (Boston: Beacon Press, 1965), p. 11.

4. Claudio Naranjo and Robert Ornstein, *On the Psychology of Meditation* (New York: The Viking Press, 1971, pp. 19–74; London: George Allen & Unwin, 1973).

5. Walpola Rahula, *What the Buddha Taught* (New York: Grove Press, 1959), p. 70.

6. P. Kapleau, *op. cit.,* p. 79.

7. B. Anand, G. Chhina, and B. Singh, "Studies on Shri Ramananda Yogi During His Stay in an Airtight Box," *Indian Journal of Medical Research,* 49 (1961), 82–89.

8. Robert Keith Wallace and Herbert Benson, "The Physiology of Meditation," *Scientific American* (Feb. 1972), pp. 84–90. Offprint no. 1242. Reprinted in Robert Ornstein, ed., *The Nature of Human Consciousness* (San Francisco, W. H. Freeman and Co.; New York, The Viking Press; 1973).

9. Ajit Mookerjee, *Tantra Art: Its Philosophy and Physics* (New Delhi: Ravi Kumar, 1966).

10. Rammurti Mishra, *Fundamentals of Yoga* (New York: Julian Press, 1959), pp. 65–66.

11. This quote is in one of the most beautiful books written on Yoga: Frederic Spiegelberg, *Spiritual Practices of India* (New York: Citadel Press, 1962), pp. 46–47.

12. Idries Shah, *Oriental Magic* (London: Octagon, 1968).

13. This and many other articles of interest are collected in Roy W. Davidson, *Documents on Contemporary Dervish Communities* (London: Hoopoe Ltd., 1966), pp. 10–11. The publisher's address is 14 Baker Street, London W1.

14. Cyprian Rice, *The Persian Sufis* (London: George Allen & Unwin, 1964).

15. Arthur Deikman, "Deautomatization and the Mystic Experience," *Psychiatry,* 29 (1966), 329–343. Reprinted in Charles Tart, ed., *Altered States of Consciousness* (New York: Wiley, 1969), and in Ornstein, *The Nature of Human Consciousness.*

16. E. Kadlovbovsky and G. E. H. Palmer, trans., *Writings from Philokalia, on the Prayer of the Heart* (London: Faber & Faber, 1951).

17. Peter Freuchen, *The Book of the Eskimos* (New York: Fawcett World Library, 1959).

18. Roy M. Pritchard, "Stabilized Images on the Retina," *Scientific American* (June 1961), pp. 72–78. Offprint no. 466. Donald O. Hebb, *The Organization of Behavior* (New York: Wiley, 1949).

19. D. Lehmann, G. W. Beeler, and D. H. Fender, "EEG Responses During the Observation of Stabilized and Normal Retinal Images," *Electroencephalography and Clinical Neurophysiology*, 22 (1967), 136–142.

20. W. Cohen, "Spatial and Textural Characteristics of the Ganzfeld," *American Journal of Psychology*, 70 (1957), 403–410. T. C. Cadwallander, "Cessation of Visual Experience under Prolonged Uniform Visual Stimulation," *American Psychologist*, 13 (1958), 410 (abstract).

21. D. T. Tepas, "The Electrophysiological Correlates of Vision in a Uniform Field," M. A. Whitcom, ed., *Visual Problems of the Armed Forces* (Washington: The National Academy of Science, National Research Council, 1962), pp. 21–25.

22. B. Bagchi and M. Wenger, "Electrophysiological Correlates on Some Yogic Exercises," *Electroencephalography and Clinical Neurophysiology*, suppl. 7 (1957), pp. 132–149. B. Anand, G. Chhina, and B. Singh, "Some Aspects of Electroencephalographic Studies in Yogis," *Electroencephalography and Clinical Neurophysiology*, 13 (1961), 452–456. Reprinted in Tart, *Altered States of Consciousness*. A. Kasamatsu and T. Hirai, "An Electroencephalographic Study of Zen Meditation (Zazen)," *Folia Psychiatria et Neurologia Japonica*, 20 (1966), 315–336. Reprinted in Tart, *Altered States of Consciousness*. Yoshiharu Akishige, *Psychological Studies on Zen, Bulletin of the Faculty of Literature of Kyushu University, Japan*, no. V (1968). Dr. Akishige can be written to c/o the Zen Institute, Komazawa University, Komazawa 1, Setagaya-Ku, Tokyo, Japan. Robert Keith Wallace and Herbert Benson, "The Physiology of Meditation," *Scientific American* (Feb. 1972), pp. 84–90.

23. D. Knowles, *The English Mystical Tradition* (London: Burnes & Oates, 1961), p. 57.

24. P. Kapleau, *op. cit.*, p. 53.

25. W. Rahula, *op. cit.*, p. 71.

26. B. Anand, *et al.*, *op. cit.*

27. Kasamatsu and Hirai, *op. cit.*

28. Arthur Deikman, "Experimental Meditation," *Journal of Nervous and Mental Disorders*, 136 (1963), 329–343. Reprinted in Tart, *Altered States of Consciousness*.

29. A. Poulain, *The Graces of Interior Prayer: A Treatise on Mystical Theology* (St. Louis: Herder, 1950), p. 272. Quoted in Deikman, "Deautomatization and the Mystic Experience."

30. Shah, *Tales of the Dervishes*, pp. 25–26.

31. William James, *The Varieties of Religious Experience* (New York: New American Library, 1958). Arthur Deikman, "Deautomatization and Mystic Experience," *loc. cit.*

32. This quote is from a subject in an LSD session. Walter N. Pahnke and William A. Richards, "Implications of LSD and Experimental Mysticism," *Journal of Religion and Health*, 5 (1966), 175–208. Reprinted in Tart, *Altered States of Consciousness*.

33. Deikman, "Deautomatization and the Mystic Experience."

34. Wallace and Benson, *op. cit.*

Chapter 7

1. This story can be found in many traditions. This version is based on Idries Shah, *Tales of the Dervishes* (New York: E. P. Dutton, 1970, pp. 25–26; London: Jonathan Cape, 1967).

2. J. R. Oppenheimer, *Science and the Human Understanding* (New York: Simon & Schuster, 1966), p. 69.

3. Carlos Castaneda, *The Teachings of Don Juan: A Yaqui Way of Knowledge* (New York: Simon & Schuster, 1973); the quote here is from his *A Separate Reality: Further Conversations with Don Juan* (New York: Simon & Schuster, 1971, p. 36; London: The Bodley Head, 1971). Castaneda has recently published a third volume on his experiences: *Journey to Ixtlan* (New York, Simon & Schuster; London, The Bodley Head; 1973).

4. Idries Shah, *Thinkers of the East* (London: Jonathan Cape, 1969; Baltimore: Penguin, 1972), p. 96.

5. Elmer Green, manuscript in preparation, Menninger Foundation, Topeka, Kansas. For many other reports, see T. Barber *et al.*, eds., *Biofeedback and Self-Control* (Chicago: Aldine-Atherton, 1971).

6. For a first-person encounter with this "energy," see Gopi Krishna, *Kundalini: The Evolutionary Energy in Man* (Berkeley: Shambala, 1970). For the caution, see Idries Shah, "The Fisherman and the Genie," in *Tales of the Dervishes*, pp. 117–120.

7. Idries Shah, *The Sufis* (New York: Doubleday, 1971, p. 430; London: Jonathan Cape, 1969).

8. Rafael Lefort, *The Teachers of Gurdjieff* (London: Gollancz, 1968), pp. 62–63.

9. Idries Shah, *Oriental Magic* (London: Octagon, 1968), p. 122.

10. Carlos Castaneda, *A Separate Reality*, pp. 262–263.

11. Rafael Lefort, *op. cit.*, p. 105.

12. Katherine Hulme, *Undiscovered Country* (Boston: Atlantic–Little, Brown, 1966).

13. Idries Shah, *The Way of the Sufi* (New York: Dutton, 1970, p. 140; London: Jonathan Cape, 1968).

14. *Ibid.*, p. 151.

15. Shah, *Thinkers of the East*, p. 122.

16. Adapted from Shah, *The Way of the Sufi*, p. 107.

17. Rafael Lefort, *op. cit.*

18. This discussion is based on Kilton Stewart, "Dream Theory in Malaya" in Charles T. Tart, ed., *Altered States of Consciousness* (New York: John Wiley & Sons, 1969).

19. See Brenda Milner, "Interhemispheric Differences in the Localization of Psychological Processes in Man," *British Medical Bulletin*, 27, no. 3 (1971), 272–277.

20. Shah, *The Way of the Sufi*, p. 16.

21. J. B. Carroll, ed., *Language, Thought and Reality: Selected Writings of Benjamin Lee Whorf* (Cambridge, Mass.: The M.I.T. Press, 1951). See the essay titled "Language, Mind, and Reality."

22. Rafael Lefort, *op. cit.*, p. 57.

23. Idries Shah, *Caravan of Dreams* (London: Octagon, 1968; Baltimore: Penguin, 1972), pp. 95–96.

24. Dennis Fry, "Some Effects of Music," *Institute for Cultural Research Monographs*, 13 Soho Square, London W1. A paper that opens up the consideration of these matters.

25. Idries Shah, *The Pleasantries of the Incredible Mulla Nasrudin* (New York: E. P. Dutton, 1971, p. 82; London: Jonathan Cape, 1968).

26. Idries Shah, *The Exploits of the Incomparable Mulla Nasrudin* (New York: E. P. Dutton, 1972, p. 20; London: Jonathan Cape, 1966).

27. Shah, *Pleasantries*, p. 67.

28. Shah, *Exploits*, p. 26.

29. Shah, *Caravan of Dreams*, pp. 180–181.

Chapter 9

1. "There is more light here" is found in Idries Shah, *The Exploits of the Incomparable Mulla Nasrudin* (New York: E. P. Dutton, 1972, pp. 26–27; London: Jonathan Cape, 1966).

2. Elmer Green, manuscript in preparation, Menninger Foundation, Topeka, Kansas. Alexandra David-Neel, *Magic and Mystery in Tibet* (Baltimore: Penguin, 1971).

3. A. R. Luria, *The Mind of a Mnemonist* (New York, Avon; London, Jonathan Cape; 1969).

4. *Swansea Medical Reports*, 1971.

5. K. M. Bykov and W. H. Gantt, *The Cerebral Cortex and the Internal Organs* (New York: Chemical Publishing Company, 1957).

6. Joseph Breuer and Sigmund Freud, *Studies in Hysteria* (Boston: Beacon Press, 1937; London: Hogarth Press, 1956. Originally published in 1895).

7. Neal Miller, "Learning of Visceral and Glandular Responses," *Science*, 163 (1969), 434–445. Leo V. Di-Cara, "Learning in the Autonomic Nervous System,"

Scientific American (Jan. 1970), pp. 30–39. Offprint no. 525. Reprinted in Robert Ornstein, ed., *The Nature of Human Consciousness* (San Francisco, W. H. Freeman and Co.; New York, The Viking Press; 1973).

8. Peter J. Lang, "Autonomic Control or Learning to Play the Internal Organs." Reprinted in T. Barber *et al.*, eds., *Biofeedback and Self-Control, 1970* (Chicago: Aldine-Atherton, 1971).

9. David Shapiro, Bernard Tursky, and Gary E. Schwartz, "Control of Blood Pressure in Man by Operant Condition," *Circulation Research*, suppl. I (1970), pp. 26, 27, 1–27 to 1–32. David Shapiro, Bernard Tursky and Gary E. Schwartz, "Differentiation of Heart Rate and Systolic Blood Pressure in Man by Operant Conditioning," *Psychosomatic Medicine*, 32 (1970), 417–423. Both reprinted in T. Barber *et al.*, *op. cit.*

10. David P. Nowlis and J. Kamiya, "The Control of Electroencephalographic Alpha Rhythms through Auditory Feedback and the Associated Mental Activity," *Psychophysiology*, 6, no. 4 (1970), 476–484. Reprinted in Ornstein, *op. cit.*

11. David Galin and Robert Ornstein, "Lateral Specialization of Cognitive Mode: An EEG Study," *Psychophysiology* (1972), in press.

12. Thomas H. Budzynski, Johann Stoyva, and Charles Adler, "Feedback-Induced Muscle Relaxation: Application to Tension Headaches," *Journal of Behavioral Therapy and Experimental Psychiatry*, 1 (1970), 205–211. Reprinted in T. Barber *et al.*, *op. cit.*

Chapter 10

1. Nasafi, in Idries Shah, *The Sufis* (New York: Doubleday, 1971, p. 401; London: Jonathan Cape, 1969).

2. Gay Luce, *Biological Rhythms in Psychiatry and Medicine* (Bethesda, Md.: National Institute of Mental Health, 1970), pp. 1–80. Much of this discussion is adapted from Luce's monograph. A more popularized version of this material can be found in her *Body Time* (New York: Pantheon, 1971; London: Paladin, 1973).

3. E. E. Von Bount, M. D. Shepherd, J. R. Wall, W. F. Ganong, and M. T. Clegg, "Penetration of Light into the Brain of Mammals," *Annals of the New York Academy of Sciences*, 117 (1964), 217–224.

4. Swami Vishnudevananda, *The Complete Illustrated Book of Yoga* (New York: Bell Publishing Co., 1960), p. 223.

5. Omar Garrison, *Tantra: The Yoga of Sex* (New York: The Julian Press, 1964), pp. 143–145.

6. S. Kimura, M. Ashiba and I. Matsushima, "Influences of the Air Lacking in Light Ions and the Effect of Its Artificial Ionization upon Human Beings in Occupied Rooms," *Japanese Journal of Medical Science*, 7 (1939), 1–12.

7. N. Robinson and F. S. Dirnfeld, "The Ionization State of the Atmosphere as a Function of the Meteorological Elements and the Various Sources of Ions," *International Journal of Biometeorology*, 6 (1963), 101–110.

8. A. P. Krueger and H. B. Levine, "The Effect of Unipolar Positively Ionized Air on the Course of Coccidioidomycosis in Mice," *International Journal of Biometeorology*, 11 (1967), 279–288.

9. Krueger's paper is probably the best review written to date. A. P. Krueger, "Preliminary Consideration of the Biological Significance of Air Ions," *Scientia*, vol. 104 (Sept.–Oct. 1969). Reprinted in Robert Ornstein, ed., *The Nature of Human Consciousness* (San Francisco, W. H. Freeman and Co.; New York, The Viking Press; 1973).

10. S. Kotaka and A. P. Krueger, "Studies on Air Ionized-Induced Growth Increase in Higher Plants," *Advancing Frontiers of Plant Sciences*, 20 (1967), 115–208.

11. These studies are referred to in A. P. Krueger, "The Biological Significance of Air Ions," in *Bioclimatology, Biometeorology, and Aeroiontherapy* (Milan, Italy: Carlo ERBA Foundation, 1969). Also see the article by Kornbleuth in the same volume.

12. A. L. Tchijevsky, trans., Central Laboratory Sci. Res. Ionification (Publishing House of the Commune, Voronej, 1933). This is merely a report and would need much verification before its contention could be accepted.

13. For the one report which considers a possible mechanism of this effect, see A. P. Krueger, P. C. Andriese, and S. Kotaka, "Small Air Ions: Their Effect on Blood Levels of Serotonin in Terms of Modern Physical Theory," *International Journal of Biometeorology*, 12, no. 3 (1968), 225–239.

14. Ida Rolf, "Structural Integration: Gravity, an Unexplored Factor in a More Human Use of Human Beings," *Systematics*, vol. I (June 1963). David Sobel, "Gravity & Structural Integration," in Ornstein, *op. cit.*

15. Roger W. Sperry, "Neurology and the Mind-Brain Problem," *American Scientist*, 40 (1951), 291–312. Leon Festinger, H. Ono, C. A. Burnham, and D. Bamber, "Efference and the Conscious Experience of Perception," *Journal of Experimental Psychology*, 74 (1967), 74, 1–36.

16. F. S. Perls, *Gestalt Therapy Verbatim* (Lafayette, Calif.: Real People Press, 1969).

17. Joen Fagen and Irma Lee Shepard, eds., *Gestalt Therapy Now* (New York: Harper & Row, 1971), p. 38.

18. Roberto Assagioli, *Psychosynthesis* (New York: The Viking Press, 1971).

19. Idries Shah, *The Sufis* (London: Jonathan Cape, 1969; New York: Doubleday, 1971). See chapter on "Miracles and Magic."

20. M. Ullman and S. Krippner, *Dream Studies and Telepathy: An Experimental Approach* (New York: Parapsychological monograph no. 12, Parapsychology Foundation, 29 W. 57th Street, New York, 1970). M. Ullman, S. Krippner, and S. Feldstein, "Experimentally-Induced Telepathic Dreams: Two Studies Using EEG and REM Monitoring Technique," *International Journal of Neuropsychiatry*, 2 (1966), 420–438.

21. Two additional experiments on this mode of communication are reported in Thelma Moss and Thomas Gangerelli, "Telepathy and Emotional Stimuli: A Controlled Experiment," *Journal of Abnormal Psychology*, 72 (1967), 341–348, and T. McBain, "Quasi-Sensory Communication: An Investigation Using Semantic

Matching and Accentuated Affect," *Journal of Personality and Social Psychology*, 14 (1970), 281–291.

22. See the works of Idries Shah listed at the end of this chapter and of Chapter 7.

Index

THE DIVIDED SELF

R. D. Laing

The Divided Self is a unique study of the human situation. Dr. R. D. Laing's first purpose is to make madness and the process of going mad comprehensible. In this, with case studies of schizophrenic patients, he succeeds brilliantly, but he does more; through a vision of sanity and madness as "degrees of conjunction and disjunction between two persons where the one is sane by common consent," he offers a rich existential analysis of personal alienation. The outsider, estranged from himself and society, cannot experience either himself or others as "real." He invents a false self, and with it, he confronts both the outside world and his own despair. The disintegration of his real self keeps pace with the growing unreality of his false self until, in the extremes of schizophrenic breakdown, the whole personality disintegrates. "Dr. Laing is saying something very important indeed. . . . This is a truly humanist approach"—Philip Toynbee. "It is a study that makes all other works I have read on schizophrenia seem fragmentary. . . . The author brings, through his vision and perception, that particular touch of genius which causes one to say, 'Yes, I have always known that; why have I never thought of it before?'"—*Journal of Analytical Psychology*.